"Gail McMeekin is such a gift. Her *12 Secrets of Highly Successful Women* gets right to the loving heart of how women are redefining success and building lives that are wildly creative and creatively successful! I'll be recommending this book for many years to come."

—SARK, author of *Succulent Wild Woman, PlanetSARK.com*

"Reading *The 12 Secrets of Highly Successful Women*, you gradually discover the one real secret of a successful life: it is yours—and yours alone. You get to find and define it. You get to create it. You get to fall in love with it. And you get to live it on your own terms. That's exciting, yes, but daunting, too. Be not afraid. Between these covers, Gail McMeekin has distilled a rich array of wisdom from thirty brilliant and successful women and her thirty years of coaching experience into 12 essential ingredients. Take them, sift them, stir them into your own brilliant and successful life."

—Janet Conner, author of *Writing Down Your Soul*

"What looks like a practical guidebook quickly reveals itself to be a fireworks display of inspiration and encouragement. In *The 12 Secrets of Highly Successful Women*, Gail McMeekin not only gives women a map toward clearer success for themselves, she also offers the wisdom of other women to reinforce her message that success hinges on heeding the voice of inspiration. She's let the cat out of the bag in her latest book: creativity is not only a part of success . . . it's the heart of success. Whatever part of the journey you're on, McMeekin's book will help you tune in, turn on, let go, and shine brighter in order to create the life that defines success for YOU."

—Mary Beth Maziarz, songwriter and author of *Kick-Ass Creativity: An Energy Makeover for Artists, Explorers, and Creative Professionals*

"Gail has done it again. What a powerhouse of practical, inspiring stories. I have flagged, underlined, and highlighted many, many passages. You will be dipping into this wisdom for years to come. Buy it for yourself and for all your friends who wonder, 'How does she do it?'"

—Jennifer Louden, author of *The Woman's Comfort Book* and *The Life Organizer*

"Gail McMeekin's new book on success secrets for creative women is even better than her first (which I loved)! She shares real stories of successful women—not just the glory but the details of how they got up from the falls, got past the slams and insults, and got through the fear. This book is a toolkit for the kind of success that comes straight from the soul."

—Barbara Sher, *New York Times* bestselling author of
I Could Do Anything If Only I Knew What It Was

"This book weds access to meaningful work and heart-based action with practical, actionable steps toward business fulfillment and success. With precision Gail calls out the chronic undermining elements in a woman's career and elevates the models for satisfaction and reward. She extracts the very best gems from her generous successful guides. It's a treasure box: open it."

—Mary Anne Radmacher, author of *Lean Forward into Your Life*

"*The 12 Secrets of Highly Successful Women* is a book for anyone who values the feminine perspective as an agent of change and healing upon the planet. Gail's creative inspiration to give voice to women, whose leadership is needed now more than ever, is pure genius."

—Brenda Michaels, radio talk show host, *Conscious Talk*

"Because it draws from the lives of successful women and because it identifies the strategies that any woman can employ to become more successful, Gail McMeekin's *The Twelve Secrets of Highly Successful Women* is a must read!"

—Eric Maisel, author of *Coaching the Artist Within*

"Gail McMeekin is a trustworthy and experienced guide for any woman wanting to cultivate her highest creative potential. She writes with warmth, wit, and wisdom. She draws to her women who are seasoned on the path of making their dreams come true. Gail knows what questions to ask, how to get to the heart of anyone's true desire, and how to guide them toward fulfillment."

—Lucia Capacchione, PhD, Visioning˚ Coach and bestselling author of
Recovery of Your Inner Child and *Visioning: Ten Steps to Designing the Life of Your Dreams*

The 12 Secrets of Highly Successful Women

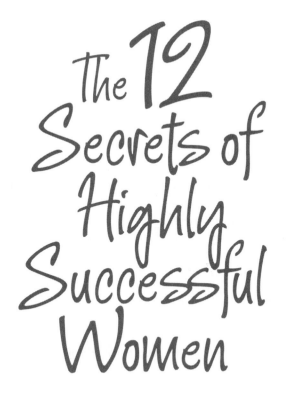

A Portable Life Coach for Creative Women

Gail McMeekin

Conari Press

First published in 2011 by Conari Press, an imprint of
Red Wheel/Weiser, LLC

With offices at:
665 Third Street, Suite 400
San Francisco, CA 94107
www.redwheelweiser.com

ISBN: 978-1-57324-493-0

Library of Congress Cataloging-in-Publication Data

McMeekin, Gail.
    The 12 secrets of highly successful women : a portable life coach for creative women /
Gail McMeekin.
        p. cm.
    Includes bibliographical references.
    ISBN 978-1-57324-493-0 (alk. paper)
    1. Women—Psychology. 2. Creative ability—Case studies. 3. Success—Case studies.
I. Title.
    HQ1206.M3697 2011
    646.70082—dc23   2011017722

Cover design by Barb Fisher
Cover art © Yulia Grigoryeva (smilewithjul)
Interior by Dutton & Sherman Design
Typeset in Warnock Pro text and Argenta and Nexus Sans display

Printed in Canada
TCP
10 9 8 7 6 5 4 3 2 1

The paper used in this publication meets the minimum requirements of the American
National Standard for Information Sciences—Permanence of Paper for Printed Library
Materials Z39.48-1992 (R1997).

To my husband, Russ Street; I thank him for his unconditional love and support—these are priceless gifts.

To my parents, Elizabeth and Herbert McMeekin; I am blessed that they taught and modeled for me a life of integrity, good works, tenacity, optimism, a strong love for family and friends, and dedication to community.

To women everywhere; claim your creativity, be your true self in the world, and trust.

Contents

Preface

Hello!

You are about to embark on a journey of self-discovery and learn the wisdom of success. I suggest that you invest in a compact, beautiful journal that you can carry with you long after you read this book for the first time. Throughout the book, you will find many special Challenges exercises to complete to make this experience more meaningful for you. Use your journal to record your responses to these Challenges.

Then, after you have finished your first reading of this book, carry your journal with you and note down your own secrets to success and your stretch goals for a happy and prosperous future of heartfelt success and a life of fulfillment. It all begins with loving yourself and extending that love to others by being the person that you aspire to be. Do creative work that nourishes you, other people and creatures, and the planet. You are meant to be here. Take advantage of it.

Just a note, as there are so many wonderful, successful women in America, I invited a diverse group of one hundred women to be interviewed for this book, with a goal of only interviewing twenty-five, although I interviewed a few more than that. The women who responded positively to my request generously and openly shared their work and life experiences and their wisdom with us. As with my first book, *The 12 Secrets of Highly Creative Women: A Portable Mentor,* I did not chase women for the book. I trusted that each woman who chose to participate and to serve as a mentor to other women knew intuitively that it was the right thing to do and that she wanted to be part of this project. We owe each of them our gratitude and respect. Their website addresses are in the back of the book in the Resources section. I thank them with all my heart.

Gail McMeekin, LICSW, Creative Success LLC
Boston, Fall 2010

Acknowledgments

Last spring, I was getting ready to pitch a few new ideas to my publisher, Conari Press, when out of the blue, Associate Publisher Caroline Pincus got in touch with me first. We agreed on two book ideas: this one you are reading, and a journal to accompany *The 12 Secrets of Highly Creative Women,* which my readers have been asking me for since it was first published. I will write the journal this winter. Caroline is a dream editor, and she feels a bit like my fairy godmother as she weaves her magic. She is smart, fast, loaded with clever ideas, and very supportive. She is a gift and I hope to collaborate with her again in the future. I also want to acknowledge Barb Fisher for designing the beautiful, playful cover for this book, which brings me joy every time I look at it. Major thanks also go to Bonni Hamilton and Lisa Trudeau and the entire marketing team in Newburyport, Massachusetts, for their efforts to get the word out about our books and for teaching us about the new world of social media and blogs.

I feel very lucky to be part of the Red Wheel Weiser/Conari Press family. My two books are still selling, and I still get emails or Facebook posts from all over the world thanking me for writing them. What every self-help author wants is for our work to endure and continue to motivate people to create better lives. The entire staff at Red Wheel Weiser/Conari Press deserve credit for birthing wise and visually appealing books. I salute them all.

I am deeply appreciative of the community of women who made the time to be interviewed for this book, shared their varied experiences, and agreed to be mentors for other women. It felt important for me to duplicate the formula that worked so well in the first *12 Secrets* book. This group of women is also highly creative, as well as kind and caring, which were criteria for selection. These are remarkable, no-nonsense women of courage who have a strong passion for life and for their mission of service. They don't "settle," but instead they take action and make big things happen. They fail sometimes, as we all do when taking positive risks, but they get right back up again and move forward on their paths. I am grateful to each of you for participating in this sacred project with me.

I also hired a team of people to help me with all the administrative details of this book, and there were many. I want to especially thank Linda Poirier for her endless patience and perseverance in dealing with many changes and challenging tasks, and for her edits. To Beverly Morrison and Clare Nielsen, my transcription team, many thanks for the hours you spent listening to the recordings of my interviews and for being so quick and accurate. I also want to thank Barbara Williams, Crissy Sutter, and Patrice Birenberg for holding down the fort with my newsletter, my website, and my clients, etcetera while I was submerged in weeks of intense interviewing and writing.

On a personal note, I must first thank my husband and soul mate, Russ Street, for once again stepping up to bat (he used to be a great baseball player) and taking care of things so that are lives stayed glued together. His support astonishes me daily. To Marilyn Veltrop, my daily email partner, our exchange gives me a daily dose of your intuition and your insights which enrich my life and ground me each morning. I am grateful to Nancy Monson and Deborah Knox for their special offers of support for this project. To Mary Headley, whom I just met in a year ago, courtesy of Suzanne Falter-Barns, thank you for inviting me to be your guest at Lisa Sasevich's amazing workshop called "Speak to Sell" in California. This invitation opened many new doors for me, plus we had great fun traipsing all around the country going to other incredible workshops this year hosted by Ali Brown and Baeth Davis, as well as Lisa and Suzanne. Our adventures were life-changing— thank you. My learnings from those workshops are interwoven into this book and several of the women in the book either ran or attended these workshops. I also want to thank my friends and family, as well as my cheering section on Facebook, who checked in on me to see how this book was coming along. It meant a lot. Of course, I am grateful to all my wonderful clients who share their creative journeys with me and whom I learn from as they grow into their own personal, heartfelt success. Lastly, I am grateful to my Trusted Source for inspiration and inner guidance which facilitates my creative expression.

Secret One

Express Your Creative Gifts and Life Purpose

> "I've come to believe that each of us has a personal calling that's as unique as a fingerprint—and that the best way to succeed is to discover what you love and then find a way to offer it to others in the form of a service, working hard, and allowing the energy of the universe to lead you."
> —*Oprah Winfrey*

Over the past ten years, I received notes from thousands of women (and men) worldwide who said that my first book, *The 12 Secrets of Highly Creative Women: A Portable Mentor,* changed their lives, gave them inspiration and hope, and allowed them to embrace their creativity again and run with it. In contrast, I have run into many women (and men) in my travels who react to the title of that book by saying "Oh, that's not for me, I'm not creative at all."

My heart aches when I hear those words, as we are all creative in our lives, not just writers, artists, and actresses. Watch a healthy two-year-old child at play while they gleefully try out new projects, like throwing sand to see what happens, running after a butterfly to see if they can catch it, discovering the wonders of glue, and sticking together everything they can find.

As we know, the definition of creativity is "to make or invent something new"—to make connections. Children allowed to engage in free play (as opposed to being perched in front of a DVD) invent and make all kinds of original creations without intimidation or self-consciousness.

But something happens to many of us as we grow up—we freeze up creatively or disown our gifts. Then we get bad advice and often get on the wrong path. Thus, creativity goes underground. Or we follow a creative path but we don't treat our work as a profession and end up living on the margin, and we don't get the recognition or financial rewards that we deserve. Other people have a creative outlet that they consider a hobby, like knitting, and choose to have a different day job. But both the job and the knitting can be creative outlets, too. Part of our creative process is to craft the life and the business that we want.

Then there are women who actively choose to pursue their creative interest (or interests, very often), and become highly creative women. But even then, they may fall prey to bad advice, low self-esteem, not marketing themselves actively, and the terror of being seen. This book will help each of you, regardless of which category you are in.

- You are creative—own it!

- You have the potential to become highly successful.

- Your creativity is an essential ingredient to building a successful career, business, and personal life.

- You can learn to be successful creatively by following the advice in this book.

- You can potentially change your entire life and lifestyle to honor your creative gifts and finally feel free, fulfilled, and prosperous.

- You have an inner brilliance that allows you to solve problems with novel and innovative solutions, help others, and profit from it.

This book is your ticket to becoming the highly creative and successful woman you long to be. But first, you have to do some healing work, learn new professional development and lifestyle strategies, and empower yourself as an entrepreneur or as a key contributor to an ethical, quality organization where you enjoy working. Even if you choose to spend some time working for someone else, you need to keep your eye on the door, your skills and your About Page updated, and a strong network going. Your best security is to grow yourself. You need to follow a special path for creative success. It will reawaken that creative little girl who either got squelched or silenced or went out on the creative path with the wrong guidance and has been stumbling along. If you are already operating as a highly creative woman, this book will propel you to the next level of growth, stretching your comfort zone and pushing you to step fully into a CEO mindset.

THE MAGIC OF TWELVE

Many of you may be wondering why I am writing another book with the title "12 Secrets" in it. In doing a little research, I discovered that 12 is the number of a whole and perfect harmonious unit. There are 12 months in a year, 12 signs on the zodiac, 12 inches in a foot, 12 face cards in a card deck, and 12 basic hues in a color wheel. And of course we have 12-Step Recovery Programs that are very powerful and teach a complete outline of what works. So my intent with this book is to share with you my model for the 12 secrets of highly successful women, compiled from my own life journey, the myriad of clients I have coached over thirty years in my business, now called Creative Success LLC, and the wisdom of the thirty women who I interviewed for this book, some of whom have been powerful mentors to me. Some of these women are multimillionaires and on television, while others value their lifestyle more than just money, and make business and lifestyle choices around those desires. Many of the women are trying to have balanced lives and be wealthy at the same time, or have already achieved that balance. They all work hard, feel strongly connected to their work, and feel called to express it in the world as a gift to others. Their stories are meant to illustrate the 12 ingredients that I outline that are essential to the soup of success for you.

DEFINING HEARTFELT PERSONAL SUCCESS

In my thirty-plus years of experience helping people to heal and create a life of fulfillment, I have been struck repeatedly with how essential it is for each of us to do the necessary soul searching to design and live by our own definition of our success. In this celebrity- and media-crazed culture we live in, it is easy to get confused about what composes a high quality and successful life for ourselves. Defining heartfelt success is a very personal and unique endeavor.

I have worked with thousands of clients who have been tortured by the agony and confusion of living according to someone else's values, misconceptions, scripts, or formulas. Just because your mother thought you were overly dramatic doesn't mean you *are* or that being so is even a liability. While the media or your family might worship fame, money, entrepreneurship, or corporate ladder-climbing, none of these pathways guarantee happiness for you unless you freely choose them. We all deserve prosperity. The starving artist syndrome serves no one. Yet fulfillment in life means knowing what we want while appreciating what we already have and having the self-worth to think independently and create a life that's original.

Webster defines success simply as "a favorable or satisfactory outcome or result." I like to add the adjectives "heartfelt" and "personal" so that you can visualize results that express your true self. Whether you are twenty-four or eighty-four, it's time to stop the lies. For example, I have a client now who keeps brainstorming with me about ideas for this elaborate international consulting business. But if you look at her overall life goals, she really wants to only work twenty-five hours a week. That means that her business plan has to be carefully designed to target the work that can be done quickly for the most fulfillment for her in terms of either impact or financial reward. It may take her several years to achieve this model. The best time management strategy in the world is letting go of fantasies and working within your own desired paradigm. Successful people focus on the outcomes that resonate for them—creating viable businesses that service their customers and clients—and so they can revel in the joy of that heartfelt, personal set of goals.

> *The best time management strategy in the world is letting go of fantasies and working within your own desired paradigm.*

I interviewed many successful women for this book. Here are some of the unique elements of their definition of success.

Ali Brown, millionaire entrepreneur, mentor, CEO of Ali International LLC, member of the *Inc.* "500 in 2009," and leader of the Millionaire Protégé Club and the Shine Conference:

> Success for me, in the beginning, and this may be true for everyone, was liking the *stuff.* I wanted the house and the car and I love my creature comforts and I love beautiful things. But once I reached these goals, I looked around and said, "Okay, now what?" I've got this gorgeous house on the beach and I have a wonderful life; what is this all about? And I realized that success is truly being just true to myself and that whatever I define success to be, that's what it is. And I think women need to give themselves permission that success can look like exactly what they want it to look like. I'm here in a big way and building a global business to empower women entrepreneurs internationally, but not every woman wants to make some of the sacrifices I have made.

Gillian Drake, serial entrepreneur, editor, writer, and publisher of many books and the *Cape Arts Review,* real estate designer and developer, and now a medical intuitive:

To me, success is living on your own terms, being who you truly are, being your authentic self. I know that the standard definition of success means a high paying, prestigious job, the perfect marriage, a beautiful home—the American Dream, I guess. But that's not for me. I need freedom, independence, and a series of creative projects to work on in order to be happy.

(You should see her villa in Italy that she redesigned and built.)

Lisa Sasevich, known as "The Queen of Sales Conversion," author of *The Invisible Close,* and leader of large workshops like Speak to Sell Bootcamp:

…The reason I feel successful the most is really that I feel blessed to have healthy children, a loving husband, and work that is meaningful that makes a difference. As I discovered a few years ago, my blessing is to help experts who are making a difference to get their message out—people who love what they do but hate the sales part—and last year my business took a quantum leap from $130K in sales to 2.2 million in sales. I also feel successful because I can be an inspiration to other women who also have a busy life, to be able to really create the lifestyle of their dreams and make a huge contribution at the same time.

Victoria Moran, author of ten books, including *Living a Charmed Life,* spiritual-life and holistic health coach:

I see my success as moving forward each day as a spiritual being having an earthly experience. I believe that this life is extremely important. I don't have the idea of "Oh well, you know, work and the body and things like that are physical so they don't matter." They matter tremendously. But when I think of success it has to be both—the here and now and the forever after.

Sheri McConnell, CEO of Smart Women's Institute of Entrepreneurial Learning and author of several books, including *Smart Women Know Their Why:*

Western entrepreneurial women will save the world and our mission is to create positive change in the world—making the world a better place.

Caroll Michels, career coach, artist advocate, author of the classic book, *How to Survive and Prosper as an Artist,* and creator of the ArtistHelpNetwork website:

I'm happy. I mean it is just as simple as that. I'm happier than I have ever been in my whole life and I just wake up happy.

Chellie Campbell, creator of the Financial Stress Reduction® Workshop and author of *The Wealthy Spirit* and *Zero to Zillionaire:*

> The number one thing I want is a business that I run, not one that runs me. I want work to get me to a life, not be my life. I want my life to be beautiful. I want to have a lot of time off for fun, to enjoy the ride of it.

Brenda Michaels, co-host of Conscious Talk Radio, emotional and spiritual coach, and author of an upcoming book called *The Gift of Cancer: Awakening the Healer Within:*

> First and foremost, I define success through relationship with myself, and how well I take care of myself. How well I nurture myself and how well I allow myself to honor my feelings and my needs, and my willingness to bring balance and harmony into my life. I believe this is important because we can't truly give to others what we withhold from ourselves. Living this way allows me to give love in such a way that there is peace and integrity in my personal relationships, as well as in my professional relationships.

Jeanne Carbonetti, watercolor painter and teacher, owner of Crow Hill Gallery, and author of many books, including *The Heart of Creativity:*

> Yes, I do feel successful and for me, success is doing what I love and being able to make a living at it and I am able to do that. It also means feeling like I am fulfilling my purpose in life. I have a strong sense that everything in my life was guiding me to be devoted to teaching the power of beauty and that's what I spend my time doing.

Dr. Elizabeth Stewart, MD, physician in Obstetrics and Gynecology at the Mayo Clinic in Minnesota and researcher on fibroid treatments:

> I do feel successful. For me it means being able to do work that is interesting and challenging and to have some element of creative fulfillment as well, and also being able to balance that with life outside of work.

Deborah George Tsakoumakis, founder/owner of Wire a Cake/HB Bakery Connections®, a company that sends cakes all over the world, including to many of our troops overseas:

> Yes, I feel successful. And as far as success, we have to define success as not exactly measured in dollars, but rather success in knowing that I have accomplished something that has had a positive effect these past twenty-three years

when I started the cake business. I see the effects that my cakes have had with respect to the families that receive them, especially my military families. I send families a picture of the cakes I ship and I'll get emails back from an army wife, for example, and she will say, "I'm in tears right now, looking at this cake, and knowing that I can send a cake to my husband who is deployed, has made all the difference in the world.

FALLING IN LOVE WITH YOUR WORK

A few years ago, I planned a wonderful Mediterranean cruise for my husband and me. It had been a lifelong dream and it was time for us to have the experience. I was charmed by the cliffs on the island of Capri, the beauty of the French Riviera, and the periwinkle blue and white buildings on Santorini. It was an amazing adventure to places of staggering beauty. It was an investment in the joy of travel.

On the cruise ship, I met an incredible pianist, Pearl Kaufman. Since the publication of *The 12 Secrets of Highly Creative Women*, a number of people have said that they wish I had interviewed more musicians, so I took the opportunity to interview Pearl. Pearl performed on the ship three times, and each performance sparked a standing ovation with cheering. People fell all over each other in the line to buy her CDs. She was adored, and she plays on cruises all over the world to enthusiastic audiences (talk about a great job!). As Pearl said to me, "everyone should experience the joy of being cheered——there's nothing like it." Pearl decided to become a pianist while watching a movie at age eight, and thankfully, no one tried to talk her out of it.

She received a music and scholastic scholarship to college, played for Igor Stravinsky, and is known for her famous movie performances with Henry Mancini and John Williams, among others. She loves all kinds of music, and believes strongly in its inspirational qualities. I asked her if she had any special favorites and she had an intriguing answer: "I'm like Elizabeth Taylor—I fall in love with everything I play." Pearl says she does not get blocked or bored and never plans to retire—just slow down a bit to enjoy her grandchildren. Her advice for aspiring creatives: "Go where the action is. You can't stay home and expect your work to be seen or heard. You have to make the effort."

Love is an essential success strategy for any endeavor. Doing work you love captivates your life force and enthusiasm. If you are settling for doing work you hate, you are missing this joy of full engagement. Falling in love with our work, over and over again, fulfills us like a great marriage. Our work is a potent relationship, and love is an essential lubricant. Pearl's love affair with her piano and its possibilities reminds us all that expressing love through our creative work is a peak experience of life.

CHALLENGE

Spend some time this month "remembering" what captivates you about your work and renew your vows.

MANAGING HIGH CREATIVITY

Highly creative women often have special aptitudes that give rise to creative intelligence, a superior ability for innovative thinking and application. In today's marketplace, our ability to think differently about problems and solve them with original and novel solutions is a key to success. Highly creative women can have problems if they don't see themselves or their abilities clearly. In my experience, some of the strengths and necessary talents of highly creative women can also be their downfall if not managed well. This book is meant to be a guide to help you to leverage your abilities and counter these potential pitfalls. These would include:

- Being overly sensitive and therefore too thin-skinned to be out in the world much

- Ambivalence about money and therefore being afraid or uncomfortable charging what they deserve

- Intuitive—getting wrapped up too much in other people's life decisions, which distracts the highly creative woman from her own life

- Divergent thinking—going from project to project—too many ideas at the same time can be overwhelming and make it difficult to focus

- Independence—being afraid/disinclined to ask for emotional support and business help when they need it

- Severely critical—perfectionism can be paralyzing and prevent highly creative women from ever releasing their completed work into the world or finishing projects at all

- Non-conforming—being scapegoated by others for being too far "out there" and not following enough protocol to successfully do business in this world—can lead to isolation and loneliness

- Not completely confident—having damaged self-esteem or lack of expertise in certain skill areas that they may need to learn or to delegate to others

- Can be workaholics and ignore their own needs for self—nurturance, serenity and relaxation

- Need for solitude—the highly successful woman must honor this and negotiate with partners and family

- Can make simple things complex due to a long list of internal comfort criteria

- Sad—often feel that they haven't met their potential or realized their dreams for this life

- Fear of being who they really are and telling the truth about it and risking disapproval

- Feeling guilty about not having chosen a traditional career path with job security, a pension, and securing people's understanding of what they do

- Feeling confused by having too many interests and not knowing what to specialize in

- Fear of rejection as being unbearable and something from which they won't recover

- Fear that pursuing their creative work will hurt the ones they love

- Being labeled by others as a risk taker or being hesitant to take the necessary risks to succeed

Fortunately, there are remedies for all of these issues, and this book is your guide to creative success and peace of mind. Most of these creative liabilities are also strengths, but you must learn how to capitalize on them and redesign your strategies of being in the world.

This is a book of hope and know-how. Let's start by looking at what inspires you.

SPARK YOUR CREATIVITY USING YOUR INTUITION

Worried that you're not creative? You are, but you may be out of touch with your creativity. Your intuition can lead you into a world of novel ideas, experimentation, and brainstorming that will perk up your work life and stimulate innovation and problem solving. Intuition is not just for New Agers. Many executives, business owners, and research and development professionals attribute their successes to following intuitive clues.

Intuition is your internal information and feeling source. It is an inner library of physical and emotional cues that can direct you onto the right avenue. It is the composite of "gut feelings" and perceptions unique to you. It is an inner way of knowing. Too often, we are trained to discount or repress that knowledge and therefore purposely neglect it, devalue it, or refuse to recognize its message. Intuition is a tool for insight and illumination. Can you recall a time when your intuition prompted you to follow a different course and connected you to a result you were looking for?

Susan recalls a time when her intuition prodded her to take an unfamiliar exit off the expressway on her way home. As she turned off, she felt foolish and almost turned around. But she followed a country road and passed an intriguing building with a "For Sale" sign on it. She stopped in amazement—this building fit her image of the gourmet shop she wanted to open some day. Here was her dream in reality; the rest was up to her.

The creative process demands that, like Susan, you are willing to step into the unknown and see what happens. Creativity is born of inspiration and your inspirations evolve from your passions. So follow your whims and see where they lead.

These excursions will stimulate new thought patterns and generate new paradigms for you. To help you to massage your intuitive talents, you can try a series of exercises to evoke creative prospects for you.

Exercise One: What Inspires You?

What do you feel excited by or passionate about? What kinds of books or magazines do you read? What kinds of people do you most like to talk with? What kinds of interests and projects are you drawn to in your leisure time? If you went back to school, what would you most like to learn about? What do you fantasize about? What are your aspirations? What kinds of activities stimulate your creative expression? Do you long to paint or write or build or sing or play something? Write down everything and anything that comes to mind.

No idea is wrong or silly. What is your internal voice urging you to explore or experience? Let this exercise be the beginning of a creative journal. You may be surprised at the wisdom and guidance stored for you in these seemingly random thoughts.

To facilitate the new, it helps to clear away the past. Think back to any regrets you have about lost opportunities. Kim wishes she had studied engineering in college instead of teaching. Karen had a chance to go into business with a friend and turned it down because she was too scared. Her friend is now a millionaire who works part-time. It may not be too late for you.

Exercise Two: What Creative Dreams Have You Abandoned and Why?

Make a list of all the things you wanted to do, but didn't. Then, think back to what your intuition told you about these options. Choose one. Are you still interested in this path? What does your inner voice tell you about this choice now? Note any patterns that are still possible or an enduring vision that you want to manifest.

You need to make peace with these cast-off dreams. What can you learn from your mistakes? Rose learned that she hadn't been ready until recently to write her play. Her vision just became vivid enough for her to tell the story, so she was able to release her regrets. Melissa, on the other hand, always wanted to become a lawyer. At age fifty, she thought she was too old, but the dream still beckoned her.

This was a choice point for her. She could either live the rest of her life with the sorrow of not having become a lawyer, or she could go to law school. Or she could leverage her skills and become a lobbyist, a political activist, a paralegal, a city official, or fulfill her dream in numerous alternative ways. It was time for Melissa to move on.

Grieve what you must and then turn the corner and make room for the next episode.

Learning to trust your intuition is the critical foundation for creativity. Think back to the times when you were clear that a particular choice was not a wise one. Your "gut" warned you against it.

Nadia, a billing consultant, recalls a phone call she received from a potential client. The woman owned an antique store and sounded stressed, disorganized, and demanding. Nadia had a negative visceral reaction to the woman's voice. But Nadia needed more business and this was a big account, so she hushed her intuitive radar and accepted the woman as a client. A year later, the woman sued Nadia for malpractice.

During the legal proceedings, Nadia learned that this woman had sued her last two billing agents and that lawsuits, not antiques, were her primary source of income. Nadia swore to heed her intuitive doubts in the future.

Exercise Three: *I Am Grateful To My Intuition For the Following:*

When has your intuition steered you right? Make a list of the times when your intuition helped you make the right decision or prompted you to try something. What have you learned about how it operates on your behalf? One of the greatest blocks to creativity is fear. Fear keeps you from exploring new ways of doing things. Fear of failure keeps you from enjoying an experimental mindset where failure is expected and welcomed as new information. Fear of being wrong or criticized also clips your creative wings. Almost everyone can remember trying something fresh and new and being chided or teased about it.

Therefore, we learn to play it safe, cease taking risks, and stop the flow of creative solutions. While most people are educated in a school system that advocates one right answer, today's workplace requires you to evoke new answers. The beauty of the entrepreneurial mindset is that it allows you to innovate and make up your own solutions. Fear of "getting the wrong answer" halts your flow of unique ideas.

Exercise Four: What Frightens You Most About Expressing Your Creativity?

What is your fear about? What creative traumas from the past still hold power over you? What do you fear from your internal critic and others? What person(s) from your past criticized your ideas and actions? Write this all down so you can see it.

Fear is a component of risk and risking is essential to creativity. When you read about writers and artists and business people, they all acknowledge fear. You will never be free of fear, but you can minimize it and strategize around it. Just don't let fear keep you from your true self. Whenever you accomplish something, you become vulnerable to criticism. Leaders are often controversial and therefore are targets for someone's arrow. Are you living your life for them or for yourself?

> Don't let fear keep you from your true self.

When I get scared to write, I pick up a book called *Walking on Alligators: A Book of Meditations for Writers* by Susan Shaughnessy. Writing often feels dangerous to me, and reading about another writer's similar terrors helps me to forget my doubt and just start typing. You need to find antidotes for your fear. That's why I developed my *Creativity Courage Cards* with affirmations matched to beautiful photos—to counter fear. Mentors, support groups, classes, coaches, and readings all offer support systems that can undo the demons from the past. Figure out what solutions will most help your fear to stay in the background, and use them.

Another form of support for your creativity is a nurturing environment. Where do you do your best thinking? Where does your inner self feel most daring and alive?

Exercise Five: Creative Stimuli

Describe the ideal environment for your creative process. Imagine it in all its detail. What distracts and what stimulates you? Are you alone or with others? Is there music playing? Are you outdoors? What tools do you need? Are you at home or at a quaint inn? Knowing what sparks your creative fire allows you to make that space. Lots of creative people talk about having a studio or room of their own.

Kay, a painter I know, can paint anywhere that's light enough if she has her female jazz singers serenading her in the background. Music is her cue to let go and play with her colors. Trudie, a landscape architect, built an office for herself above the garage. As she lives in the city and doesn't have a view of trees, her office walls are plastered with pictures of plants and trees and gardens, and she has silk flowers all over. Her outdoor carpet spreads out like a lawn, and her desk is a table inside a rickety old trellis with strings of vines and garden tools attached to it. She keeps bags of dirt and peat moss in the corner so she can smell them and pretend she's in the garden. You know what business she's in by looking at her workspace. Even if you only have a small space, make it your own and fill it with personal catalysts.

Sometimes when you have a business problem or feel stuck on a decision, nothing seems to help. Sit quietly and ask your intuitive guide for suggestions. You can also write yourself a note requesting an answer and put it in a drawer and let go for a while. Or you can change the format of your project or question and see what happens. I often find that drawing a picture of what I'm trying to write about opens up new angles.

Other innovators try techniques like turning a project upside down or sideways, miniaturizing it, making it into a story, photographing it, or discussing it with a child. These configurations often cut through the haze. You've heard tales of inventions that were actually mistakes or the result of a hairbrained scheme. Experiment with your dilemma and watch the solution appear.

Comparisons are also helpful. For example, Barbara's intuition urged her to ponder how her

> *Experiment with your dilemma and watch the solution appear.*

decision about whether or not to cut staff was like a tree. So she bundled up in her parka and went out to look at the oak in her front yard. She finally realized that her employees were like the roots of her company; they held the tree up. Cutting an employee was like chopping off a necessary root—yet she had to cut the payroll. So she went back into the house and began to draft plans for reduced hours, part-time positions, and job-sharing. Honor your intuitive messages and allow them to help you.

<center>~~~~</center>

Exercise Six: *Your Creative Saboteurs*

Write down all the things, people, places, activities, or thoughts that diminish your creative energy. What would you like to subtract from your life that interferes with the clarity of your intuitive channel?

Your intuition is a valuable asset; you can't afford to have it compromised by clutter, other people's needs, or busyness. Even if you only find the time to write in your creative journal or sit quietly for fifteen minutes a day, you are connecting with your intuition. Preserve the messages and insights.

From the above list, what can you subtract from your life to free up more creative space for yourself? What life choices support your ingenious energy? Honor your individual cravings and notions. Do you thrive in tranquility or excitement? Diligently restructure your lifestyle to cultivate your intuitive knowledge and its creative offshoots. Enjoy the new and exciting adventures that will result.

Take an hour to reflect, identify, and write down your own definition of success that expresses your self-knowledge, your loves and dislikes, your energy level, your recipe for balance, your values and life purpose, and your chosen lifestyle. This foundation gives you a guiding light of clarity to rely on daily as you transform your life, one success strategy at a time.

FINDING YOUR LIFE PURPOSE

One of life's universal questions is "Why am I here?" My clients and I work together every day to find the right answers. When we can grasp the meaning of life for us as individuals, we can create a travel itinerary for our life's journey. It provides a focus and a framework from which to make life choices and direct our creative efforts. My definition of purpose is an intention with meaning. What is meaningful to us personally becomes the center point for our circle of life.

When I work with clients trying to help them find their perfect work and get their creative genius out into the world, I take them through a series of exercises just like the ones you just read, plus a number of other ones. I also use career and personality tests like the MBTI, the Campbell Skills and Assessment Test, and the Strong Interest Inventory Test as scanners to see if other options surface. I have also just been trained in scientific hand analysis, a tool that helps people to discover their life purpose that I now offer to clients. The results are amazing. The information from my client's self-assessment, testing, and personal development exercises, plus my intuition and years of experience, usually combine to give us a plan and target a few options. Then I send people out to do some strategic experiments to test out our hypotheses about what they are destined to do next in their lives. I have them keep a journal about how they feel and think about their experiences. Most of the time, we can find a clear path or maybe two paths to choose from. But sometimes people are still lost or conflicted, so we try other techniques like visualization, active imagination, my positive choices program, etcetera to try to shake loose what they may be resisting seeing.

CHALLENGE

1. Write down and/or make a visual representation of personal and heartfelt success for you. Include your thoughts on career, money, health, friends and family, romance, personal growth, fun and recreation, organization, home and, of course, your creativity! If you are stuck on this exercise, please refer to either of my books, my visualizations, or my website for an abundance of stimulating exercises to facilitate a vision for you. Even if you have done a similar exploration before, do it again. Our world has changed significantly, and so have you, so it's time to update your vision.

2. Meditate on what contentment is for you and see if you can discover a symbol of success that will serve as a metaphor to guide you. One of my clients sees success as a wild kangaroo running free in Australia, while another one sees success as a cushy lounge chair. Once you find your symbol, figure out a way that you can interact with it daily. Then watch how much clearer and focused you are!

A couple of years ago, I was on a teleclass call with Ali Brown. She talked about how a hand analysis reading with Baeth Davis had changed her life. Baeth had told Ali that she would become internationally known and help women all over the world to build businesses and happy lives. At first Ali didn't take this seriously, but now she does and is living that life. Baeth Davis is known as "The Hand Analyst." She helps people to find their life purpose, runs mentoring programs, and founded The Hand Analyst, Inc. A number of other women in the book also had their hands read by Baeth and found the information was a breakthrough for them. So, being committed to helping people to find their life purpose and create businesses and lives that are glorious, I had to learn the hand analysis technique.

When I went to one of Baeth's workshops and had my hands read, I was stunned by how accurate the information she gleaned from my handprint was. I did some research, and apparently hand analysis is a science with very specific outcomes that has been around for thousands of years.

Like Ali, Baeth has a huge vision. As Baeth says, "My intention is to reach hundreds of millions of people and help them discover their life purpose. I want to make the language about purpose commonplace in the world dialogue so that families wonder, 'what's my child's life purpose.' It's one of the first things they find out in order to nurture and support that child to truly actualize what they've come here to do."

Baeth believes that one of the major reasons that people struggle in their relationships and in their work is because they are not connected to their deepest self. She says, "The work I do quite literally offers you a spiritual plan, a set of spiritual tools to understand the 'why' and the 'what for' of your life on the planet, what you are here to express and accomplish in your lifetime. Because we have not only our own life purpose to fulfill, our own evolution, but we are working together to evolve the purpose of humanity." As Baeth says, she cannot read everyone's hands herself, so she is training a group of us to help her bring this tool out into the mainstream. I've always been a great believer in prevention, and if parents can use this technology to discover their own life purpose and live it, and then help their child to grow in the right direction toward his or her life purpose, then we can prevent the stress that so many people who are not in touch with their life purpose experience." I love big visions and this is one that I am thrilled to be part of; it fits my life purpose of Passionate Guide and Mentor in the Spotlight.

So many people show up in my office upset that they didn't have a miracle in their lives where a voice told them at a young age what kind of work or creative expression they ought to pursue. We do a terrible job in this country of helping young people trust their inspirations and pursue work that truly fascinates them. Someone usually tries to talk you out of what you know inside to be true, and then you get into the wrong career and struggle. The Challenges in this book are meant to help you to tap into your inner knowing, your creativity, and your commitment to serve, and point you in the right direction toward your purpose. If you know your purpose already, this book will deepen it and give you powerful tools to unleash it.

Secret Two

Sift Through Your Ideas to Get Heart-Focused

"The best and most beautiful things in the world cannot be seen or even touched. They must be felt with the heart."
—*Helen Keller*

EMBRACE YOUR FLOW OF IDEAS

I was recently searching for my winter clothes; I found my fluffy white suede jacket and threw it on to go to a meeting. After I got home, I was digging business cards out of my pockets and discovered this quote from a fortune cookie:

"Ideas not coupled with action never become bigger than the brain cells they occupied."

How timely for me, and for all of us with creative ideas popping in our heads. I just cleaned out some file drawers and found papers with all kinds of ideas written on them—book ideas, marketing ideas, big vision ideas, joint venture ideas, watercolor painting ideas, and the list goes on. I put all those papers in a pile (after putting many pages in the recycling bin) and it is now one and a half feet high.

I noted that some of these ideas were written down numerous times and some of them I didn't remember writing at all. My first reaction to this pile was dread. Yet, I stood back from this pile and gave thanks instead.

Many years ago, I took the Johnson O'Connor Aptitude Tests and scored in the 99th percentile on ideaphoria—the rapid flow of ideas. I like to define the word as the ability to generate lots of thoughts and ideas quickly. It is an experience where one feels a constant onslaught of new ideas, creating a euphoric state of idea creation. I should mention that I flunked spatial relations with blocks, which is why I never became an interior designer on the side, even though I love color. My ideaphoria is a true gift—I suspect many of you reading this book have it as well—yet it has to be managed.

It's all about choices. From this abundance of ideas, I get to choose which ones I will do this year and which ones I will postpone until next year or three years from now. Some of these ideas will never happen—I don't have enough time to dance with them all. People with ideaphoria have to learn to take action and execute their ideas, not just let them sit in piles. Idea books and idea folders are wonderful tools. But at some point, we have to use our good sense and intuition and commit to a plan of action and explore one or more of the ideas to their fullest.

This past year I moderated a panel on "The Next Big Idea" for the Massachusetts Women's Conference. We talked about how to activate our ideas and then craft them into something original and useful. Your ideas are your most valuable asset. Write them down somewhere, review them regularly, and tune into which ones you are most passionate about. Be thankful that your brain clicks into gear and that you think of new ideas. Even if they are wild and crazy, these ideas may lead you somewhere.

Each year, in the quiet of December, I take my pile of ideas and select those treasures that are calling to me the most for the coming year. These ideas will be cultivated and nourished. And I will take a moment to express my gratitude for these ideas. I will also carefully make a new file for the next batch for the following year.

I recently purchased four new, lovely, ivory wooden file cabinets with sixteen file drawers for my office. It was a reluctant purchase, since we already have file cabinets all over the house that have been cleared out of junk. But I had to face the fact that I needed these new files to be truly organized. My husband put them together for me, and then I had two wonderful women take my piles of papers (we right-brainers like to make piles so that we can see things, but then we spend too much time going through the piles and get overwhelmed) and make several hundred new folders with printed labels. They put the piles into files where they should be. My desk is now clear except for my Treasure Map of goals, which I use as a blotter, and a small, three-shelf tray with current to-dos.

I feel immense relief, but I do have to remind myself to check the files regularly so that I don't lose touch with the gems in them. As a writer, I collect articles of interest and research about things I want to write about, and I have files on book ideas, book marketing, social media, all of my clippings from fifty-plus magazines and other periodicals, business articles for my clients, and so on. This is valuable information to save. I religiously throw out and recycle anything I can. So while it is a lot of paper, I bless these files now because they are my creative resources, not something to be embarrassed about, especially since they are now organized. Know that your ideas are the keys to your creative gifts and service in this world.

I must sheepishly add here that when I interviewed Shama Kabani, the award-winning online marketing expert who was named one of the Top 25 Entrepreneurs Under Age 25 by *BusinessWeek* in 2009 and is the President of the Marketing Zen Group, she told me that she does not do anything with paper. Shama said, "No, I can't remember the last time I wrote something. The only time I hold a pen is when I sign checks. If someone wants to send me something, I ask them to please send it digitally because I don't want any paper. I don't have an office and I don't have anywhere to keep it. Even when I get business cards, I take pictures of them, and then throw away the cards." I know for me, and for many of my older clients and the older women that I interviewed for this book, we grew up with paper and real books, and still work that way. Even when I write, I have to print each chapter out on paper; sometimes I even use different colors, because the words look different on the printed page than they do on the laptop screen. I take my hat off to Shama and her generation for being able to really work paperlessly.

MANAGING IDEAPHORIA

Ideaphoria is also called divergent thinking. Many jobs, careers, and educational programs teach the opposite model, convergent thinking, which is critical thinking. This is the kind of critical and logical thinking used to evaluate ideas and choices. The SATs are convergent, which is why many brilliant idea people don't do well on them. In fact, there is one study that indicates that teachers do not enjoy working with divergent thinkers. That is interesting, because Johnson O'Connor themselves write that "the best trait of a teacher is ideaphoria." Ideaphoria is an important aspect of creativity, but originality, flexibility, and elaboration are important too. The ideaphoria part is often about word association, fantasy, story-telling, and analogies, linking unrelated things.

The challenge for people with ideaphoria is choosing what to focus on and getting it done without changing your mind or moving on to a new project. Focus and execution are key skills that those of us with ideaphoria need to learn. People with ideaphoria can often have multiple careers—copywriters, novelists, teachers, inventors, designers, entrepreneurs, artists, sales people, marketers—any career where they can express their rapid, ceaseless flow of ideas. Therefore, they may have erratic career paths, feel unfocused, have closets full of unfinished projects, and may not stay with things long enough to be successful with them. Successful people open the windows of opportunity to generate ideas and then close the windows securely to evaluate those ideas. People with ideaphoria see connections among things that other people don't see. They are big picture people, change agents, generalists, and can have trouble specializing. This can hurt them financially, as they need to settle down and work on one thing at a time and not get distracted. Barbara Sher refers to people with ideaphoria as "scanners." When I see clients with ideaphoria, I try to brainstorm with them about ways to have what I call "umbrella careers" that combine a variety of things that they love to do. But they have to focus on a limited number of projects at a time. Being an entrepreneur can be a good route, as you have flexibility and can focus on the big picture, but you need to have people to help you execute your vision.

Highly creative people quite often have ideaphoria combined with strong intuitive skills, high emotional intelligence, and a keen awareness of their senses. They can absorb things like a sponge, which can make them tired, anxious, and overwhelmed. Issues of self-esteem, lack of self-acceptance, and weak problem-solving skills can undermine the careers of people with ideaphoria, leaving them under-employed, unhappy, and underpaid. Sometimes highly creative people are misdiagnosed with anxiety and depression when they simply need outlets for their creative ideas. They need people and projects that can benefit from their highly productive capacity for new ideas—it is creative imagination.

There are six strategies that I teach people who have ideaphoria to help them avoid its pitfalls:

1. Celebrate your talents and heal from your misunderstandings. One potential pitfall is negative self-talk, with you wishing that you were more focused. Acknowledge that you need meaningful projects in which to express your creativity and that you may have multiple careers and identities, and that is okay. There is nothing wrong with you, but you do need to learn how to control it. You are also vulnerable to burnout and sensory overload.

2. Be sure to come up with an effective way to record your ideas daily; then look for patterns or themes. Your ideas are valuable. Then focus on which one to three ideas excite you the most right now.

3. Learn to say NO, not now. You need strong filters so that you don't get overloaded with too much input. You need to put up formidable boundaries. Unsubscribe from magazines, blogs, newsletters, etc. and make a decision about what new data you are willing to receive right now and delete the rest—for now. Look at the short-term view of what you are working on at the moment and beware of the lure of bright, shiny, new objects. Note them down and file them away until later.

4. Clear the clutter in your life. Keep one or two books by your bed, not fifteen. Find someone who can help you to get organized and clear away everything that you are not going to complete. A personal organizer who is very structured can be a life changer.

5. You must develop a decision-making process for yourself, which is why a coach or a mentor is essential. Think in three-month quarters, and plot out what you will do during that time to support your big vision and your life purpose. Then cut down your list so that it is realistic. Can't decide what book to write? Start with the one that you most want to write or one that is almost complete that you still feel passionate about—but choose one. Several support systems may be needed to keep you on track.

6. Design a daily centering process to review your goals and affirmations each morning, so that you remember what they are. Because you are so attracted to the new and the novel, you may forget your current plan and not reap the benefits of your idea generation and execution.

Convergent thinkers are creative too, but they may need a push to learn to tap into their creative ideas. Start by keeping an Excitement List. For two weeks, write down anything that excites you—a color, a word, a concept, a person— and then have someone help you look at the patterns. Then try the Creativity Catalysts at the end of the chapter for a jump-start. You can train yourself to notice your creative ideas by journaling about them with your Excitement List, and by having novel and interesting adventures every week to stimulate new ways of thinking.

Take a different route home from work, wear a color that you never wore before (that's in your color chart, of course), talk to an intriguing person in a favorite store, travel to someplace you have longed to see. Shake up your life and see what emerges. It's all about making new connections between concepts.

INFUSING YOUR MUSE

It is vital that you make a connection with your inner muse so that she or he can become your personal Idea Manager. You need tools and assistance that will help you to capture your ideas so that you don't lose your inspiration. But you need your muse to walk you through a system that leads to evaluating and deciding about these choices. Ultimately, you must choose only one to three creative projects at a time or your energy will be much too scattered.

A lot of my coaching work with clients involves taking them through a research and decision-making process about each of their precious creative ideas and helping them to choose the wisest and most compelling one to focus on. Our first step, though, is getting acquainted with our inner muse. My muse, Tiffany, is a lovely, blonde, classy lady who lives in a luxurious cave high above the Coral Beach Club in Bermuda with a view of my beloved beach with its clear blue water, gorgeous grape leaves, and caves to explore. I discovered her many years ago in a meditation at EST and she has been my inner guide ever since. She meets with me whenever I like.

Here are some tips to help you find and build a solid relationship with your muse.

My friend Deborah Knox sent me an amazing book called *Sleeping with Schubert* by Bonnie Marson. It is a story of the transformation of a bored female lawyer, Liza Durbin, who was inhabited by the composer Franz Shubert's spirit. Her life became a creative journey extraordinaire. All of a sudden, she was playing concerts, listening to all kinds of music, co-composing music, and launching into a career as a performer. While there were many anxious moments and lots of controversy, Liza had the opportunity to dance and converse with a musical genius, and she became immersed in her own creative gifts and explorations. It is an engaging tale of passion, love, and creative risk-taking. While it is a fictional story, there are many lessons woven into the story for those of us with creative souls. These lessons include:

- Read about the lives of creative people you admire in your field, visit their houses, look at their original works, and study their contemporaries in diverse fields.

- Take a day or a week to pretend you are one of your muses and dress like them, visit their city, or adopt their creative schedules or habits. Get as much insight as possible into their lives and talents.

- Make a collage about your muse and study it. Then, at the right time, choose his or her best success strategies and incorporate them into your own creative practice.

- When you are ready to grow again, move on to a new mentor and begin the process anew. It will be life-changing!

An interesting note: this was Bonnie's first novel, and film rights for the book were recently purchased by Paramount Pictures. Bonnie is a long-time artist, and her own adventure with a muse has brought her great success.

WHEN I MET MY MUSE

"I glanced at her and took my glasses off—they were still singing. They buzzed like a locust on the coffee table and then ceased. Her voice belled forth, and the sunlight bent. I felt the ceiling arch, and knew that the nails up there took a new grip on whatever they touched. 'I am your own way of looking at things,' she said. 'When you allow me to live with you, every glance at the world around you will be a sort of salvation. And I took her hand.'"
—Wilma Stafford

Now is the perfect time to connect more deeply with your inner muse and invite new mentors and colleagues to support your creative growth. Consider the following questions:

1. What actions can I take to spend more time with my inner creative guide?

2. What inner messages do I need to honor to make my creativity a priority right now?

3. What kind of creative skill development do I need to tackle? What will take me to a higher level of expertise?

4. Who am I attracted to who could potentially be a new mentor or colleagues, and how do I access these people?

Enjoy your adventures!

Now that you have your muse to be CEO of your ideas, you need to review the ideas that are lurking in your life. Go through all of your files and piles of paper at home and at work and pull out all of your scraps of paper with genius written on them. Go into all of your closets and collect the unfinished paintings, quilts, sweaters, flower arrangements, photos to be organized, proposals never completed, new business ideas, joint ventures that never manifested, and all other creative initiatives. Then look around your home and office and take note of rooms that are only half decorated and either photograph them or make a sketch of them. Dig up catalogs of courses not taken, workshops not attended, novels and poems unfinished, e-books begun, things not built, and so on. Collect everything in one room if you can. If you can't, find representations of the "ideas" that are revolving around in your head, write them down on note cards, and add them to the pile.

Carve out a day when you will not be interrupted to begin dealing with these ideas. Use your intuition as your guide for now. Sort the ideas into three categories:

1. Ideas that I love that I want as part of my legacy

2. Ideas that I used to be excited about but now I'm not sure about

3. Ideas or projects that I feel repelled by, bored by, embarrassed by, or that elicit some negative emotion

Start with pile number three. Throw out, donate, or give away—no kidding—any unfinished project that you really don't want to complete. Clear them out and get rid of them. Many dumps have "gift houses" where people would love to pick up your pattern for a sweater or your collection of poetry books or your art easel. Recycle everything you can. Give things or project ideas or books to others who have that interest. The old projects that you are not committed to are taking up valuable real estate in your mind. They are negative stressors that I call Serenity Stealers—let them go. This process may be hard. You may cry, or start a rap of negative self-talk about how you should finish them now or you would have finished them if only you weren't so lazy. Turn off the tape—we all try things and do creative experiments that don't click with us. Throw out all of your old work proposals, marketing materials, and planning notes that you know in your heart are never going to happen. Releasing all these old ideas and projects is absolutely necessary to making your work a creative success. So close your eyes and move on.

If you can't bear to part with something and you must save it, put it in a box or a file marked "review in three months" and put it out of sight.

Look at pile number two—"ideas that you used to be excited about but now you are not sure about." Go through this pile and remove anything that doesn't make your heart sing. If you are really ambivalent, you can put it in the "review in three months" box.

Now, it is time to explore pile number one—"ideas that I love and are part of my legacy." This will be a treat! Put these ideas and projects in order, beginning with the premier idea that you are most excited about. The last one on the list should be a project that you know you want to complete but that is the least appealing right now. Now look at this group.

1. Are there any projects here that are close to completion? Estimate how much time it would take to complete them. This includes services or products that are done but that need to be sold or marketed.

2. Of any of these ideas or projects that are close to completion, would it benefit you to pick one or two of these and get them done and out into the world right now?

3. Identify the top three projects that you love. Which one(s) most reflect what you are known for or want to be known for? For example, I have an idea for a book called "Watercolor Woman" that I would love to write, but it's not a top priority for my business like this book is—plus there is a novel by that title already, so I have to come up with a new name.

We all try creative experiments that don't click with us. Throw out your old work proposals, marketing materials, and planning notes you know in your heart are never going to happen. Releasing these old ideas is absolutely necessary to making your work a creative success.

If you are unsure about your top three ideas/projects, do some research on Google and Amazon on those topics. What's already out there? How is your idea different? Does it look like there is a market for this service? Talk to your clients and colleagues and ask them if they would be interested in a product like yours, being careful not to tell them too much about it unless you know and trust them.

Do your research in depth. My first product was an audiotape workshop with three meditations and a mini-workbook, all on a cassette tape called *Positive Choices: From Stress to Serenity*. While I spoke with several bookstores about packaging, etcetera, I didn't get enough good information. With the limited knowledge I had at the time, I created one tape and tucked the nine workshop exercises into the cover case. I loved that it was all so compact. What I learned later, however, was that I probably should have done a four- to six-tape box series to get the big catalog companies and bookstores really interested. Fortunately, people loved the single tape, and several companies sold them at tradeshows and in stores. I only have a handful left, but they keep selling, and I plan on reissuing it as an updated CD soon.

Part of what you have to decide about your top three ideas is which one you love the most and which one is the most relevant to your work or least expensive. Ideally, we want to choose the idea or project that fascinates us and that we strongly believe will serve others and reflect our professional or personal mission.

Sometimes our favorite idea is ahead of its time or it's a very long-term project. So we have to decide: do we want to spend a few months working on one or two projects that we can complete and put out into the world right away, or do we respond to our "calling" to do idea or project number one?

Now is the time to gather up the top projects and put them in a circle, if possible, and sit in the middle. Find a quiet time where you can meditate and talk to your muse about your decision. When you are ready, sit in the circle and notice where your attention is drawn most. Sit comfortably with your palms facing up, close your eyes, and ask your inner guide this question: "Which idea or project will best serve me and others in the world at this time?" Listen to whatever answer you get. Go pick up that idea or project and hold it in your hand or your lap. See if it feels "right" to you. If not, look around and see which one idea or project you really want to work on and bring that into the circle as well. If there is still a third idea or project that is calling to you, bring that third one in close to you as well.

Now, close your eyes and invite your muse into the circle to join you. When he or she arrives, open your eyes and describe in detail each idea or project and how you feel about it. Tell your muse who would use it and how it would help them in their lives. Be as complete as possible. If your muse asks you questions, answer them. Then close your eyes and ask your muse for guidance—and listen to what he or she tells you. Do you feel like you have the information you need to decide? If so, write out your commitment to your one to three projects, putting a realistic timeframe on each. You may decide to focus on number one exclusively for now, and that is fine.

JJ Virgin, celebrity nutritionist and costar of the new reality TV show *Freaky Eaters* on TLC, had Baeth Davis do a hand analysis on her. One of her life lessons is "overwhelm." Finding her focus is a challenge for her, as it is for me. As JJ says, "I download so many things from my brain, I wonder where the dimmer switch is. So then I think: Stop! If you look at those who are truly successful, they are focused; they don't have fifty thousand different things they're doing. One of the things I'm working on is focusing, and not working on ten thousand things at once. If I have a thought, but if three or four days later I'm not still thinking about it, because if you're going to build a business you have to live it and breathe it, then I let it go. It has to be 'Oh, I have to do this' before I embrace an idea. It's really matching that idea with your passion and what the marketplace wants, in a format that's going to work. All those things have to work. There has to be return on investment; the margins have to be there. You have to be able to market it, you have to want it and stay excited about it, and if it doesn't meet all of those tests, don't do it."

Congrats if you have found your focus! If nothing feels right yet, try doing this Creativity Catalysts Exercise and start over. This is a great exercise to stimulate new ideas or check the decision you just made.

Exercise: Creativity Catalysts Exercise

We know we are creative beings. Yet we are also very aware that sometimes our creativity stalls, plays tricks on us, or appears to have vanished completely. It is at those moments that we need to reconnect with the vitality around our creative process or project and leverage our inspirational powers to stimulate our ability to make new connections.

The following tips are meant to arouse your natural creative gifts so that you can surmount the obstacles in your journey and achieve maximum potential. Have fun with them, and enjoy the wonder of discovery as you expand your imagination and allow yourself to be a conduit for excellent work!

- Keep a daily excitement list about why you are passionate and committed to your exploration or creative project or hypothesis.

- Visualize your end result and make a collage of images that support that vision and post it where you can see it regularly.

- Take a field trip relating to your project to explore a particular facet of it.

- Experience your project using the three learning styles of visual, auditory, and kinesthetic experiences.

- Draw a picture of it, make a mind-map of it, or take a photo of it and play with it on Photoshop.

- Talk about your project on a tape or video recorder or teach a real or pretend class on the topic to an audience or to your friends.

- Act it out with props and maybe even other characters.

- Record and follow your intuitive clues relating to your project.

- Go to a toy store and select a toy that reminds you of your project and let your inner child play with it.

- Set up a series of experiments related to your project with hypotheses to test out.

- Exercise regularly to clear your head.

- Find someone who is an opposite thinker (a devil's advocate) from you, tell them about your project, and let them challenge or stimulate your thinking.

- Select inspiring music that resonates with your project and play it at the beginning of your work time.

- Create a water experience—sit in a hot tub, go swimming, take a shower, or visit a spa to increase your flow of ideas.

- Take your project away with you as a companion and see how it changes in a new setting.

- Meditate or pray about your topic.

- Find a symbol of your creative process and keep it close by when you are working or contemplating.

- Initiate creative rituals, such as lighting a candle or reading before you begin, to invite your muse into the project.

- Look at visual representations relating to your project, like paintings, special destinations, or actual products related to your story.

- Send your inner critic to a foreign land so you feel free to make mistakes and cast about for new connections.

- Change your location—work on your project in bed, outside in nature, in a museum, or simply change rooms.

- Take a day or two off so you can take a fresh look at your project when you return.

- Keep a file card packet in your office, car, etc. to jot down all related ideas and thoughts, even if their meaning is a mystery.

- Read related books and articles and take notes to jog your inspiration.

- Look for the metaphors—how is your proposal like an artichoke or a trolley car?

- Keep a separate journal or computer file for each project and keep track of new impressions.

- At the right time, share your project with trusted others and gather new insights.

- Take creative risks using your fascinations as a guide to unique explorations.

GETTING HEART-FOCUSED

The word "passion" is often thought to be an overused word these days, however it does help you to get heart centered on what you want your work and your life to be about. The messages that you get from your heart chakra are a guide, and those messages emanate from your life purpose and your fascinations. Dr. Gayle Madeleine Randall, MD, is a physician, scientist, medical professor, cross-cultural practitioner, and a writer. Madeleine says, "One of the secrets to my success is always following my passion, and listening to what my heart tells me to do. Whether or not it conforms to what other people think I should do or other people think they should do. Early in my cross cultural exploration at UCLA, I helped set up a series of conferences on what we then called 'alternative medicine.' It was considered pretty out there. However, surprisingly, it was so well received that it just grew and grew. I think that one of the secrets is to follow your passion, because it's trying to tell you something. Yes, of course, you should use your mind, logic, and knowledge that you can't run after everything. Because then you're just going to be running, from thing to thing, diluting your energy. In my experience almost everything I have done has gone toward the same core purpose, and that is ultimately to help people and myself, and to heal the planet. Don't forget about Mother Earth and that we make up nine-tenths of the planet."

Multimillionaire mom Sheri McConnell, CEO of the Smart Women's Institute of Entrepreneurial Learning, is an expert on helping women start businesses and build associations or membership sites. When I asked her where she first got the idea for membership sites, Sheri said, "You know, it came from passion. I was at home, I had just had my third little girl, and at that point in my life I totally needed other adults. I was seeking other women to hang out with so I could be a little sane, since it was the first time in my life that I wasn't working toward a degree or working in the corporate world. It was the first time I gave myself permission to relax and look at my passion, and I was about twenty-eight at that point. I had left Verizon Wireless after two or three years and so I had time to think, 'what do I love?' At that point, having already gotten my master's in Organizational Management, I knew it was writing, because that's all you do in your master's program is write, write, write. I became the regional representative for the International Women's Writing Guild in the Dallas/Fort Worth area. I was doing all this work for them and then I decided that I ought to do all this work for my own business. So that's how I got started with the association model, but I took the traditional model and put it on the Internet and merged the best of both models."

As one of the hosts of Conscious Talk radio, along with her husband, Rob Spears, Brenda does weekly interviews that bring forth new ideas that help people live a more conscious life in a down-to-earth, boots on the ground style, while empowering her listeners to live in accordance with their deeper values. Brenda began her career as an aspiring actress and television host, but was removed from that limelight when she was diagnosed with her third bout of cancer. After her diagnosis, and upon deep reflection, she began a non-traditional healing journey that ultimately healed her body, mind, and soul. Besides her soon to-be-published book coming out, her passion now is communicating through the media outlets. Conscious Talk has been on the air for nine years and is being expanded into more markets through syndications. Conscious Talk, where I have been a guest several times, is an informative and compelling alternative talk show that was one of the first radio shows in the Seattle area pioneering a shift in consciousness. The show topics cover politics, money, conscious consuming, spiritual and alternative healing, as well as social, environmental, and relational issues. Brenda and Rob are cancer survivors and do individual sessions with people, along with webinars and workshops on Conscious Living. As Brenda says, "I am passionate about creating, speaking, and communicating through terrestrial radio, the Internet, and television in order to get our message out." Brenda also sits on the Board of Advisors for a new nonprofit cancer foundation called Emerald Heart Cancer Foundation, and is an anchor writer for a beautiful online women's magazine called *Sibyl*.

A long time ago, I read Victoria Moran's early book, *Creating a Charmed Life*, and wrote her a letter telling her how much I enjoyed her work. She was still living in Kansas City but she was plotting to move to her beloved New York City, because writers live there. We met shortly after that when we were both in the city and she invited me to meet her for high tea at The Plaza. We've been friends ever since, and we help each other out whenever we can. As Victoria says, "I am first and foremost a writer, and I am a writer with a mission. I really believe that I have something to share, both about living with this childlike sense of magic and also living in a way that is compassionate and astonishingly healthy. So that's how I see everything first. When people ask me, 'What do you do?' I always say: 'I write books.' I've said that for a long time. I've thought about trying to train myself to say some of the other things, but it's just automatic. What do you do? I write books. This is my legacy. This is what I came to the earth to do. But while I'm doing something else, I'm focusing on that. I mean I love speaking; I just love it, it's the most fun. The one thing that I really want to get more clear on as I go along, and as the new media progresses and is easier to understand, is where *not* to put energy and emphasis. Right now, as part of a platform for being a writer, it's very important to be able to say I do this or that online, but there's also the reality of how much good is that really doing? How many people are my efforts really reaching? I need to weed out what doesn't really have a return and focus on what does."

Victoria and I often speculate on what will happen to books and writers in the future with e-books, Kindles, etcetera in our midst. But we know in our hearts that there are many of us who were born to write and love to hold real printed books in our hands.

Sometimes our passion can even be a bit unconscious. My colleague Caroll Michels is the author of the classic book *How To Survive and Prosper as an Artist* as well as an artist advocate and career coach. She identified strongly with her creative father, who earned his living as a graphic designer but was actually a painter who had other interests as well. He always had a million projects going on at any one time. Caroll inherited his tendency to work on many things at once, although at the moment her passion is dance, especially the tango, and a fusion of ballet, modern, hip hop, and jazz. I get great holiday cards from her every year that depict her decked out in her dance attire doing some daring move. Before she became a career coach to artists, she was a sculptor herself and had a number of jobs, including a job in advertising. Her father was an important support system for her. But as Caroll says, "When it came time for my father to take his art out into the marketplace, this is where he froze. It wasn't until I was in my fifties that it hit me—look at what I do for a living. I am helping artists do what my father was unable to do. And that was a real mind-blower for me."

This next story speaks to the value of experience in helping young people zero in on what they want to do and what they are truly fascinated about. Kathleen Dudzinski, PhD, is the founder and director of the Dolphin Communication Project in Mystic, Connecticut. She attended a high school with programs in vocational agriculture and was part of the Future Farmers of America. There, she was able to blend her passion for animals and science. She worked at a veterinary clinic, raised chickens, and did petting zoos for local schools. Her love of the ocean and the coast came from summers with her family on Cape Cod and the Connecticut shore. While she was accepted to a number of prestigious colleges, she chose to go to the University of Connecticut because she did not want to start out her adult life in debt.

When she got to college, Kathleen says, "I knew I didn't want to go to veterinary school because I don't really like microscopes. I didn't know how to make a career out of what I wanted. I loved science and I could tell you the name of every single science teacher or professor I've had since the seventh grade, but in college I didn't know how to make a science career work. So I participated in as many internships as I could, doing labs and field work. During the summer after my sophomore year in college, my internship was with a whale watching company out of Gloucester, Massachusetts, and I was there from Memorial Day to Labor Day. We worked seven days a week, twelve hours a day, and I thoroughly enjoyed it and knew, okay, this is what I want to do. I started reading everything I could on mammals and I was drawn to communication and social behavior. I started applying for scholarships after college and was accepted into Texas A&M without a master's degree because I had published as an undergraduate. I went straight for my PhD and was awarded a National Science Foundation Pre-doctoral Fellowship.

"Then, in 1997, just after I finished my graduate degree, I was invited to participate in a film that Macgillivray Freeman Films was making for IMAX theaters called *Dolphins.* I put together a website that people could go to after they saw the film. Both Alejandrao Acevedo, another scientist in the film, and I spent a year visiting forty museums and theaters to introduce the film and develop programs for kids, again funded by NSF. During this time, I was also able to create my nonprofit, which allows us to do research in four locations and then take the research directly into the schools."

My favorite watercolorist and the author of a number of thoughtful and beautiful books, Jeanne Carbonetti, came to painting very early, she says, starting on her own with scribble pictures but taking no classes. It wasn't until she was a senior in high school that she took her first art class. "I remember doing the first oil painting that I was so excited about in that class, and going to the teacher at the end of the day asking if it was dry enough so that I could take it home. The teacher said, 'Oh, God, yes.' I think that's probably why, when I got to college, I minored in art history, not studio art, and majored in English literature."

Jeanne became an English teacher and her plan was to paint in the summers. But it wasn't enough. So she and her husband built a house and a gallery in Vermont and moved there. Painting became a key part of her life, as it had been when she was a child.

All of these women were guided to their passions; one by an illness, one by an internship, one by loneliness, and so forth. When we know our life purpose and tell the truth about what we love to do, we find our rightful place in the world and are able to make our unique and creative contribution. Too many women chase security or obligation until their soul starts screaming at them to change. We each have a gift and a chance to focus on the field or the ideas that make us want to get up in the morning and to begin every day with joy and an agenda.

Secret Three

Heal Your Self-Esteem and Your Fears

"When one woman honors who she is, all women collectively move closer to becoming what they are capable of being."
—*Unknown*

In order to be highly successful women, we have to treat ourselves with complete and total respect. Let me say that again—complete and total respect. Too many women underachieve, or play too small (when that's not what they choose), don't get paid what they are worth, belittle themselves, and walk around feeling wounded. Even women who are deemed successful can frequently be caught thinking that they are neither gifted nor special. While we have made great strides in many areas, this self-esteem injury that women have to deal with dashes too many hopes and dreams.

We want to be able to share our authentic selves in our creative work and in our lives. Step number one is to dismantle the limiting beliefs that we carry around that have been indoctrinated into our psyche. I have been amazed at how many of my individual clients, as well as the folks in my Out on a Limb Club groups, Creative Courage Catalyst groups, and Creative Success and Positive Choices workshops, have been haunted and daunted by myths. These axioms of "how life should be lived" have a range of origins—family, friends, colleagues, social theory, outdated norms from the past, old stereotypes about men and women, internal demons, or the projection of other people's fears. All of these myths and distortions eclipse your ability to claim the life that you are uniquely meant to live.

Common myths seem to be:

1. Your perfect job or career path will hit you like an epiphany at an early age (or else you are a lost soul).

2. You don't have the right to save your sanity and your health by leaving a horrible job, marriage, partnership, or business.

3. You need to underachieve or play "small" in your life so that your friends and family members (or their ghosts) will not be depressed or threatened by your talent and your success.

4. You have to do more than feels reasonable for you in order to achieve your goals and be recognized.

5. It is not okay if you don't know what your next step is (you need to be in control and have everything together at all times).

6. You will never recover from getting fired or divorced or rejected by anyone.

7. You can never fail at anything and, if you do, you should hide it.

8. Whatever the truth about your personal, creative work style, it can't be right, so you can't honor it.

9. You have to do things perfectly the first time, which denies that creativity is a process of experimentation and discovery.

10. If you can't be absolutely brilliant or the best at something early on, it's better to quit than to allow yourself to learn how to do it—skill by skill.

11. Criticism by anyone makes you lose your power.

Pay attention to which of these myths are operating in your life and undermining your personal power. You can't be the great businesswoman or professional that you are meant to be if you are afraid of making others feel insecure. Reclaim your own destiny. If you are miserable in any area of your life, choose a more positive direction. If you are afraid to confront the early stages of professional growth, tap into your beginner's mind and give yourself permission to learn the basics. Develop your own list of guiding principles that honor the human spirit, the imperfections of life, and the challenges of fear and change.

Women who are successful can get slammed—and it stings. But it comes with the territory. Ali Brown is a marketing whiz, runs $100K coaching programs and multiple businesses, and has a big vision to empower women to run viable and profitable businesses worldwide that make a difference. She is a generous and strong woman, but when I asked her about criticism, Ali said, "It hurts, though, because as women, we are so sensitive. One thing that comes from success that is nonnegotiable is that you have to accept the fact that not everyone will like you and you may even, in some cases, be detested by some people. This is just a sad, dark side that comes with success and it's such a minor part compared to all the joy, power, excitement, and happy benefits. People look at me and they think, 'She's fearless. She's got tough skin. Look at her go.' And then some little thing will happen or some woman will write something and I will just break down in tears."

After Shine (her annual women's business conference), some woman wrote Ali a lengthy letter saying that it was an insult to the audience that Ali looked so good on stage. The writer said "You've obviously been working out, you had beautiful clothes on, and it made me feel like I should be doing more than walking the dog." "Can you believe that?" Ali said. Ali said she cried, not only because it was an "ouch" but because during the whole time at Shine she was saying that you should do what's good for you. She told the women in the audience to shine their own light. That was the whole point. What made her sad is what women will do to each other.

Ali went on to say, "You know that's going to happen sometimes, and that it's going to hurt. It's more because of the bigger picture, that women sometimes do that to each other. It's the tall poppy syndrome. What frightens me? I think (and I'm happy to share this), that I am single. I have not had good, strong relationships, and I think that the last missing piece for me is the right guy. I remember seeing the cover of *People* or *InTouch* or something, and on the cover were Jennifer Aniston, Cameron Diaz, and another beautiful actress, I think it was Oprah, and the title said, 'Rich, beautiful, and alone.' And I thought 'ooh, ouch.' Deep down I wonder, am I going to be single forever? I know I'm not, but that's a fear for me. What if I never meet the right guy? I have a good feeling that he's coming soon. In the meantime, I just need to stay positive and open, because if I close myself off, that's not going to help. So I just have fun, and I know that I'll attract the right guy at the right time, whatever God has planned."

When I talked with Shama Kabani about her new book, *The Zen of Social Marketing,* some guy had just written a terrible review of the book on Amazon. This reviewer accused Shama of having made up all forty of her five star reviews, because no book could possibly have that many perfect reviews. Shama says, "I think a lot of entrepreneurs face this. Ten people can validate what you are doing, but if one person says, 'I don't think so,' that critical person can have more impact than your ten strongest supporters."

JJ Virgin, author of *Six Weeks to Sleeveless and Sexy,* had someone write a mean Amazon review about her book that brought her rating down from 5 stars to 4.5 stars. JJ says, "I know as I get bigger and bigger this will happen more; it happened when I was on the *Dr. Phil* show regularly, and I know it happens with TLC, too. There will always be people who will be critical of you. I mean, my gosh, there is a website called 'I Hate Rachael Ray.' How could anyone hate Rachael Ray? It would be like hating Katie Couric. There are always going to be people out there who are going to call you a freak or a quack or whatever. You've heard the saying, 'well-behaved women do not make history.' You have to be controversial. If you start giving everyone vanilla ice cream, who cares? They've already got it. So if you really want to get out there, you can't be saying the same old stuff."

Pat Schroder was certainly controversial during her days in Congress, and I remember always seeing her on TV and in the papers back then. Pat was the Democratic member of the United States House of Representatives from Colorado from 1973–1997 and then went on to become the CEO and President of the Association of American Publishers for eleven years. As Pat says about her days in Congress, "I was always so high profile. I kept warning myself to engage my brain before starting to speak, but there were some days that I didn't quite follow my own advice. I would end up on the front page of the paper for something I said and my mother would say, 'I can't believe you said that.' The classic that almost put my mother over the edge was when about the fiftieth person said to me, 'how can you be a mother and a congresswoman?' And I finally lost it and I said, 'I have a brain, I have a uterus, and they both work, next question.' You know, of course, I have had to eat those words forever. I often got in trouble that way."

Pat talked about how she worked hard for programs for the people, especially women, children, daycare, and veterans, and that the guys in Congress and the press would just roll their eyes when she brought up these topics. As she says, "They really should be issues for both men and women and yet, somehow in our culture, they're not. I used to always say to the guys when they'd say, 'Oh there you go again,' I'd say, 'Well look, if you want to bring it up, fine, I've got all the talking points right here. I understand their hesitation because they never had anybody in Congress talking about family issues. They felt those were kind of girly man issues or power issues. I don't know what they wanted me to talk about, but it was always a constant struggle that way. But I think, to be honest, that women find this in the workplace all the time."

We need to free ourselves from the limitations in our minds and support ourselves and other humans in the quest for fulfillment. Exploding these myths and having the courage to craft your own path mandates support. Whatever personal challenges you may face, you increase your likelihood of success if you admit you need support systems to stay focused and brave. More about that later.

The world is changing so quickly that it has us all reeling. Everything is changing in terms of how we work, how we communicate, how we spend time (or not) with people we love, having multiple careers and not retiring, and so on. It is a lot to absorb and can put extra stress on us. Change is constant, we know, but we are living in a time of radical changes—and that can be unnerving.

I mentioned earlier that Victoria Moran moved herself and her family to NYC because that's where writers live and thrive. She is a popular speaker, and she speaks all over the country. She has a radio show and takes a special interest in spirituality and health. She also writes about being a vegan, and she knows every good vegan restaurant in the city. Anyway, she is a sassy woman who has been independently self-employed for many moons. When I asked her what she still feared, she said "financial insecurity." When I asked her more about that, as she has clearly been successful as a writer plus other things, she said, "I have been preparing for the idea that old writers don't retire, they just die. But now, writers young and old are having a lot of trouble getting paid. I mean, the magazine work I used to do is largely gone, the Web doesn't pay, and opportunities for speaking have been depressed for a couple of years. The need for revolutionary reinvention in order to be financially viable is a big challenge. But I look around my life and I think, 'Oh my, this is amazing. And I think the most important thing about feeling good that is to keep that overall sense and not let what goes on in any particular day shake that."

Victoria wants to do more with TV, radio, and as a corporate spokesperson. She is writing a new book she is passionate about called *Main Street Vegan: Everything You Need to Know To Eat Healthfully and Live Compassionately in the Real World.* She will reroute herself just fine. Anyone who is a writer now needs to pay attention to what is happening with e-books, apps, video, and social media and develop some new strategies. Whatever field you are in, change is happening—things are disappearing and creativity will give you a real edge in the marketplace right now. Think about how you can make or invent something new.

I asked Victoria for her intuitive sense of what is happening out there in the world right now and she replied, "We went to the Museum of American Finance on Wall Street last weekend, which was so interesting. The overarching impression that I left with was how cyclic the economy is. It goes up and down; it always has. I don't understand the fine points of economics, but I do have a very strong belief that we are generally taken care of. I understand that there are people who fall through the cracks, but when I look around at large groups of people—you go to a sporting event or a concert and you're looking at a few thousand people—I want to look around and say, 'Oh my goodness, these people are all being taken care of!' And I see the New York City pigeons and the squirrels in Central Park being taken care of and I just keep that in my mind."

Once you can let go of these outrageous limiting beliefs and embrace a "can-do" attitude, you can move into action mode and make a space in your life to let more of the "real you" emerge and create. In my training classes with creativity coaches, as well as with my regular clients, the question often comes up of how much to reveal about yourself on your website, in your business name, in your artwork, and in your life. Creativity is about personal expression, and our creative efforts should be directed at things we feel called to do and are strongly connected to. Our choices reveal what we value and what we are thinking about.

Authenticity is a key dynamic in relationships and support systems of all kinds. People want to feel that they know who we are and what we are about. When we live a false life, it is tedious and unfulfilling, and can even be dangerous.

Olga Aura is a Master Your Destiny Mentor who empowers women entrepreneurs to unleash their "gold" power in the form of a bestseller, a big event, or even a blockbuster. She calls herself a modern-day shaman. In 1996, Olga's team won an Olympic gold medal in Atlanta for rhythmic gymnastics. She'd come from Ukraine, where she had been training since the age of five. She came to America at age fourteen, and she didn't get back on the bus. Instead, she accepted the invitation from a family in North Carolina to stay in the United States, go to school, and learn English. After finishing high school, Olga went to college. Then the challenges began.

Olga says, "In my freshman year of college, I had an identity crisis that most people encounter in mid-life. I had retired from professional competitive gymnastics, and my body started changing. I gained weight. For women especially, a lot of our identity is woven into our body image—whether you are a gymnast, a businesswoman, or a mother, it doesn't matter. That is just the culture of women. I hit a big depression. Well, I had been depressed for a long, long time—but that's a whole other book and story about Soviet oppression, domestic violence, and alcoholism in my family and how that inevitably propelled me to become a victor and not a victim in life. If I can share one thing with women who are making a difference in the world, it's that most of us don't know how to express our needs, so we suffer silently for too long and then hit a wall and collapse."

Olga went on to say, "We don't want to burden anyone with our troubles, and I was following that same perilous journey. It's the archetypal heroine's journey for all of us who are highly successful women. You go through the dark forest, you go through the dark night of the soul, and you fight the dragon in the cave. I attempted suicide when I was eighteen. That crisis, I see now, was really a jolt to true spiritual awakening. I overdosed on three big bottles of pain medications, but I didn't actually want to die. What I wanted was to fall asleep and not have to wake up to such a harsh world, where my family in Ukraine still lived on a household income of $100 a month. I wanted to break free from oppression, but I did not know how.

"Historically, women have rebelled against the status quo to the point of hurting themselves in the process—burnout to breakdown. In retrospect, I was to pioneer a new way for all of us. While I was asleep, I had a dream. All the walls and rooms disappeared, and there was just white light as far as I could see, both backward and forward. There was no past, no present, no future—nothing. Those seeking enlightenment would call it an Ego death. And I felt a weight lift off my shoulders, and a voice said, 'No matter what mistakes you think you have made, the truth about who you are is unchanged.' I thought, if the truth about who you are is unchanged, then my slate is always clean. So, I figured I may as well dream big and write a brand new awesome story for my life. And that's exactly what I did."

What happened next is another lesson for us all. Olga asked for help from her university professor, because she still couldn't figure out exactly what she was born to do. She was journaling and trying to put the pieces together. Olga's teacher told her to go to Naropa University in Boulder, Colorado. She had a colleague who taught dance at Naropa and suggested Olga go there because, she said, "it seemed like you are searching for something that is not available here at a Christian college in business management." Olga went, and it changed her life.

Here are some guidelines to help you tap into your creative self and authenticity in your work and personal life.

1. Write down your top five values right now. Are you engaging with them in your life currently? One of my clients wrote down philanthropy and realized that she was not giving any money away, so she sent a check to The Audubon Society immediately.

2. Look in the mirror. Does your "look" support your tastes and delights? If you love cool colors, are you wearing them? How about your love of teak earrings and capes? Dressing for fun and to express your unique preferences lets people know more about your inner self.

3. If you have a business or career, how are you revealing your true self in your day-to-day work? If you have your own business, are you still doing work you love, or is it time to make some changes? If you work for an employer, are you asking for learning experiences and for new projects that speak to your new interests or to what's hot in your industry? Work is a powerful form of self-expression, and we need to keep looking for opportunities that evolve as we do.

4. How are you spending your time? Are you having the adventures you have dreamed of or are you watching too much TV? Are you seeing friends and family that you dearly love, or are you working all the time? Are you spending the time you want to on your quilting or volunteer work? We all have the same amount of time and we need to try to use it in a way that tells people what kind of person we are.

5. Many of us have been criticized for being ourselves. As we age, we (hopefully) get more comfortable taking risks and expressing our views and feelings to trusted others. Whether we are an artist or sell long-term care insurance, not everyone will like or resonate with our work. That's okay, as long as we are in our truth and telling a story that is meaningful to us. We need to keep some inner armor available to use when we get attacked. We need to stay centered as a creative person so that we can express what fascinates us and learn to care less about what others think.

Becoming ourselves is a lifetime journey with peak moments and pitfalls. Each of us has an original presence on the planet. Share it and celebrate it! We all benefit from being able to get to know the real you.

I wrote a newsletter called "Know Thyself" where I presented a list of healing questions that help us to mend and move on and to be more ourselves in the world. Many people wrote in and thanked me for the questions (which I will share with you) and told me that answering them had been a powerful process for them. I also got an email from a well-known writing teacher who told me that people needed positive inquiries to build their self-worth and that my questions would only bring people down. I'm all for positive, proactive thinking, but in order to heal and learn to completely value ourselves, we need to dig up the dirt so that we can release it.

Therefore, I think this is a good time to ponder some questions. If possible, take a day off and think about yourself and your life. On my recent day off, I got a spa treatment, lounged around, and wrote in my journal. I had some tough decisions to make about my business, as it is growing in new directions, and I have to integrate all of the social media and YouTube videos into my business plan. Personally, I am always working on decluttering my house and my mind, walking every day, spending time with friends and family, and working on new projects like trying out a highly recommended watercolor teacher or developing new ideas to write about. I do need to make a short list, though, not an overwhelming one.

> *We all have the same amount of time and we need to try to use it in a way that tells people what kind of person we are.*

My current Creative Courage Circles are such a great reminder of the power of a support group in helping us take major leaps in our lives and stay focused. You might want to gather one or more like-minded souls together to keep you focused and challenge you to think.

Here are those questions to try to answer or explore:

1. What do you feel most ashamed about and how can you heal it?

2. If you were much braver, what challenges would you tackle this year?

3. What kinds of filters do you need in your life to screen out negative thoughts, people who are "downers," the media, the Internet, stress overload, and anything else that you need to protect yourself from?

4. What have you been putting off in your life that you want to do/be/have now? How will you make that happen?

5. Have you thought about your legacy lately? How do you want to make a difference?

6. Lastly, what self-imposed limitation do you need to dynamite through and free yourself from?

These are big questions. Give yourself time to ponder them and let the truth be revealed.

Mary Hayden, PhD, is married to a man, John, whom I went to high school with. And John became one of my husband's best friends in college. Mary is a scientist at the National Center for Atmospheric Research in Boulder, Colorado. She works on the intersection of climate change, climate variability, and health issues. She travels all over the world and works with communities to help them handle challenging climate and health issues. She has just returned from Uganda, where she had the opportunity to do work on the plague and collaborate with witch doctors there. She was recently in Phoenix trying to better understand people's vulnerability to heat and promote solutions for those folks. She has a dengue fever project in Mexico that is funded by the National Science Foundation and a meningitis project in Ghana that is funded by Google.org.

I asked Mary if she felt successful in the work she was doing, and she said, "It's funny, we talk about this a lot where we work, how in academia you never quite feel like you're good enough and that you can always be just a little bit better. But I'm very happy with the work I do, partially because it is work that reaches out to help other people and also because I can see that it makes a difference in people's lives. I like to remind myself occasionally of what I teach my children all the time: if you are doing the best that you can do, that's it. That's great. You can't do more than that."

I asked Mary what her biggest fear was and she said, "I think as a parent that you always worry about your kids. It's constant. You think that once they grow up and leave the house, that's going to change. Well, it doesn't change—you still worry about them all the time. I see them every week and I like to hang out with them, but I think my worst fear is that something will happen to one of them and I'm sure John would say the same thing."

In many management studies, when employees are asked "what is the one thing that you want the most," they answer that they want positive recognition for their work. Some organizations are very competitive and workaholic, and no matter what you do, the message is that you could have done more and could have done it better. This leads to burnout and disillusionment. As women, we tend to fall into the trap of working harder in hopes that someone will notice and promote us. If we are entrepreneurs, we work harder in hopes that someone will give us key client contacts. We have to decide for ourselves what is "good enough" so that we maintain our personal power.

Chellie Campbell talks about the "100% Club." She had a history of overachieving and overworking and was always being asked to lead organizations, events, and so on. "Finally," she says, "I started to take it easier in life. In my 100% Club, I had to be perfect all the time. My email had to be 100 percent perfect and 100 percent of the people I met had to like me and admire me. I'd go to a party with one hundred people and ninety-nine of them would like me. One wouldn't, and I'd follow that one around. It's so silly. So I thought, who are the most successful, famous, loving wonderful people in the world, and do 100 percent of the people in the world always like them? The answer was No. Then I re-prioritized my life."

Shame is a creativity murderess. Fear is another. We need to deal with our demons in those six questions to free ourselves to create and to feel joyful.

As many of you know, I love Cape Cod and relish the beauty and the solitude of miles of perfect white sand, dunes, and glorious views on the private part of Nauset Beach. I feel blessed every time I visit. I also have some special friends on the Cape whom I enjoy catching up with each season. I had hot chocolate (she had iced coffee) with my friend Gillian Drake recently, and she reminded me of the power of taking risks with our creative interests. Gillian has done numerous ventures on her own, including creating two print magazines, running a publishing company, and renovating a villa in Italy that is now a beautiful rental spot for vacations and retreats. She took one of her print magazines, put it online, and passed it off to a new owner. Nothing seems impossible for her; she just does it. She just embarked on an innovative unique path as a medical intuitive and she is developing tools that can possibly improve our health. Stay tuned.

> Shame is a creativity murderess. Fear is another.

Gillian grew up in England at a time when women were not encouraged to go to college, but her brother was allowed to go. She did go to art school and then secretarial school and she admits that she can still type "like the wind." When I asked Gillian about the secret to her success, she said: "To really KNOW myself, know my rhythms, idiosyncrasies, strengths, weaknesses, and true goals. I found out at the age of twenty-one that working a 9-to-5 job was not for me, or even working for other people, and I have been self-employed ever since, in one way or the other. I prefer the freedom. It suits my energy, which comes in extreme spurts, and then I need a fallow period to recover and regroup. I have a form of ADD and instead of feeling sorry for myself, I have learned to focus on my strengths and realize that there are certain things I'll never be good at, such as keeping a strict routine, building up a business after the initial exciting, creative part, or speaking in public. I don't waste my time focusing on them, or feeling bad about myself because I am not good at those things. I am better as a behind-the-scenes person. And that's fine. We can't all be Oprah."

Part of your healing process is learning to take positive, calculated risks that feed your personal, professional, and creative growth. I have done a lot of writing and teaching about risk-taking and its benefits.

Are you ready to take some creative risks yourself? Here are some guidelines for you to follow as you traverse the potentially treacherous trail.

1. Make certain that you are passionate about what you are doing. If you don't have the zest, you won't have the stamina to stick with it.

2. Know what talents you have and what you will need help and support with. While some people like Gillian can manage to do most things themselves, many of us aren't quite that daring and adaptable, so we may need to enlist other resources.

3. Give yourself the time and the space to focus on your learning curve. It takes time to learn something new. I just started painting peonies, which I adore, but my hundredth painting will be far better than my first.

4. Realize that, as a risk-taker in the marketplace, you are going to have to sell your idea, product, or service to someone in order to get it out into the world. Brush up on the self-marketing skills that we have talked about and put together a plan that you can enjoy and stay committed to.

5. Lastly, know when it's time to move on. Some risks don't pan out and we need to cut our losses and let go. Other risks nourish us for a period of time and then we need to wave a "done" wand and advance. These transitions can be daunting, but they are totally normal and to be expected.

Decide what risk you would like to take and get started. Release your fears and inhibitions, take the plunge into the land of creative abundance, and enjoy!

STOP TOLERATING PAIN

What are you tolerating in your life? Whatever it is becomes a challenge to conquer. As creative vessels, we need to take exquisite care of our bodies, minds, and spirits so that our channels are clear and open.

After a couple of years of putting up with intermittent neck and shoulder pain, I finally signed up for physical therapy, which is time consuming and pushes against my non-jock edges. Yet, after many weeks, the pain is now gone most days, which is fabulous. In order to keep the pain from coming back, I have to watch my computer posture and do neck exercises daily. (What a reminder that most things have to be worked at regularly as opposed to being magically fixed.) But confronting this pain has been a powerful metaphor that has stimulated other life changes for me.

I completely redesigned my home office with luxurious leather chairs and artwork so that I can see in-person clients here and have everything in one place.

I have totally changed my project filing system, so that I can better manage my idea mania. In addition, I have declared one day a week as my Creativity Day, and am leveraging the power of morning time for big-picture business planning, new product development, and writing. I've also worked with a dream group and am instructing my dream genie each night to support my creative projects. More additions and subtractions are in the works as well, and I feel empowered and excited. Yet, like keeping my neck relaxed and strong, all of these changes will require commitment and refining. But like the pain in my neck, I no longer want to tolerate anything that does not support my body, mind, and spirit. Only when we face the "pain" in our lives can we create new habits and structures.

CHALLENGES

What kinds of physical or emotional "pain" are you accepting in your life? Do you need to discover more fulfilling work? Do you need to redirect your creative energy? Do you need to get healthy? Do you need more friends? Keep a journal for a month and use it to take a personal "pain" inventory of what is not working in your life. Choose three action steps to complete this year, remembering that you will need to carve out time to initiate your new intentions. Conquering pain that we can fix is proactive and is a signal to the universe that we are empowered!

As we grow, we must deal with losses. Just as we do balance sheets of profits and losses in our business, we need to take time regularly to acknowledge our blessings and release our failures and disappointments.

Some of you had creative dreams that failed to manifest or were delayed. Still others feel stuck or had to deal with an unexpected life crisis. I remember a time when I lost my astrologist of fifteen years to retirement, my intuitive advisor of many years died suddenly of cancer, my virtual assistant of seven years and my web designer both moved on to new opportunities, and my hairdresser, Mandy, went out on maternity leave. I also had a number of new health challenges that year and was not able to move ahead as rapidly as I had hoped with my business.

We must remember that with every loss there is growth, but we need to take the time to decipher the lessons. Although sometimes a loss is simply a painful reminder that we all have limited time on the planet and that relationships have time limits, too, we must let go and embrace the new. I did hire a new business team and found a spunky new hairdresser as well (although I eventually went back to my beloved Mandy). New relationships take us on novel adventures and expand our resilience. Often we resist the process and want to hang on to what is illusively secure. Take the time to thank the people or projects that have left you this year and embrace them. Celebrate and note all the new gains you have created, small or large. I have one client who is finally exercising daily for the first time in her life and liking it, and is also doing stained glasswork with a group every Sunday evening. These two gains have been life-changing for her and she glows with empowerment. Look through your appointment book or your Blackberry and note what you have gained this year in learning and forward movements. Then take a moment to mourn the things you have been unable to manifest as well as the relationships that can comfort you no longer.

Light a candle for your future and burn up a note card on which you have written anything that you will not be carrying forward. Allow yourself to heal and begin again with optimism and a clean pathway.

What do you do when you get burned out or lose your spunk? In the past few months I have seen so many clients and talked with numerous colleagues, all of whom were complaining about feeling disconnected from their life purpose. "The passion is just gone," one successful writer moaned. "I'm out of ideas," lamented a corporate consultant. "I've done it all before." "I know I have another chapter to my business, but I can't figure it out yet," complained an entrepreneur. All three people are showing signs of burnout, but are also ready to grow.

There is a myth in our culture that we should have our lives "together" at all times. It doesn't allow for the pain of change, creative experimentation, dead ends, or personal development. We often feel discouraged or even depressed when we don't know what's next, but we know that we can't keep doing what we are doing any longer. As we live and work for more years, it makes sense that we will desire numerous transitions. In addition, today's marketplace demands that we keep up with the needs and desires of our customers and clients for different and better services and products.

Lisa Sasevich is a hugely successful entrepreneur who went from making $130K to $2.2 million in one year and then she doubled that amount the next year. She helps people to sell without being "sales-y." Lisa says she is living an abundant life with a wonderful husband and two children, a huge new house in La Jolla, and a business that she loves, but she admits that she still has fears. Lisa says, "I still have a fear of failing, like most people. When I get an inspired thought and I know it's right, I move very quickly. Then there are times when I am not clear yet, and I let things percolate. Probably the biggest fear is losing the deep connection that I have with Source, because that is the darkest time in my life when I don't feel like

I am getting these direct downloads. Right now I am in a place where I am getting lots of downloads and it is so divine."

JJ Virgin talks about being full of fear. She says, "I have had more fear this past year than I've ever had in my life. But I think that if you're not a little scared, you're not doing it right. If you want to get bigger, you've got to stretch. I am so scared of looking at my life and thinking, 'what did I accomplish? Who did I impact? Who did I serve? What did I help? Did I really make a difference?' To me, the most scary thing would be to turn around at the end of my life feeling like I hadn't done what I was put here to do. I look at my mom, who has raised two kids and plays golf. And so her accomplishment is to raise two kids, but is that really what she was brought here to do? Really? That's it? That's the legacy, how many times she played golf? I don't get it. That would be my fear—not fulfilling my destiny. I look at people in my field who've done things that will live so far beyond them, and that's what I want to do. I'm full of fear but I totally fake it. I take myself out of my comfort zone on a daily basis and I just do it, over and over and over. I get knocked down, I get up, down, up, down. I kept thinking when I'm on TV that someone's going to find me out —I have the imposter syndrome severely. Baeth Davis told me that I had to be a celebrity; that's what it says in my hands, that I am meant to be famous. I just need to get out of my own way, step into that power, and own it."

As we evolve and our life cycle and priorities shift, we desire more chapters or changes in our career path. Passion and purpose are fueled by what excites and intrigues us at the moment, and that shifts as we travel our personal path.

To help you to rediscover your passion and purpose, try the following strategies.

1. Note down what interests you on a daily basis.

2. Look for the patterns and themes over a two-week period.

3. Talk to people who share those same interests, and see if you can determine whether or not this is a hobby or a potential vocational track for you.

4. Experiment with something at the top of your interest list—take a class, try it on your own, or read about it.

5. Zero in on how to incorporate this interest into your current career or what steps you would need to take to start a business, or just indulge this interest as a personal pursuit.

Have fun with this process!

INVITING IN COMMENTARY

"Saddle your dreams before you ride them."
—*Mary Webb*

In my books and teachings, I am always reminding readers and clients to protect their precious creative ideas and to surround themselves with people who truly care about their well-being. There are dangerous saboteurs out there who will give you terrible advice due to their vindictiveness, jealousy, or limiting beliefs. It's a sad fact of life that we cannot trust everyone. I want to present you with a different challenge. Armed with your own passion and people who love you and your work, I challenge you to find at least one person who thinks totally differently from you and have them comment on one of your projects, business strategies, or dreams. By "polling" opinions from opposite types, you will learn something valuable.

For example, I have a client who runs a very successful administrative services company. Most of her clients are small- to medium-sized businesses. For those of you who are familiar with the Myers-Briggs Type Indicator, she is an ISTJ, which is a great fit for detailed work. Understandably, the economy has impacted her business and those of her clients, and she needed to take a fresh look at her vision. Since I'm an INFJ, I brainstormed with her about strengthening her personal relationships with her existing clients, marketing to companies that personally interest her (like spas, hotels, and restaurants), and rewriting her materials so that they are more upbeat and positive.

As a result of our brainstorming session, my client was able to feel more excited about meeting new people with similar interests, consciously dialoguing with her existing clients for input on improving her services, and adding some "fun" to her marketing materials. By hiring a coach who thinks differently than you do, you gain a whole new perspective. I also sent my client out to ask three diverse people what they would most value in an administrative service. Her hairdresser said she wanted someone to "hold her hand" so she could learn to double-check the books to ensure accuracy, her auto mechanic said he wanted to buy software so that he could do it himself, and her banker confirmed what I said about personal service and advising, but added that she should add online tutorials to her website.

Now my client has lots to ponder in redoing her business plan, and she feels reinvigorated. By daring to ask people whom you may perceive as non-supportive or oblivious, or who are using your competition, you can learn a lot. Some of it may sting a bit, but that's the point. So, stoke your courage and invite new information into your world. Assimilate the best of it and enjoy pursuing new directions!

CHALLENGE

1. Who do you know who is successful at the personality or professional traits that you are weakest in? Seek them out.

2. Who has felt to you like a "critic" in the past, whose advice turned out to be right? Talk to that person.

3. Identify a great idea you are interested in doing, and ask for objective advice from people with different value systems, educational backgrounds, or professions, and listen carefully to their input.

4. Discard advice that is "way off" but look carefully for any hidden messages worth paying attention to.

5. Summarize your new insights and play with the possibilities.

6. Thank your new "advisors" and offer to help them with a dilemma of their own.

Secret Four

Learn New Mindsets for Courage and Success

"Life shrinks or expands in proportion to one's courage."
—*Anais Nin*

SCRIPT YOURSELF FOR SUCCESS

You cannot be successful if you cannot control your thoughts. You must tune into your passion, remember whom you are here to serve, eliminate negative programming and people, and change your internal dialogue—drastically. The mindset of success is learned behavior, just like chronic failure. The world is full of empowerment training programs, self-help books, business books, inspirational events and materials, etcetera. There is a buffet of options for you to study and learn about how to be successful, including creating the new heartfelt personal success. But the success philosophy has to get into our brains way before we take any actions. Successful women are always learning new strategies and proactive ways of thinking. Even in a recession, successful people are looking for opportunities, not sitting around complaining with the "ain't it awful" club.

Successful women turn off the TV and the media and all the bad news and work on themselves and their business instead. They try to find their edge in the market, as well as the right people to support them.

International intuitive consultant and speaker and the author of a number of books including *Listen* and *Divine Intuition*, Lynn Robinson was once described by a roommate as "pathologically positive." Lynn took it as a compliment because her roommate was endlessly pessimistic. She says, "I don't really like hanging around with people like that, as they bring me down. We have all had friends that have gone through a difficult time and we may feel that we've got the right words of wisdom to share with them to help them. And if they're being extremely negative about the situation, they are not going to be open to whatever it is we have to say. This is also true of our intuitive creative spirit, that when we are being overly negative, our intuition and creative ideas have a hard time getting through."

When I asked Lynn if she felt successful, she brought up a really important point. She said, "Most of the time I feel successful, but I have to confess that sometimes I don't, but that's rare. I think that is such a good question because sometimes we look at successful people and assume they have no moments of doubt, none whatsoever. We think that they are always happy and cheerful and that everything always goes their way. I know from doing the work that I do with people that it simply isn't true. Everyone has what my friend Laura indelicately calls 'saggy diaper days'. All of us who are human beings and still live on the planet have moments of doubt, fear, and anxiety and all those other horrible emotions. What I find, though, is that most of the time they don't last too long for me. It might last a day or two, but not weeks or months. But I think it's important for people to know that everything doesn't go my way 100 percent of the time." This ability to deal with a crisis or a failure—when you get stunned by a blow but still process your emotions and recover quickly—is very present among successful women. They have accepted that they are imperfect and that life is challenging, and they get up and back into the flow.

Ali Brown talks a lot about how we need to shift our mindset to embrace success. She says about herself and her entrepreneur clients, "There is no better personal development tool than starting your own business, because it brings up all of your issues. Anytime you are trying to up-level your business you are up-leveling yourself, and stuff bubbles to the surface that has to be dealt with, mastered, or moved through. That's where a lot of people quit, because sometimes it isn't pretty. This brings up all of your stuff, everything from the boyfriend who left you in the eighth grade to your alcoholic father, anything, and it makes you grow as a person. There's a great quote from John Rohm; when I first heard it, it changed my life. He said, 'You don't become a millionaire for the million dollars. You become a millionaire because of the person you become. It's the person that it makes you in the process.'

You cannot be successful if you cannot control your thoughts.

I value much more the person I have become than the money that I have made because I know I can make that money again and again."

One of the things I see that really holds women back is waiting until everything is perfect before they launch something or change careers. Because of our intense fear of criticism, we are vulnerable to over-working and waiting too long to launch something new. When I help people either start a business or repackage themselves for another career, especially people who have "SF" as their middle letters on the Myers-Briggs Type Indicator, they have a hard time believing in themselves enough to try it, goof up, and master it. I attended Lisa Sasevich's fabulous workshop "Speak to Sell" this year and she has a great spin on this issue. Lisa says, "One of the secrets of my success has been to take imperfect action. I was once somebody who used to research everything ad nauseum and think about things for a long time. In the last couple of years, I started to really invest in myself and take action when I get the inspiration, so even though it wasn't perfect and I didn't know how to do it, I would take inspired, imperfect action. I find the more I did it, the more confidence I would build, and I would do it again. Now I'm taking imperfect inspired action on pretty big choices, and it's moved us forward very quickly in my business."

I remember as a young girl watching Congresswoman Pat Schroeder on TV talking about equal rights for women, day care, family leave for families, and services for our military families. As I alluded to earlier, she was passionate, yet logical, and spoke to improve the quality of life for everyone in this country. She lasted twenty-four years in Congress. When Newt Gingrich and Tom Delay showed up, it wasn't fun anymore. When I asked her what kept her going for those twenty-four years, her answer was interesting: "I never thought of myself as a politician and so, when I won, I thought, well, any time I could lose, so while I'm here, I may as well make the best of it and do whatever I possibly can to make change. It's not going to be the end of my life if I am not in politics. And it's no secret that it's a tough lifestyle if you've got kids and a family and you're traveling back and forth for the weekend, and dealing with two homes. But I did get through it and the kids came through it and they all seem to be perfectly happy and have gone on to perfectly normal lives, because at that time, people told me I couldn't do it. I remember Bella Abzug calling me, saying 'I hear that you have young kids; there's no way.' So I do think to have been able to juggle it all and come out the other end was very good."

Take imperfect inspired action.

She went on to say that this was not an issue that the men in the House and Senate struggled with in the same way at all, as so many of them had household help and stay-at-home wives.

Pat talked about her willingness to take on all sorts of issues that no one else would take on because there was no money in it. She says, "I did an alternative defense budget every year which the guys thought was beyond ballsy. I did all sorts of things for women—getting them into the military academy, letting them fly missions, getting them fully recognized, getting military and federal pensions to be split upon divorce, and the Family Medical Leave Act, because it was terribly important to do them for the whole country. Everybody says it was wonderful, so why don't they increase it? All the work on women's issues and children's issues I thought was very important because those were all the issues that had no political action committees behind them, no big special interest groups ready to pay big bucks for them. We set out to try to prove that the federal government could be a model employer and show the private sector that they could incorporate work and family and not lose productivity, and people liked it." Pat is an example of a woman who led with her values and stood up for what she believed in even in a male-dominated institution; she pushed through legislation in spite of it.

Another challenge for women is the fear of being found out as a fraud. JJ Virgin admits to having this issue, like so many of us do. JJ says, "This is not about me being a celebrity diva. Yes, I can be the number one fitness and nutrition expert in the country. It gave me the clarity—the permission—but also the realization that it really isn't up to me; that it's really me stopping, listening, and realizing that this was why I was put here. I am a big believer that we have spiritual gifts to give to the world and we are supposed to leave this world a better place than when we found it. I am a healer and I empower people and I cannot continue to diminish myself to make people feel more comfortable around me." As of this writing, JJ's new reality show, *Freaky Eaters,* was just renewed by TLC! In the show, JJ has a chance to show her compassion, but also to illustrate how the "science" of food ingested in our bodies holds lots of health info and warnings that can help people to change their habits, one step at a time.

PROACTIVELY RUN YOUR LIFE AND YOUR CAREER

Now we are going to accelerate your self-reliance. We are living in an unprecedented time in history and are being asked to make up new paradigms and develop novel strategies for managing our lives and our careers. Except for a select few, corporate America is not going to take care of us long-term. Abandon those fantasies right now. In this age of downsizing and shrinking benefits, you now own the responsibility for your life and your career success.

The new workplace requires flexibility, multiple skills, constant retraining, sales and marketing facility, creativity, technological expertise, and an entrepreneurial mindset. As for your lifestyle, you have options there too. Do you want to live and work at home or do you crave group energy? If you have a family, what kinds of relationships do you want to have with them? If you long to find more time for something you love to do, can that thing become your work?

Having to take responsibility for your own life can be daunting at first, but here are a few guidelines to help you navigate the challenges:

1. Review your family history and extract the wise lessons you learned about life from the people you respect. Then release the axioms that are simply out of date or don't apply to you. Many people got messages from their parents such as "you should trade your happiness and freedom for security" or "do whatever it takes to please your boss." I sometimes tell my clients that they may want to temporarily shield their parents or relatives from the ups and downs of a career transition. I often say, "Don't expect your parents to think this is a good idea to start a business (or change careers or quit an awful job)." If you've been laid off, even though you did a great job, some people may not understand that you might be a victim of the times. In this time of change and turmoil, lots of excellent people have had to retrain or start over and make new choices. You need people in your life who can cheer you on, not give you advice based on fear or a lack of understanding of the new workplace. If you do keep getting laid off repeatedly, you may want to do some soul searching about whether or not you are in a dying field or one that doesn't suit you. Face the facts and make a change. Successful people don't stay stuck for too long. They analyze, intuit, and decide.

2. If you have a job you enjoy, don't get too comfy. I tell people to keep their resume updated, network continuously, stay up-to-date in their field, and keep their eye on the door. You never know. You also need to stay very tuned into the company priorities so that you can position yourself in alignment with the organizational goals. But even if you do everything right, your job or contract may still end. Award-winning TV anchor Cindy Morrison got

laid off from her station, despite having great ratings and a strong following in Oklahoma. As Cindy says, "I was planning to spend my whole career as an investigative journalist and TV anchor. I joke that I planned to work there through two facelifts. I was stunned when I was let go after such an accomplished run." Do not have all of your professional contacts at one organization. Find a network group that resonates for you or start your own Success Team. In Cindy's fun new book *Girlfriends 2.0*, she talks about how her network boosted her up and helped her to reinvent herself as a sought-after speaker, spokesperson, and author.

3. Even if you are currently working for someone else, you need to think of yourself as an enterprise. It is likely that at some point you will have to deal with a change that you don't like. Expect it and plan accordingly. If you have your own business, choose it. Don't just think of it as a "second choice" because you lost your job or have not been able to find the right job. It is an opportunity, so invest in it. As many of us will be working well into our seventies and maybe beyond, having a business is a great edge against age discrimination. Learn how to play your strengths and get help from people who excel at what you don't.

4. If you allow yourself to think of your lifestyle as part of your career decision-making, then you can tailor your jobs or your business to your life priorities. Are you a single parent who wants to be home in the afternoon? Have you had it with traveling every week or office politics? Do you have a passion for solving some world problem or trying an experiment? Technology has given us multiple freedoms, so leverage them and develop options that fit your lifestyle and your personal values. Since 9/11, my clients have been looking carefully at their lifestyle issues and choosing to think about living where they want to and about what truly matters in their lives.

5. Seek out new mentors or role models. Read about career transitioners, talk to business owners about their successes and failures, research what's "hot" in your field. Be open to new locations, flexible schedules, or projects that stretch you. Take the risks necessary to go after what you truly want.

INVEST FULLY IN YOUR WORK

Like it or not, your career is a business. Whether you are working for someone other than yourself (for the moment) or have your own business, you are the CEO of your professional development. Realizing your creative ambitions and funding your retirement accounts is your domain. Delegating your career path to corporate mentors or enlightened superiors is simply a dangerous fantasy. Although I have had my own business since 1982, I never stop learning and reinventing myself, which is part of the fun and the challenge. This past year I have traveled all over the country to attend six major conferences to give me new ideas about how to redesign my business once again, and to research this book. Many of the women who led those conferences are in this book. It was a rich experience. I came away more focused in my own work and full of creative ideas for my clients, too.

Committing to your personal and professional growth is a cornerstone of creative success. There are perils to not being fully in change and taking positive risks with your career. I saw a client last week who is writing a book that she has put off for years. I asked her how she planned to learn the craft of writing, as she's a sales gal. She had never thought of the book as an investment requiring start-up skill-building. If she does not invest money as well as time in this project, she will likely fail. I also had a call this week from a

You are the CEO of your personal development.

female CEO who hates her job and is in the wrong field, but plans to stay in the same situation. Her request was for me to help her to learn how to be "tough and immune to the stress." This is another recipe for failure. She needs to find work she loves that will support her health and well-being and give her a strong chance for happiness in life. We have to take care of ourselves to do work that directly helps people so that we do not get compassion fatigue or disheartened.

TAKE THIS CAREER/BUSINESS CHECK-UP QUIZ

1. Am I investing in a positive future that reflects my talents and interests (or am I hiding out and settling for less in my life)?

2. Do I have a long-term plan for my career or business, given that I may work into my seventies or eighties by choice or necessity?

3. Am I actively investing time and resources into my business and creative projects?

If you answered "no" to one or more of these questions, it's time to recommit to an updated plan for your future.

SELECTING THE RIGHT PRIORITIES

Many of us who are drawn to success and advancement have a gift for coming up with a myriad of ideas. While this is an amazing talent, it can also be incredibly overwhelming, lead to confusion, and result in a lack of focus. Therefore, learning to let go of possibilities and prioritize what is most important as well as realistic for that time-frame is an essential success strategy. As a coach, helping people to envision and prioritize is one of my primary roles. For example, how many of you made a long list of New Year's resolutions? The stats are not in your favor for accomplishing these resolutions. Most people have failed by February. You need to begin with a Treasure Map.

TREASURE MAPS

They are called Treasure Maps, prosperity maps, wheels of fortune, wish collages, etcetera. The purpose of the exercise is to make a collage of images that you want

to create in your life. You can draw the visuals or cut pictures out of magazines or use mixed media of any kind.

Many writers have given prescriptions for how to do this, and your own creativity plays a major role. I have been rereading one of my favorite prosperity books, *Open Your Mind to Prosperity* by Catherine Ponder. I had forgotten that she has her own ideas about this strategy, which I will share with you today.

1. Keep your pictures quiet. Do not speak of them and instead have this be a private prayer.

2. Use big colorful poster board and color pictures and do not clutter the space. Make several boards for different phases of your life, if you need to.

3. Colors have special meanings. You can use this guide:
   Use green or gold for job or career success.
   Use yellow or white for increased spiritual understanding.
   Use blue for intellectual accomplishments.
   Use orange or bright yellow for health, energy, and vitality.
   Use pink, rose, or warm red for love, harmony, and happiness in
      relationships.

4. On your financial board, put money on the board, not just the things you want. Use play money, real money, or checks.

5. Put a spiritual symbol that is meaningful for you on your board for spiritual protection.

6. View your treasure map every day, preferably before going to bed. The more you study your map, the sooner results will manifest.

We must always remember that sometimes things don't manifest as quickly as we would like because there is another divine plan in store for us. A powerful affirmation to use is "This or something better will manifest for me in its right time" to demonstrate that we trust the process.

So, get focused on your goals and wishes and put them in tangible form so you can meditate on them daily and wait for results. Remember, action in support of our visions is a key component.

Take some time to cut up magazines and other periodicals or materials and make a Treasure Map of all of the things that you are hoping to create in your life. Use the guidance from the above instructions, your personal and heartfelt success vision, your resolutions for this year, and your answers to all of the Challenges in this book as guides for your Map. Make your Map as meaningful to you as possible and keep adding to it if you need to. What is most important for you in terms of life fulfillment or your rendition of success right now? Successful people know that pacing, prioritizing, and clear decisions make all the difference in results.

Can you write and sell a symphony, start a business, remodel your entire downstairs, fix your marriage, start working with a personal trainer, learn to fundraise for a community organization, and work on a remedial program for your struggling ADD child all at once? No, unless you subtract sleep and peace of mind from your days. You have to pick one recipe, one path, and give it your all. Think of the year in three-month quarters of twelve-week blocks and schedule your plan. If you don't actively select a set of priorities, you will be writing down the same goals next year. Commitment and focus are essential to support your dreams.

CHALLENGE

For the next thirty days, select your priorities and post them on your mirror. Study them as you brush your teeth daily. For each priority, outline three steps and schedule them into a specific time slot. For example, if your priority is to create a new product, then step one may be to research similar products, step two may be to build a prototype, and step three may be to show it to five friends for feedback. This may not sound glamorous, but it works.

I have noticed that many people are walking around rather dazed these days. We are bombarded with daily news that is almost unbelievable. There are the staggering numbers of lay-offs that have people fearful about security. And those paper number reductions in savings and house values are hard to face as well. Consumers are holding back their spending due to fear of what might happen to their income. The media is having a heyday with all of it.

Our challenge is to keep things in perspective, build on what we have, and use our creativity to design new services and products that people want. I aim to spend my time with people who are focused on creating new opportunities and finding their special market in the new world of business. Many people are on a news "fast" and don't listen to too much negativity. Others are being careful to avoid the people that Cindy Morrison calls the "Debbie Downers,"—those people who can't move from complaining to action. Indeed, these are some really difficult times for people who can't sell their house, have large medical bills, or have been laid off. We want to be compassionate and lend a helping hand to those folks when we can. But we can also help by listening and then encouraging them to solve one problem at a time and be proactive, not passive about their situation.

Prosperity thinking begins with gratitude for what you already have. Make a list of all the assets you possess, including your talents and your loved ones, and post it where you can see it easily during the day. Think of that as your foundation for new growth. If your business is slow, do a project that you've been putting off that will generate income and hopefully give you enjoyment. If you are unhappy at your job, start networking, volunteering, or taking classes to prepare for your next step. If you are looking for work, do your job hunting diligently, but take time for yourself and your significant others to have fun and enjoy life.

We can choose how we handle the cycles in the marketplace. Every change holds promise if we leverage it. Look at how you can invent or make something new and useful. Let go of the fear and replace it with novel ways of doing things. Try to speak in positive terms, and don't whine about what's happening. Our words are very important as they direct our thinking and our actions. Find other kindred spirits who are dedicated to finding the silver lining in the new reality and support each other. Prosperity is a mindset that starts from within.

As I mentioned in the last chapter, if you have unresolved confidence issues, old family scripts, or have to dig yourself out of a mess, your creativity may be distracted temporarily. All these stimuli can rob us of our creative ideas of possibility and promise. If our heads are too filled with negative talk, there is not room enough for the exploration of our fascinations, creative experiments, new relationships, and adventures. While we need to deal with the realities of our lives, we also need a sacred space in our minds that fertilizes creative thoughts and positive thinking.

So how do we protect ourselves? We must be vigilant about subtracting negative influences and replacing them with positive life choices and growth-enhancing thoughts. Therefore, we need strong filters to sift through the media downers and the people who want to play in a negative space. Here are some strategies to help.

CHALLENGES

1. Collect positive words and quotations and read them regularly.

2. Sit quietly in front of your Treasure Map daily and make sure that it feels right to you. If not, fix it. We are always changing.

3. Practice a technique called "thought stopping"—when you get a negative thought you don't want, erase it from your mind. This takes practice, but it works. Replace it with a proactive thought that supports your vision of life.

4. Avoid negative people and news whenever you can. Meditate daily on your connection with the planet and all the people on earth and the goodness in the world.

5. Lastly, put your energy into changing what you can in your life and the lives of others. Focus on improving things and making a contribution of your creative presence in the world. Join the folks who believe they can institute positive change in the world and who don't waste their valuable time focusing on the negative. You can subtract the negative from your life by actively solving your problems and the problems of others with passion, integrity, and joy.

FIGHTING OVERWHELM

Look at your options and make positive life choices. Tune into your heart center and follow its guidance. You know which choices call to you and stir your passions. That is your best defense against dilly-dallying between too many options and never getting anything done.

How do we prevent ourselves from getting overwhelmed, frustrated, immobile, scattered, or otherwise dysfunctional? Here are some tips to keep you on track.

1. Pull out your list of annual goals or your business plan, if you have one. If you don't, write a one-page description of what you are trying to accomplish with your creative urges. Start with your own personal "big picture" before you make a move.

2. Take some time to make sure what you say you want is, in fact, what you really want. Have your goals changed? Is your heart somewhere else now? Are you going in a direction that fascinates you and calls to you? Often we feel overwhelmed when we lose our sense of purpose or mission.

3. Focus on what you feel is right for you and then start by visualizing all the steps you need to take to get there. As you go through the steps in your mind, ask yourself these questions: Are you enjoying the process? Do you need help from someone? Are you satisfied with what you are doing? Tune into your intuition and note what messages you are receiving about your idea.

4. If your idea doesn't feel right, then go back to item number one and start over. If your idea suits you as a next project, write down the action steps you identified in your visualization. This is your creative project roadmap. Try to estimate the time it will take to complete what you are trying to do.

5. Make your creative project a priority in your life. Every morning, read through your action plan and remind yourself of why you are doing what you are doing. Focus your intentions and trust that you will find the resolutions to the snags you encounter as you engage with your plan.

    There will be challenges to resolve and conquer. You can count on that. Your determination to stay the course will make the difference between success and failure. Problems can be resolved if we engage our creative self and pull in the brainstorms of trusted others, as needed.

6. Lastly, celebrate your results! Note what helped you to make this project work and what undermined you. Life is about continuous learning and mastery. Good luck!

GET YOURSELF GROUNDED

While I've been on a "subtracting" tear (see my books for information on the power of subtraction) recently and have made great progress, more layers keep appearing. But I now have files in the right places, so I can more easily find things.

Progress is energizing! Once we clear out the old, the outgrown, and the dysfunctional, we can examine the systems and practices that support our well-being and our creative inspirations and thus create our foundation. As always, you must first identify the essence of what you truly desire, and then make it happen. Take an inventory in the following categories: work space, idea generation, administrative support, and creative time commitments.

CHALLENGE

1. How do you feel in your office or home spaces? Are you comfortable and inspired or overwhelmed and distracted? If your current office is Starbucks, are you bringing along what you need? I've had two clients this week commit to carving out a creativity corner or to fashioning a create-wherever-you-go basket, so they can work effectively. As creative people, our work space is very important to our process. If you don't have a supportive space, find one, and if you have one, improve it.

2. Are you "cooking" creatively or are you stuck? If you are in the flow, make a note of what's working. If you are stuck, change your medium to shake up your process. I often paint to jump-start my writing. I have a client who choreographs her business challenges and comes up with great new solutions. Allow your intuition to guide you. There is always a gateway if you look for it.

3. Do you know where your money is? Do you know your quarterly income and expenses? Are you investing in your business or your creative self? Do you need to hire a numbers person to keep you on track or barter your gifts for theirs? I know from my clients and my own experience that this is often an unappealing area of focus. Yet without the facts, our decisions can be uneducated. Knowledge is truly power. While I am the first to support people in pursuing their dreams, and adore watching the universe support targeted action plans, we need to be clear that we can take care of ourselves. People often come to me who want to

write a book or start a business and "forget" that they have to invest in their learning, whether it's in classes, coaching, or raw materials. Grant yourself a sum of money to support your goals.

4. Find your ideal creative time and make a commitment to use it. If two hours on Saturday morning or Thursday night is the target and you miss your time this week, schedule it again. You owe the bank. When you don't engage with your process or project, you lose significant ground. Set your creative time as a priority in your organizer and tell everyone you know that this is protected time and that you need their support to keep your promises to yourself.

5. Lastly, identify what other strategies serve to keep you grounded and inspired and round them up to support you in being focused this year.

WHAT DO YOU NEED COURAGE FOR RIGHT NOW?

Courage is essential to self-expression and that expression, regardless of its form, is creative. Anything that we want to change invites in the creative process, whether we are changing careers, starting a business, going on a diet, or writing a book. We have to be able to imagine the ingredients of what we want in order to bake the cake. To begin, we take a calculated risk and start experimenting with options until we find a formula that works for us.

All of these aspirations and changes require courage. The biggest obstacle to our achieving the changes we want in our lives is the negative mindset that we put on ourselves like a plastic sports helmet. We need guidance and support to take that helmet of "no can do" off once and for all—and start our change action plan today.

The reason I developed the *Creativity Courage Cards* was to be able to visually guide you and your personal and professional creative growth on a daily basis in the comfort of your own home or office; to build up your courage muscles, to get you actively working on your goals every day. I use the *Cards*, too, as I am always reaching for the next inspired product or service to develop. If we are stretching and growing, then we always need courage and a willingness to be wrong, get nowhere, or try something new and learn from it. The *Cards* remind me daily to honor the magic of the creative process and to keep that negative helmet off my head. It works—I just keep inventing.

If we are willing to get out there and live our life purpose, we are going to have moments of terror. It comes with stretching. As Lynn Robinson says, "Whenever you do anything new, you get scared and nervous and wonder whether you can do it. Gosh, when I first went to Japan to speak, I had never spoken to two thousand people before, never worked with a translator before, never spoken out of the country before, and my knees were knocking—I was really nervous. I don't think I looked that way, which helped, but it was scary. But now that I did it, I feel really good about myself. What I observe so often, especially as women, is that we want to have the confidence to do the thing that we are scared to do. What I have observed, at least about myself, is that usually the confidence comes after I actually do the thing I fear. The self-esteem, self-confidence fairy doesn't come and sprinkle her fairy dust before the event; it's usually *after* when I can say, 'atta girl, you did it.'"

Madeleine Randall is a seasoned Integrative Medicine doctor with clients all over the world. I first met her at a workshop at Rancho La Puerta, the heavenly spa in Mexico. Madeleine was teaching the Medicine Wheel and her workshop was rich with content and knowledge. She's the person many patients go to when no one else can figure out what is wrong with them. She has been trained in Western, Ayurvedic, and Chinese medicine, as well as by Native American teachers. We talked about the difference between calculated risk and impulsive risks and how to manage them. This is Madeleine's formula for deciding whether or not to take a risk in your life. She teaches: "This is the way it works as I was taught by my teachers. First you see it and you feel it with your heart. Okay. Then bring down that powerful mind and wrap it around your heart and see what comes up. Courage is something that you need to use your mind for taking risks. Some people just take risks for no reason. But you have to really feel it. If it does not pass the heart test, it is out. If you feel a sinking feeling or you feel drained then you know it won't work out. If your heart lifts, opens, and says, 'Yes, that's it,' **y**ou know that's your path, and when you bring your mind down, the combination of wisdoms will help you to stay on the path.

"When you are on your path, it will bring you exactly what you need. You don't even have to go and get it, it comes to you. And that's when you are functioning at your highest vibration, right there."

Madeleine also talks about the skill of quick recovery when we take a risk that we feel is right. She says, "You have to have courage, because if you fall down, it's really not a big deal. So what you do is you just get up. I mean what's the worst thing that can happen? Make opportunity and wisdom from failure. I've crashed and burned so many times that I'm not afraid of it. I have the power to pop out of it now, as I've learned how to land and learn the gifts from my experience."

Mary Hayden talks about the value of feedback and acknowledgment as fuel for a courageous mindset. She says, "Well, I guess I don't even think of myself as courageous, but I think that when you have some success, it really helps to make you feel that you're on the right track, and if that success is going back to the Public Health Department and being able to say, 'Hey, here's some information that we think might be useful.' And having them say, 'This is really helpful for us. I think that part of that feedback stems from working with our stakeholders right from the beginning, too, so we are steering our research toward what they need, and that also helps to have that reinforcement that yes, this is working. And if it's not, then we go back and adjust our game plan until it does work. I think that's part of it too."

> *Make opportunity and wisdom from failure.*

There is an old saying that our thoughts are like prayers. If we are filling our thoughts with garbage, we will get poor results in life. If we retrain ourselves to think differently about ourselves and think that we deserve success and the courage to make it happen, our lives change. That is one centerpiece of creating success. But we also have to take action, which we will talk about in detail in the seventh section of this book. But for now, may I remind you of what financial stress reduction expert Chellie Campbell teaches, which is that we need to keep "sending out ships" daily to have a successful business. Chellie means that we need to be reaching out and calling people, which she calls sending out ships, because you can't just wait for your ship to come in—you need to keep sending your messages out there. So part of our mindset shift has to be a willingness to go out and meet people and sell our products and services. That is much easier if we feel passionate about what we are doing and if we are connected with our life purpose and the change we want to make in the world.

Secret Five

Design Action Strategies That Work

"You must have control of the authorship of your destiny. The pen that writes your life story must be held in your own hand."
—Irene C. Kassorla

PROSPERITY AND GOAL-SETTING

What is prosperity for you? A key element in my Positive Choices strategies program that is outlined in my book, *The Power of Positive Choices*, is the addition of positive choices to your life that reflect your prosperity goals. Prosperity for most people is not simply money in the bank. Your health, peace of mind, and well-being all count. Think about combinations of fulfilling work, great relationships, a sense of community, healthy lifestyles, harmony with nature, personal growth, and creative expression. You are the author of your own life, and your prosperity plan reflects your uniqueness.

I once met a photographer at Yosemite National Park who lives in a tent (a very nice tent) and sells her numerous photographs of the park's stunning mountains and streams to the local gift shops. She told me that she's living her prosperity dream—fresh air, intimacy with nature, and a serene lifestyle. When she talks about her slides of the park, her joy radiates. She is living the life that she relishes. Successful people know what they desire and set about making it happen. Success is different for each of us, and it also shifts as we progress through the cycles of life.

What do you want? While I loved visiting Yosemite, after three days I couldn't wait to move on to a quaint California town with art shops and cafes, while my husband could have stayed there taking photos for another month. We are each unique. Forget reality for a moment and tell the truth. Write down a paragraph describing a favorite day in your life so far, and then add to it what you would really like. Be as specific as possible. Do the pictures fit together? If not, what needs to be shifted?

As a workshop leader, I see many people roll their eyes when I mention goal-setting. But writing down your personal, professional, and creative goals is a proven success strategy. It works. Also, if you add visuals, like a collage, a mandala, or a significant object as a symbol of what you are trying to accomplish, the process works even better. Change is experiential, and we have to long for it on an intense emotional level. We have to "crave" it in our bones. It has to be urgent in some way, not just another "should" on society's list of do's and don'ts. Goals have to be personal and desired on a body, mind, and spirit level to warrant the challenges of changing our behavior, breaking old habits, and taking risks. So, before you skip this chapter, let's make this simple for you.

WHAT IS A GOAL?

A goal is a statement of intention—a target.

Goals are supported by:

- Writing them down

- Stating them clearly and specifically

- Making them realistic and time-limited

- Conceptualizing them positively and in action language

- Working with an accountability buddy, coach, or team

- Your craving to achieve this result for yourself and/or for others

Here are a few key tips to help you to write powerful goals:

1. Be specific. State the exact result you want in detail. For example, Jane wrote, "I want to complete a master's degree in computer graphics at my state university by December, two years from now, so that I can start my own

business designing websites for nonprofit organizations that help promote eating local organic foods."

2. Be realistic about time and ability. Carmen wanted to be a rock star but couldn't sing, so achieving that goal was unlikely. So she found an aspect of the music business that matches her skills. Barbara wanted to raise a million dollars for her child's school from the profits of her PR company. Some prosperity experts advise writing down what you really want, even if it's unlikely, and seeing what evolves.

3. Break down each goal into detailed action steps. These action steps help you make continual progress on the path. Develop a framework that spells out what you can do today or this week to further you along.

4. Be clear about the challenges of your goal. Fill out a Personal Success Contract (coming up shortly) to follow for each one.

5. Select only ONE multifaceted goal for the next three months.

   Example: As part of my marketing plan, I am going to license my artwork to a giftware company, I am going to set up exhibits of my artwork in three new galleries and personally invite one hundred people to the openings, and I am going to teach a new workshop on art and business at two summer conferences, where I will sell five paintings.

6. Write a history of your past "close encounters" with this goal and identify what has worked before and what has failed so you can leverage your strengths and resolve your resistance.

   Examples: I have licensing info but have not been able to get to the decision-makers, I haven't found the right galleries yet, I'm not sure which pieces to sell, I don't have a mailing list, my art teacher told me to contact Mary at Gallery X who liked my work, but I never followed through, the last workshop I did had poor attendance, and so on.

   Now you know where to target your attention and which problems to solve.

7. Write your goal in a place where you will see it first thing every morning, journal about your progress, and visualize your success.

8. Schedule in *red ink* your goal time each week in your calendar or Blackberry. If you don't keep that appointment, double up the following week. You owe the "goal bank" when you miss your time.

9. Put a time table in your action plan with specific target dates. If you miss a target, back up and do it.

10. Try to leverage times when your energy is best. Are you an AM person or a PM person? Does your project need lots of open days to complete or can you block out several hours a week on different days?

11. Be flexible with yourself and your goals. When we are making changes, we need to allow ourselves to experiment. If your goal was to get physically fit and you joined a gym, but you hate going because it's not that clean, switch to Plan B and try doing DVDs or exercise shows at home. If that doesn't work, get a buddy and try Nia or Tai Chi. Eventually, you will find your best match.

12. To make room for these new goals, you must *subtract* things from your life. Stop being a Type E woman—everything for everyone else first—and let go of anything that is unsatisfying for you, whether it is volunteer work that you don't enjoy or people that you have simply outgrown. Change is constant. Go with it.

Setting goals is positive risk-taking. The word "risk" is derived from the Greeks and means "to sail around a cliff." It beckons you to travel into the unknown for the benefit of adventure, growth, excitement, or purpose. You can't grow unless you risk, and goals can help you to approach that risk in a prepared, strategic manner.

Preparation demands talking to other successful risk-takers, researching your project, and experimenting. Factor in your own strengths and weaknesses and allow for the unexpected. Jane's husband lost his job while she was in computer graphics school and she had to take a semester off due to finances.

It always helps to be flexible and have a back-up plan. Barbara's fundraising efforts proved overwhelming as a sideline effort, so she decided to take a sabbatical for a year and fundraise full time. Stay tuned to your intuition about your goal. Sometimes we don't really want what we thought we wanted in the first place.

Carmen explored the music business and decided she disliked the constant travel. She's now the entertainment booking agent for a major local restaurant and singing in a chorus for fun.

PERSONAL SUCCESS CONTRACT

1. My Top Five Goals for this year are:

   Goal   Deadline

   a. _____

   b. _____

   c. _____

   d. _____

   e. _____

2. My one sentence life purpose statement is (as you know it to be):

   _____

3. I am committed to my five goals because:

   _____

4. My Top Three Strengths as a successful woman are:

   _____

   _____

   _____

5. The barriers to achieving these goals are:

   Goal Barriers

   a. _____

   b. _____

   c. _____

   d. _____

   e. _____

6. I need to do the following (usually develop skills, support, or courage) to ensure my likelihood of success with the above goals.

   _____

Support Systems

What kinds of support systems or skills do I need to achieve the next steps for the goals in my life or my business?

Options:

New skills _____

Information _____

Classes _____

continued on the next page

continued from the previous page

Groups _____

A Buddy/Partner _____

A Mentor/Role Model _____

Therapy/Coaching _____

Contacts/Connections_____

Resources: Books, Tapes, Online Chats, Other Professionals _____

_____

Time _____

Peace of Mind _____

Inspiration _____

Rituals_____

Spiritual Practice _____

Schedule or Structure _____

Healing work _____

Solutions for your personal stressors (Refer to my book The Power of Positive Choices to help you with that):

_____

_____

_____

7. When I achieve my five goals for the year, I will celebrate and reward myself with:

_____

8. In the midst of this "stretching" process to achieve these goals, I will do the following three things to take care of my emotional, spiritual, and physical health:

_____

_____

_____

I agree to complete the steps of this Personal Success Contract by _____ (date)

and I will share these goals with the following people _____,

_____ , _____ to help keep me clear and accountable.

Signature _____ Date _____

Marilyn Tam, successful corporate executive (former CEO of Aveda, President of Reebok Apparel & Retail Group, Vice-President of Nike), speaker, humanitarian, and the author of *How To Use What You've Got to Get What You Want,* was guided by her life mission when she decided to come to America, alone as a young girl. She says, "I was focused on saving the world. So at eleven years old, I decided I would focus on saving one continent, Africa, by helping them learn how to better run their government and to feed themselves. . I knew I needed an education before I could do that. You need to embrace your mission, and proceed goal-by-goal until you achieve your mission. With that in mind, I asked myself, what do I need to accomplish my mission? I need an education in economics and nutrition because these are the two areas I want to work in. Marilyn came to America and completed her college education, achieved great success in the corporate and entrepreneurial world, and now helps people all over the world with her nonprofit organization, the, Us Foundation (*www.usfoundation.org*). In her book, Marilyn teaches four Principles as the key to success: "Tell the truth all the time, Make me your partner, Make big mistakes, and Die by your own sword, which means stand by your own convictions." Her life is a testament to the power of what she writes about in her book—following your life's mission and your principles.

Write down your goals.

VISUALIZATION

Visualization simply means creating a picture in your mind of the results you want while you are in a relaxed state. Relaxation exercises or meditation are meant to calm you and put you in the alpha/theta state. Visualizing your goals allows you to prepare yourself to receive them.

It's like practice. It also elucidates the basics: if the goal is truly right for you, it may stimulate any emotional baggage you may have about not deserving it. Treasure Maps, as we've discussed, illustrate your vision so you can "see" the future. Mental imagery helps you do the same.

One of my clients, Maria, had the goal to double her income in the next twelve months. She had ten years of experience as an interior designer. For the past two years, she had worked as a general manager with a team, but found supervising other people irritating and inefficient. She finally admitted that she only wanted work she could do herself.

She liked having her independence. But if she continued to do general design jobs solo, she couldn't meet her goal. Her monthly average net income was $6,000.

Maria and I met and designed a plan for her. She began to sit quietly every morning and evening for ten minutes and imagined depositing $12,000 into her bank account every month. She imagined receiving checks from her customers and going to the bank, inserting her ATM card, pushing the right buttons, and receiving a $12,000 deposit slip back. She also pictured buying new office furniture for herself and hiring a housekeeper, a landscaper, and a personal organizer for her own home. She also mentally set up an IRA account for her retirement, something that she hadn't been able to do before.

Not much was happening except that Maria was getting very excited about having the extra income. She asked me if I had any suggestions to improve the impact of her visualization. I suggested that she focus on the faces of the people who were handing her the checks and having them say "thank you." After two weeks, she told me that, in her visualization, they all thanked her for designing their sunrooms. "I love sun rooms," she said. "Maybe I could specialize in that and double my income."

And that's what she did. Visualization enhances the way you are able to tune into a dilemma and sometimes surfaces new information that propels you in the right direction. It took eighteen months instead of twelve, but Maria did double her income.

Pick one goal that you want to visualize and follow all the previous steps we've discussed. Pick two times a day to focus your complete attention on this goal and its outcome. Some people create an altar or sanctuary somewhere in their home or office, in their car, or on the beach. Select a location that will foster your results.

In your quiet place, begin by focusing on the words of your goal and then move to associate a picture or pictures of what you want to manifest. Let your mind go and take whatever images you get. Nothing is set in stone; you can change the slant when you want. See what clues you can pick up from your creative mind about how your goal may happen.

Pay attention to key people who show up, specific locations, or symbols that arise. Tune into how you feel having achieved your goal. Another client, Tina, pictured herself living in St. Thomas and enjoying warm weather and tropical drinks all year long. Yet, her eyes filled up with tears when she suddenly realized that she would be all alone in St. Thomas; she felt overwhelmed with affection for her friends and family. She later decided that she only wanted to winter in St. Thomas and needed a mobile career. When she visualized that configuration, a laptop image showed up and she knew that technology held the answer.

Visualization allows you to experiment with your ideas on a daily basis. Statistics collected on athletes and other performers support the concept that visualization works. Use it to enhance your path to creative success and prosperity. So, as you make your list of goals and action steps, take a moment to visualize the results you want. Picture your business thriving, new friends, or having an abundance of healthy energy. Let your dreams come through.

Focus on your goal at least two times a day.

KEEPING YOUR PROMISES TO YOURSELF

For years now, I've had the luxury of spending part of the summer months at my Cape Cod house, enjoying the quiet tranquility and the mellow pace of life and working, too. No parking meters, people have time to chat—and relish it—and my corner of Nauset Beach can be mine, except for sharing it with the nesting piping plovers. The wonder of the Internet has made all that possible.

While I was at the Cape, I interviewed acclaimed oil painter Katherine "Ann" Hartley whose stunning still lifes done in the style of the Dutch masters sell for $2,200 to $15,000 and up. As I sat in her second floor studio, I was entranced by a just completed painting of roses in a pewter dish. The piece slowly seeped into my soul and became one of my new favorites. Ann's studio is cozy and dark, and she covers one window with cardboard to maximize her natural light from the north. She grew up in an old jailhouse which is now a restaurant and learned to love old bottles and bowls, and her collection of intriguing objects circles her studio and beckons her with new ideas for arrangements adorned with natural fruits and flowers of the season.

While Ann loved to draw as a child, she left high school without a direction and lived for many years in the Southwest, Alaska, and other places, with waitressing as her main vocation. Then, in her late twenties, she felt inspired to take one class in drawing in Arizona. She mentioned her artwork to an old restaurant contact, John Court, an accomplished artist, and he offered her a house-sitting job in exchange for art lessons in the Azores. John nurtured her talent, and after a few months he sent her to study with the famous David Leffel at the Art Students League of New York. Ann stayed and studied, still waitressed, and eventually got a studio in Union Square, where her work began to sell. She gathered around her a strong community of artists and friends, and her natural warmth networked her into both awesome apartment deals and gallery connections.

Ann feels fortunate that she had the chance to completely focus on developing her own still life painting style. She avoided looking at other people's work and didn't talk about what she did—she just kept learning. She was given two great pieces of advice. Her mother told her to keep her ego out of her art to counter the fear of failure, and another mentor advised her to "just listen" to accelerate her ability to master her craft. She never initially expected to make a living at her art, but she certainly has. Her focus has always been on beauty and the joy of creating it.

Now Ann paints four or five hours a day and has a studio on Cape Cod (and just let go of one in NYC). She enjoys being a wife and the mother of an energetic and joyful daughter. Ann has none of the hesitation or ambivalence that so many women struggle with around their creative work. When I asked her about this, Ann said that people make lots of excuses about not doing what they say they are going to do. "If you don't do it," she says, "nothing will happen."

Ann is absolutely committed to getting better and better at painting, and her fascination with learning and mastery drive her inquiry and fascination. Each time she starts a painting, she ponders how to begin, what objects and light to put together as her set, and what's compelling enough to keep it challenging and exciting for her. The process of learning new things fuels her and grounds her focus. If she does not paint for a while, she gets antsy and craves getting back to her work.

Ann's work seems to sell itself. She very recently got a website, but she is represented by a number of prestigious galleries. She rides her bike seven miles daily to her studio and is always "looking" for the vision for her paintings everywhere in her daily life. She says that often when she is not in the mood to paint, she actually gets the most done. When she is engaged with a painting she paints intensely—as often her natural objects (flowers, fruit, etcetera)—wilt quickly. Ann loves teaching and mentoring other artists, which she enjoys as another adventure in learning. Her advice for aspiring artists is to "just learn to paint," and she raves about the Art Students League of New York as a place to study. I asked her about her most exciting sale, and she lit up; she says she always feel thrilled when she sells a painting and once sold three in one day! One of Ann's paintings was recently installed above the mantle in the new and very prestigious Oyster Harbor Club in Osterville, MA. It led to two additional commissions.

For Ann, success right now is feeling happy, doing what she loves to do every day, and advancing her craft. Her goal is to continue to learn, always learn, and to keep getting better at what she does. I share Ann's story with you to remind you of the power of focus on learning your "art" and engaging with your work on a daily basis. It's all about intention and joyful creation.

THE NEED TO UNLEARN HARMFUL PROGRAMMING

In order to establish a new self-image and an empowering belief system, we often have to unlearn the "wisdom" we were taught as a child. Olga Aura, the Olympic-class gymnast, had to work extremely hard to wipe out the strict Olympic indoctrination so that she could learn to love herself as a woman and heal her soul. We talked earlier about her arduous journey of terror, and it was her time at Naropa University in Boulder, Colorado, that provided the medicine she needed to reclaim her personal power and to go on to help other women claim theirs.

As Olga says, "My love affair with Boulder and Naropa lasted five years. I literally entered a cocoon. That's what Boulder is—a cocoon surrounded by reality. I went and I unlearned everything I thought I was. I unlearned all my high ambition that was burning me out at both ends like a candlestick. It was in this small university founded by a Tibetan monk that I chose to unlearn all that Olympic training, so that I could learn gentleness and kindness for myself and learn self-value from within, not from outside. It was torture—I hated it! My first year at Naropa, I thought it was a colony of lazy bums who were meditating and proclaiming that they have the key to happiness. Where I came from in the Soviet Olympic gymnastics training, you don't sit on your butt and meditate, you work hard. It was such a duality flip-flop. It stretched my mind and my heart so wide that I was able to encapsulate such a wide range of the spectrum from go, go, get, all the way to allow, receive, and ask for help. Learning those skills was a real challenge."

Affirmations are another antidote to negative programming. When I discovered Chellie Campbell's first book *The Wealthy Spirit*, I found it loaded with daily affirmations to counter negative self beliefs and our culture's confusion around money and prosperity. I keep her book by my bedside and read it before I fall asleep. It reprograms you to get you clear on what prosperity is for you personally and in your business, and then it teaches you to get moving. Chellie writes that her affirmations are very effective for herself and for her clients, if done regularly. In fact, when she hears from people that things have not been going well for them, the first thing she asks them is if they have been doing their affirmations. Most likely, they will say "No," and when they start again, things improve. But in addition to affirmations, Chellie teaches women to be proactive and to follow through with people.

She says: "One of the big problems I have been working with all my life is helping women business owners to be able to support themselves, to make good money, to price themselves adequately, and to actively sell their products and services. Women want to be in the good girl box. They don't want to bother anybody, so they don't make sales calls. I was talking to a friend of mine who went to a networking meeting and she told two women there, 'I want to buy your services/ products, call me tomorrow.' And neither of them called her. That's absurd. What are women networking for? But people have this idea that all they have to do to network is to go out and pass out their cards and brochures and that if people are interested, they will call them. It doesn't work that way, and they can go out of business very quickly with that strategy."

So, as women, we need to unlearn our self-esteem issues around earning and enjoying money. We need to make connections with people in a meaningful way before we can expect that they will buy from us. Beware of people who will try to make you feel guilty as you become successful or who devalue your work and the fact that you are running a business. There are plenty of other women out there who you can befriend, women who will support you and your business and who are plugged into prosperity consciousness thinking. These are the buddies you need to be successful. Also, tape your affirmations on the mirror and read them every AM and PM while you are brushing your teeth.

> *As women, we need to unlearn our self-esteem issues around earning and enjoying money.*

THE POWER OF SCHEDULES

One of the fantasies of owning your own business is that you can control your time and are free to get up when you want and work when you feel moved to. While there is no question that most entrepreneurs can modify the 9-to-5 routine, we are still plugged into when our clients or customers are available, to some degree, depending on the business we are in. It was interesting that four of the women I interviewed talked about how a set work schedule was a critical success strategy for them. Schedules allow us to maximize prime CEO-thinking time and grant us the space that our creative ideas need to flourish. They give us a solid way of setting boundaries and not getting burned out.

Caroll Michels has a multifaceted business and also is passionate about dancing. She does lots of community projects in the arts in Sarasota, Florida, so she needs a schedule that accommodates all those things. She says: "I am a good morning person, so I get up early and do client work or homework then. I am a multitasker, so I can go from one thing to the next pretty easily. I focus very well. I have a rigid dance schedule so I work clients around that. I find that, with a rigid schedule, time management just falls into place. I take a few hours off in the middle of the day, sort of the European snooze, between one and four o'clock. I don't sleep, but I take time to get away from things and feel clearer when I come back. Weekends are my spontaneity days."

Jeanne Carbonetti paints regularly, writes books, runs a gallery, teaches private clients and classes at her studio in Chester, Vermont, and teaches a limited number of workshops on painting and creativity around the country. Her home and gallery are nestled into a hill, surrounded by lovely maple trees, and she has a separate studio and a Japanese tea house, too. She and her husband designed and built these lovely spaces with gorgeous glass windows so that you feel like you are close to nature in every room. It is a beautiful setting, and my goal is to start spending time with Jeanne to work on my watercolor skills and begin to get my work out into the world. Jeanne has carefully designed her time to maximize everything that she values: "Having time to be alone is so incredibly important to me. I also feel that routine is the absolute pulse of all creative life and I very much love routine. And people always laugh when I say that, but I have a fairly strict routine. Monday is about my books and bills, Tuesday is studio chores like matting and framing, Wednesday through Friday is painting, no office work, nothing except painting. Saturday is whatever needs me most and Sunday is none of the above." Jeanne also stops traveling and teaching from January until April so that she can focus on her writing and painting exclusively. She sets aside special dates to work with her students and plans out her schedule a year in advance. She is also shifting to self-publishing her books with her own imprint after she had four successful books with Watson-Guptill publishers. She was divinely guided to set out on her own now.

Patricia Aburdene, who is best known for her series of books on "megatrends," is one of the world's leading social forecasters. She spends most of her time writing books and speaking . She divides her time between Colorado and the beautiful North Shore seacoast of Massachusetts. She is currently finishing a new book called *The Power of Conscious Money* and is very involved and interested in the development of conscious capitalism. After analyzing her biorhythms and selecting her most productive times, Patricia has set up a very strict schedule, which she says she keeps to like a Prussian General. As she says, "Being self-employed and working at home, I get up and put on a cotton T-shirt and pants, make a cup of tea, and I'm at my desk. So no pantyhose, no commute, nothing like that. Before I work I indulge in an enormous amount of journaling and personal time. My primary spiritual practice is journaling, which I feel is the best way to be present to myself. So I'm usually at my desk by 7 AM and journal until about 8 AM and then I work until about noon and then I go out and do an hour of movement. Then I take a nap after lunch every day. Absolutely heavenly! Then two days out of the week I might have appointments in the afternoon, and then two nights a week I work until 8 PM. I make all my personal appointments and lunch dates on Thursdays, or maybe Monday or Tuesday, but not on Wednesdays or Fridays when I work late. I really believe this schedule helps my creative process. It's like spirit knows when I'm going to be ready to take a download. I show up, and they can make contact."

Victoria Moran says that she loves deadlines and schedules too. She told me, "I think, as a writer, that when you have a deadline for something as part of your day, it changes your relationship with time. We took a cruise recently and one of the greatest things was that they put a little leaflet under the door every night and it told you what happens tomorrow at 7 AM, 7:30 AM, and 8 AM. I loved that. I would probably make a good marine. I just love knowing exactly what's happening at 11:45 AM." Order can be comforting, especially to those of us who work for ourselves, as it means that we don't have to structure absolutely everything.

FIND GREAT CONNECTIONS

Cindy Morrison self-published her book *Girlfriends 2.0* and sold one thousand copies through social media in three weeks. Her book now has a publisher. She also met Tory Johnson from *Good Morning America* through Twitter and is now a speaker at Tory's new workshop series, Spark and Hustle. Cindy says: "I am really big on surrounding yourself with the best people possible, and sometimes meeting those people isn't always as close as your house or your neighborhood or your town." As an award-winning journalist, Cindy uses those skills in her networking. She says: "When I think I am doing business with someone, I do a background check on them and I have a sort of sixth sense about whether it could be someone that I should not do business with. Before I approach a company, I am a research geek, so I go in fully prepared with anything that you could possibly find out about them. Also, if I need to find someone, I can always find them." Cindy's natural ease with an audience has made becoming a speaker a positive choice for her. She loves helping people to have "Ah-ha" moments and believes, along with Zig Zigler, that "if you help other people get what they want, in return you will get what you want, and that is very fulfilling for me."

Debora George Tsakoumakis stumbled upon her idea for her cake business. She had tried two other businesses before that didn't click, but then she tried to wire her Dad a birthday cake for his birthday and found out that no one would do that for her. So her dream was born. She is an avid and persistent networker, and after much trial and error has set up a system that works well. She used to have a network of bakers all over the country, but now she works with one local baker. They use a special kind of cake that does well on long trips, and she just picks up the phone to make things happen. She is also active on blogs and talk shows like the Army Wife Talk Radio, Enlisted Spouse Radio, and Think Like a Black Belt Radio. She got herself featured in *Entrepreneur* and *Family Circle* too. She has now networked her way into the college market. Building key relationships has been a cornerstone of her business growth.

Lesley Bohm is a Hollywood photographer in Los Angeles who is also doing a lot of work with spirit-rich entrepreneurial women. Her work is stunning, and she uses a stylist and a make-up artist to enhance the shots. Lesley focuses intensely on the person and the message that they need to project for their business. Check out the video on her website and you can see what a major event a shooting with Lesley is. Her studio was specially picked because it maximizes the use of natural light. Lesley's business has thrived because she understands the power of authentically connecting to people and helping them to be real in front of her camera.

Lesley says: "It is the connection with people that is the key to my business, especially return business. I want people to have a great experience while they are with me and I have learned to do follow-up with them to keep the connection alive. But people call me because they love me and I make them feel important. The reason I use natural light is that the eyes come more alive and there's more energy that pops out. It enables me to make people more comfortable, nothing flashing in front of their faces, so they can relax and their true spirit comes out. That's really one of my secrets." Lesley's service orientation and caring personality make her photography very much in demand. In fact, people are begging her to do some shooting on the East Coast too, but because she is also a devoted mother, she is resisting most travel requests for now.

DECISIVENESS

I just spent a week in Las Vegas to attend Ali Brown's annual Shine conference for women entrepreneurs. Ali was just named one of Forbes' Women to Watch in 2011 and was selected as one of Ernst & Young's 2010 Entrepreneurial Winning Women. She also won the Enterprising Women of the Year Award. Ali provides a fabulous venue of speakers and rich content in all of her events and she knows how to throw an amazing party, too. She rented the Tryst nightclub at the Wynn Hotel one night with an open bar and dancing in front of a huge waterfall for her V.I.P. guests. It was a stunning night and lots of fun. Ali has been an inspiration and a mentor to so many of us.

When I interviewed Ali for this book, one of things she talked about is how important it is to make good decisions, and that as you become more successful, you have to make decisions a lot faster. She generously volunteered to share her five-part decision-making model with us. Ali recommends asking yourself five questions when you are coming up to an opportunity:

1. Is this something I want with my heart? (Does this feel good to me?)

2. Is this something I want with my head? (Does this logically make sense?)

3. Does this align with my long-term goals and my short-term goals? (So, is this part of my path?)

4. Does this excite me, even if it's a little scary? (It should be more "wahoo" than "ugh.")

5. Am I making this decision from faith and not fear? (So, is it inspiration or desperation?)

Ali says, "You want yeses for all five questions. If there is a no in there, then it is a NO. This is how I operate."

Ali goes on to comment, "Sometimes there will be something in front of me and I'm not sure how I'm going to do it. I may not have the funding to do it or the know-how to do it. But if I made a decision to go forward, I'd say 99 percent of the time when you step into that decision wholeheartedly and you say 'Yes, I'm going to do this,' things suddenly start lining up. Details take care of themselves. Resources appear. It's just phenomenal."

Lynn Robinson has another technique to get focused that helps her to prevent getting overwhelmed. Lynn says, "I try to start every day with a decision about what three things I will focus on that day. My intention is to take the action steps that feel enlivening or joyful or that I feel enthusiastic about. I feel that those are the ones that are intuitively guided. If I feel dragged down by an idea or the action step has no energy to it, I ignore it. If I am in a rut, that gets me out of it because I can say okay, here are three things I can do. It seems like a manageable number. And also at the end of the week I can say, look I've done fifteen things to grow my business or attract more money or whatever my intention is. These three daily tasks are my priorities." It works, as Lynn is one of the most incredibly organized and productive women I know. Interesting, while Lynn is very technically savvy, she and I both make paper lists of to-do's so that we have that portable visual. A lot of the women I interviewed for this book and who participated in a LinkedIn survey that I did still rely on paper lists, at least as a back-up plan.

VICTORIA'S TRIO

Victoria Moran is most adept at how to live the writer's life, philosophically and practically, and I knew she would have some great success strategies for us. Her first one is action partnering, as she calls it. In her words, "Every single day my action partner and I talk at 6:45 AM and we tell each other what actions we are going to take that day to further our goals, dreams, and aspirations. It's a commitment. I love the idea that someone is involved in my life and I am involved in hers. Even though we are in two different fields of endeavor professionally, it's as if the success that we're both striving for is held by both of us." I have a beloved e-mail buddy and we try to support each other each day as well. It is a comfort to not forge this journey of conscious living alone.

Victoria and her husband recently bought a new condo in NYC, and she had a feng shui expert work on it before she moved in. Victoria believes that "When the energies in my home are in balance and working right, I have more creativity and better decision-making abilities." The feng shui expert had a prescription for her and her husband. The best part of the condo for her husband is the master bedroom; the best part of the space for Victoria is the guest room and part of the living room next to the guestroom. It works. As Victoria says, "I find that this little guestroom is so delicious to me; I can come in here and get a whole different attitude."

Her third strategy she calls "rebooting her psyche." When she needs to get away from thinking too much, she goes out to the bank, the post office, the gym, anywhere. She says, "It is kind of like shutting off your computer and rebooting it;

and then it magically works again. I need to get away and reboot myself and then things seem less complicated."

THE MAGIC OF HUMOR

I asked former Congresswoman Pat Schroeder about the best skill she used to get done all the legislation and programs that she accomplished in her twenty-four years in a male-dominated Congress. Her answer was a surprise. Pat said, "I honestly think humor is a wonderful way; you don't get angry, which never pays. You tell other people that you know that you take the issues very seriously, but that you don't take yourself all that seriously. And you are willing to laugh and enjoy life a little, and that helped. If you tell people, 'Oh God, you had better listen to me,' that doesn't work too well." How true that can be.

REFUSING TO GIVE UP

Mary Hayden, our world scientist, claims that not giving up is her best success strategy. She got a PhD at mid-life with three kids, a husband, and a house full of assorted pets. She encountered lots of challenges, but she prevailed, and she gives her husband a lot of the credit for supporting her efforts. Mary talks about her path:

"I think perseverance is key. I don't think I'm brilliant. I don't think I have superhuman skills. I think I'm a person who perseveres—the old adage of where there's a will there's a way. I guess I don't take no for an answer in the sense that it doesn't stop me dead in my tracks. I may hear 'no,' but that just means I take a different path. And I think that's what perseverance is, it's continuing on in the face of obstacles. I also think you need to step back and say, 'Okay, I want to do this. How am I going to do it?'" Whether she is collaborating with witch doctors in Uganda to fight plague or hunting down old tires with water in them that allows mosquitoes with dengue fever to breed in Mexico, Mary is determined to find a way to have an impact on public health, and she does just that.

All of these success strategies are proactive and empowering, and they come from a place of determination and strategic thinking. They also demonstrate self-awareness about what works for our personal style. Successful women push past the fear and the roadblocks and keep forging ahead so that their businesses and their lives have compelling meaning.

Secret Six

Commit to Your Muse and Your Intuition

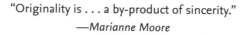

"Originality is . . . a by-product of sincerity."
—*Marianne Moore*

Our capacities for change, innovation, and heeding our inner knowing are powerful tools for success. We have to dedicate time and energy to listen to our inner voice and pay attention to its messages. So often when clients come to me in crisis, it's because they have been running away from or hiding out from their truth. For example, they took a job that they knew was wrong for them, they continue to repeat the same addictive or self-destructive behaviors over and over, or they minimize their need for change, whether it's firing an employee or ending a marriage.

In addition, in this era of so much overstimulation and too many choices, reserving time for your own growth and self-awareness takes commitment and planning. It is too easy to stay cruising down the river of action and not make the effort to stop and take an inventory of your feelings, your brainstorms, and your need to face a transition of some sort and initiate positive but extreme measures.

A key strategy for opening up your inner channels is to de-clutter your life on all levels. In order for your inner voice to speak to you and initiate new plans, you must spring clean your life first. This often calls for what I call Extreme Subtractions. I do this process each quarter. Because I get over stimulated, I need to filter things out so that I can stay focused, and to do that I need to regularly clear the decks.

An example of a recent Extreme Subtraction process for me was taking the following actions:

1. Released fifty possible marketing opportunities from my collection of notes

2. Postponed six creative projects to next year—or maybe never

3. Ended two professional affiliations

4. Closed a brokerage account that we don't need

5. Donated a huge pile of unread magazines to the YMCA for people to enjoy on the treadmill

6. Changed phone plans, then changed back, and ended up with an even lower monthly bill

7. Hired a professional organizer to help me reorganize my office and creative projects

8. Threw out & recycled eight trash bags of old files

9. Cancelled subscriptions to three book clubs, four magazines, and thirty e-zines and blogs

In this world of information overload and infinite possibilities, setting boundaries is a constant challenge. Therefore, our multitasking heads are filled to the brim with too many projects and details. We have to learn to filter out the onslaught of other people's issues and ideas and become super-selective and protective.

You must subtract anything that you have outgrown to pave the way for new growth and transformation. Get out your sword of discernment and start hacking away at all the distractions and less-than-satisfying experiences in your life, and do it today. You need time and peace of mind to accomplish your dreams.

Shut off the noise and shut down the unnecessary.

Whenever I do this, I experience a wonderful sense of freedom which continues until the next purge. I also spend about twenty minutes per day recycling things to block the incoming flow. I open my mail in the dining room and immediately put everything I can into the giant recycle bin that the City of Boston gave us, which gets filled up every week (which is amazing for only two people). Setting boundaries and keeping our defenses up is essential.

FILTER & FOCUS

I have been busy with many new clients and opportunities to work with people with lots of brilliant ideas and projects in the works. It has been very exciting, and it reinforces why I love the work that I do. In the midst of all this talent, these folks are feeling overwhelmed by the flood of ideas in their own minds, wanting to be born. On top of all that internal combustion, there is the constant onslaught of information from media, social media, email, video, cell phones, and so on that has everyone in a tizzy. No one can keep up with it—it's impossible.

In order to nurture our precious seedlings of creativity, we have to shut off the noise and shut out the unnecessary. Just like a dryer filters out lint (so we can throw it in the trash), we need a circle of filters around us to repel the unwanted stimulus. We have to turn off, tune out and say "no" to the many intrusions into our musing time. I often tell people to find a spot away from their computer/cell phone/mp3 player to think on a daily basis. Creative ideas need time and space and silence to evolve.

So what data or influence in your life do you need to filter out? Try an experiment for the next month and subtract or delete the irritating things that are more than you can handle. Would I like to read thirty blogs a day? I'm curious and I love to learn, but I can't fit all those new thoughts into my head each day. So I now read a few blogs and appreciate them, and then I rotate when I get bored. Un-friend people, or do whatever you need to in order to stop the flow of information to the "inbox" of your brain.

Even after this filter cleanse, for most creative people choosing what to focus on involves losses. As discussed earlier, if you have a list of ten projects, you can only focus on one to three at a time. This means letting go of aspirations and enticements for now, to be revisited later. I have also been noticing that many people are focusing on the wrong projects or their fantasy projects first. We often have to start with the critical building blocks of our business and get those in motion before we try out our wilder side. Focusing on the right goal is incredibly powerful. It can be life-changing. What needs to be top priority for you right now? Embrace it, and do the very best you can with the challenge. Focusing will give you freedom.

After you have done your Extreme Subtractions, take a look around you. Your mind needs care. If you want to be able to act on your original ideas, you need to clear the channels in your brain so that you can receive your inspiration, new schemes and initiatives, and plans for your well-being. Just as with your garden, you need to clear out the weeds and then get the right soil mixture in which to plant new seeds and nurture them to bloom or harvest. Just like seeds need good soil, water, and fertilizer, your mind needs care and attention as well.

Is there anything stuck in your mind that you need to pull out? A client of mine just tossed an essay that she had been working on all winter because she decided that she was no longer inspired enough about the topic to go through the magazine submission process. That's okay— she learned something, practiced her craft, and is telling the truth. She is a published author, so she has a history of finishing things (unlike the perfectionists who can't let go as nothing is ever good enough), but she feels done and is ready to move on. Another client of mine has three websites, and we decided on a new umbrella domain name for her that will encompass all three businesses and greatly simplify her life. Managing three sites with three blogs, three email boxes, and three marketing plans is a mountain too tough to climb. Still another client decided that she had too many part-time people working for her and she was doing too much human resource work, so she selected the two best people and expanded their roles. Successful women pay attention to their "pain and discomfort" and strive to eliminate it, if they can.

> Successful women pay attention to their "pain and discomfort" and strive to eliminate it, if they can.

GETTING HOOKED

When you are dancing with possible ideas to develop, you have to see which idea seduces you into a romance with it. Getting hooked is very much about letting your heart guide you toward ideas that resonate with your life purpose and the work you are intended to do. It may end up being a love affair that fizzles, but you have to try it so that you will know what to do next—and that's okay. Some ideas, like some relationships, don't have enough solidarity to keep us connected and content. So we need to follow our energy until we find the right answer.

Peggy Whitson is an astronaut who has accumulated more hours in space than any other woman. She is currently the chief of the Astronaut Corps at the NASA Johnson Space Center in Houston, Texas. While up in outer space, Peggy Whitson got inspired. As she says, "I enjoy writing, and during my missions I share some of my writings, like my letters home that I wrote to folks on the ground; these are publically available on the NASA website." But there was more. Peggy went on to expand her communications from space. She tells us, "Space is incredibly beautiful. On my first mission, looking back at earth, I used the analogy that being in space and looking out the window for the first time was like having lived in a semi-dark room my entire life—and then someone turned on the lights. Then, doing a space walk is like going out into the sunshine for the first time. During my second flight, I got tuned into photography—we do lots of earth observation photography, but you are usually shooting specific things, like urban growth, etcetera. But on this flight I took a lot of pictures that were just what I considered attractive features of the planet, either in color or in texture or all different variables that struck me while looking at the planet. I decorated the walls of my house with all these earth observations shots to show just how beautiful it was and how different places change in the seasons, or under different lighting, for example."

I suggested to Peggy that it sounds like she has the ingredients for a fascinating book. It's interesting that Peggy's personal creativity is focused on landscaping her yard. She loves plants, digging in the dirt, getting things to grow, and being physical at the same time. It satisfies her aesthetically and keeps her in great shape, which is essential for an astronaut.

A few years ago, I ended up growing a large fibroid and had to decide what to do about it—have surgery or hope that it shrank during menopause. I read six books on the topic and asked my trusted gynecologist of twenty years if I could have an MRI to check it out more closely. When we got the results, he said, "If you were my wife, I would have you get it out." But, alas, due to health insurance hassles, he no longer performed surgeries or delivered babies. I had just read a magazine article about Dr. Elizabeth Stewart at Brigham and Women's Hospital in Boston, my hospital, about how she was doing research on fibroids and alternative treatments. It turned out that my doctor and Dr. Stewart knew each other, and so off to Dr. Stewart I went. To make a long story short, I did not qualify for her research group, so Dr. Stewart took my uterus out with the fibroid and left everything else. It turned out that it was a really good idea for me to have the surgery based on what she found. Dr. Stewart was a wonderful, caring doctor and came to visit me in the hospital every day, and it was the most seamless surgery I have ever had. I am forever grateful.

When it came time to do the research for this book, I looked up Elizabeth and discovered that she was now a professor of obstetrics and gynecology at the Mayo Clinic College of Medicine in Rochester, Minnesota. She's also published a book: *Uterine Fibroids: The Complete Guide.* I wanted to know what it was about fibroids that hooked her. She said, "It started as a research project at the beginning of my fellowship, because fibroids are a little bit of a peripheral field to my work in reproductive endocrinology. Most people who go into reproductive endocrinology work with eggs, sperm, or embryos. So fibroids is a somewhat different field, but there was a good amount of work going on in the field. As time went on, it was a good fit for me. It was a field that involved surgery as well as medical aspects. It was a disease where women were not getting the kinds of options and counseling they needed in a lot of places. So it was a really good niche for someone to occupy because no one else was trying to integrate all the different approaches."

Elizabeth has been studying the new focused ultrasound treatment, among other methods, to reduce the number of fibroid surgeries. She loves the variety in her work and spends time traveling, grant-writing, seeing patients, and teaching. I asked her about her greatest creative challenge and she talked about her writing: "I think particularly with my academic work and writing that, even though it is scientific writing, it is a creative process. Trying to find the right analogies to explain something, especially when you are trying to translate scientific concepts for the lay population, is a difficult and creative process. We've just finished writing a manuscript about fibroids and how the diversity of the disease process is so much greater than the variability between other disease processes. You can have a fibroid that's the size of a dime or one that's the size of a basketball. I think there is still a lot of art to medicine, and to find the right fit for the right person and the right explanation is very much a creative process."

Chellie Campbell says that she never gets a creative idea while she is working on her to-do list. She says she gets creative ideas while napping, watching TV, or driving. She says, "If I am driving, I'll grab a piece of paper and a pen or pull over and send myself an email on my Blackberry. All I have to do is put in one word and that reminds me. I got the idea for *The Wealthy Spirit* in the car. I was thinking, I am writing a book, but how am I going to make it different? I went to the bookstore and went to the financial section and all those books were dull and not what I wanted to do. So I am driving in the morning, having read my *Daily Word* newsletter, and I thought, well, what you do in your workshops is to teach by story, and you've got lots of stories. You could do a page-a-day like the Daily Word . . . and then I was so excited!" It was an excellent idea, because with Chellie's book, you can just open it anywhere and read a story and the affirmation for the day and feel prosperous!

Mary Hayden likes her creative challenges in her multidisciplinary sciences. As she says: "Most of the work that I do is sort of a giant puzzle. There are so many components that come together and, really, the goal with each of these projects is to crack the nut, to try to better understand disease transmission and what we can do to mitigate that. I'm constantly thinking of ways that haven't been approached yet, and about how can we do this better? How can we improve on what's already been done? I'm not operating in a vacuum here. There's tons of great work that's been done before, and taking that work and building upon it is really crucial to what I'm doing. The whole idea is to try to solve the puzzle, or at least a piece of it. You can't just take what other people have done. You have to come up with your own ideas and you have to try to implement those. I also work with a team of people who are great. It's so wonderful to be able to sit down and brainstorm with people and come up with different ideas. Anytime I want, I can call and say, 'Hey, what do you think about this?' And she can laugh at me or she can say 'Oh, here's what I was thinking.' It's important for me because I'm much more of a people person, not a person who likes to sit in front of a computer all day long by myself." Mary is truly an extrovert and values being on a creative team. In fact, in the midst of National Science Foundation and other program cuts, Mary offered to take a pay cut herself so that her colleagues could stay in their jobs. Now that is dedication and appreciation for one's peers.

JJ Virgin has a big vision for her business, and she is stepping into it more each day. As JJ says, "My mission is to empower people to take charge of their lives and to do that through taking better care of their health. My whole business is about being creative and finding new ways and developing new programs for people so they will be able to accomplish that. So whether it's going to be about the delivery, like a teleclass or an mp3 or a video download or a different kind of membership club, how do we get people to be accountable, to be able to take action, and what's going to make it work? How do we satisfy what clients want while giving them what they really need? That requires incredible creativity."

When I asked JJ how she gets her ideas, she said that her creative fire is always on (I can relate, as mine is too). So, as JJ says, her process is as follows: "I carry a book around and I download my brain all the time, because my biggest challenge is that there's too much in my head. I don't have to sit there and think up ideas. It's really deciding what I should pick to do. So one of the things I do is I download all those ideas and I see which idea comes up again. If it doesn't, I figure it's really not that big of a deal. Where I'm really focusing now is hearing—to clearly listening to what people say they want. I am really letting the marketplace drive me into creating things. I don't believe in surveys, because even if people say they want something, it doesn't mean they'll actually give you money for it. But, if someone sends you an email or posts on your Facebook page or walks up and tells you, they must really want it because they had to make an effort. And that's what I'm looking for, not information I had to bribe someone to get. I'm also very much a fan of the masterminds, and I've been in a coaching group for two years, and I have a group of people that I run ideas by and work on things with, so most of my creative process now is very collaborative."

ENHANCERS

For each of us, we need to discover our own personal creative/idea generation *enhancers.* These are strategies we use to connect with our intuition or our higher self or the divine—however we choose to envision it. Stress is a creativity killer, so many of our personal enhancers involve a respite from stress and negative people and places. When I asked the women in this book what strategies they used to increase their connection with their creative reservoir, I got a wide range of answers.

> *Discover your own personal creative enhancers.*

Lisa Sasevich trained with Tim Kelley, author of a wonderful book called *True Purpose* that is filled with fascinating exercises to help you discover why you are here. One of Tim's well-known techniques is "active imagination," which I learned this year from one of Tim's colleagues. Lisa talks about how it works for her: "I stay connected to my creativity and my passion through this process of active imagination, which is really just a writing process. It's almost like writing a script between "Trusted Source" and "I." So I'll just write my name and two dots and then I will write what I want to say, like 'Hey Source, hey God, can we talk tonight?' And then I'll write 'God' and then I just trust whatever the pen writes in response to my questions. I will say in the last eighteen months, as I have taken this nearly $3 million leap in my business, so much of the guidance that I've received has been from taking the time to check in with Source and follow the guidance I get. I'll give you an example of this. I was doing a big launch for a product I have called *6-Figure Teleseminar Secrets*, and I remember not knowing how many people should be the first to get the bonus items. I had always made it a small percentage. But this time I asked Source in my active imagination process, and I got the answer '250'—the first 250. I had never even sold 250 units of anything online. So I went with it and, lo and behold, it was our first quarter million dollar launch. We sold 250 units at $1000 each, so that to me was a real affirmation about the process." I know that I dialoged many times with Trusted Source (this is the term that Lisa uses and Tim teaches in his book) to identify the women that I wanted to interview for this book and the lessons that I wanted to teach. It is a very powerful technique to use regularly.

Marilyn Tam also teaches people about innovation and has worked with many corporate leaders to spark and strengthen their creative insights. "Innovation and creativity are the Holy Grails of business and life that everybody's looking for. But how do you get creative? It's not just by reading a book. It's being able to observe, listen, integrate, and step back and ask for the underlying reason and cause. Everything has a reason for being and a natural flow; learn to understand the dynamics, pull all the relevant pieces together, and foster their development and synergy. The results will then just emerge naturally, and the next thing you know, you've got a piece of poetry or a solution to your problem or whatever you are working to create. For me, I meditate every morning, and that helps me to allow information and creativity to come in or bubble up."

Pele Rouge lives her life in harmony with Mother Earth and the rhythms of life and family. She helps people to honor events, transitions, and celebrations by leading groups of people in ceremony. Her tagline is "Life as Ceremony." To do the work that she does, she needs to be connected to herself and spirit. She and her husband, FireHawk, are carriers of an ancient body of earth wisdom teachings who have just launched the Center of Timeless Leadership. As Pele tells the story, "Timeless leadership comes from knowing who one is. It comes from knowing what you are here to do and the determination to do it, no matter what. And the medicine teaching wheels that we carry are tens of thousands of years old. So the essence of this training is to teach people how to walk in wholeness and balance no matter what, no matter where they are, no matter what's coming at them, and to use themselves as what we would call an instrument of healing."

When I asked Pele about things she does to enhance her creativity, she said: "Well, there's journaling and meditation and that pretty much covers daily practice. There is also a dance of alignment, balance, and prayer. We also have a time of annual retreat every year, typically in December, where we do ten days that we take for ourselves—we call it our dreaming time. It's a time to reflect on the year that's passed and to dream about the year or years to come. We also have a practice of what we call declaring a national holiday. We can do this, since we don't have a set pattern of work. It's not like we work Monday through Friday. It varies. And so every once in a while we just look at each other and say, 'you know, today is a national holiday' and we just declare it a day to do whatever it is that we please. We don't answer phones or work on computers. We mostly just be."

For her sixtieth birthday, Pele went on a retreat in the mountains of Colorado by herself for forty-six days. In the course of her time alone, she encountered a bear who frightened her and kept returning to her camp, but then became a great teacher to her. The story of their relationship is chronicled in her DVD, *Never Shout at a Bear*, which is a teaching story of nonviolence and harmony with all the creatures on this planet. For many women, retreats with a long expanse of profound solitude and healing are life-changing.

The opposite of meditation and retreats is an increase in your connection to other people. Shama Kabani talks about spending time with intelligent people, especially women entrepreneurs, as being a catalyst for her creativity. She says, "When I go to conferences I'm surrounded by really smart people, and that is always inspiring for me. I get motivated by seeing other people working hard and making things come true." She is someone who gets bright ideas while doing the mundane and knows enough to take notes.

Brenda Michels is loaded with energy and novel ideas. When I asked her about her creative process, she said, "My way of tapping in is to take walks in nature, which is one of the things I love to do because we live in such a beautiful area here in Seattle. That is probably my first and foremost. But I'll let you in on a little secret that is probably going to sound funny to a lot of readers,--I also get a lot of creative inspiration when I'm vacuuming the house. I deliberately make it fun and sometimes I listen to music, which adds to my creative experience. I also tap into a lot of creativity by learning from those guests that we interview, and this in turn inspires me to be more creative." Actually, Brenda and I have had numerous long conversations on the phone while she is vacuuming, and she is sharp and articulate, and passionate about her philosophy of life and what she is trying to accomplish. She never misses a beat, or even gets out of breath. Amazing!

Jeanne Carbonetti uses what she calls her "tummy jump" as well as her well-developed inner knowing to guide her creative "children" out into the world. Jeanne went through a transition period with the original publisher of her first four books, and she decided to explore other options for her new material. She has incredible patience and a real trust that she will know the right moves to make. As she says, "I really have a feeling about my books that they go out when they need to go out: the universe calls for them and then it's time. I actually wrote *The Heart of Creativity* in 2004, and I very specifically had not sent it to the publisher until it was completely finished. Because of the transition in the publishing company, we ultimately decided we weren't a good match for this project. So there was quite a period of time during which I didn't feel any kind of pressure to do anything. I sent the book out a few times and went back and forth with an agent, but was content to take my time. Then, in October of 2008, I was standing by my french doors in the living room. That's where all kinds of things seem to come out of the sky and hit me in the head. When I was standing there, I suddenly knew why I had waited until now. It was because in the very center of the book I talk about Martin Luther King and the dream, and how that is the very moment *when imagination literally becomes inspiration* and the light moves from outside the self to inside the self. We had to wait until Barack Obama became President Obama. As soon as November came, I had this incredible push of 'now' and that was when I decided it was time to do it myself. And as it turns out, I have a very nice printer right in the next town that I had done some prints with, and it was a most beautiful experience."

Jeanne's story reminds me of the teachings of the Rune on beneficial outcomes, *Jera*, which teaches, "Remember the farmer who was so eager to assist his crops that he went out at night and tugged on the new shoots. There is no way to push the river; equally you cannot hasten the harvest." We must learn the art of patience and trust, because sometimes things don't bloom because they are not meant to, or because they need more nourishment and will flower next year.

THE IMPORTANCE OF SPACE

Take a look around your office and your home. Is it working for you? Do you have everything you need to be effective and happy? Is it time to buy five pairs of scissors so you have them when and where you need them, or to get a new desk or software or learn feng shui and create a serene space? Where and how we work is really important. What do you need to add to your work or home space that will either charm you or streamline your operations?

If you have your business stashed in a closet, that is probably not enough space to run it well and get your products or services out into the world. I have had so many clients over the years who have set up a home office or studio in the basement, especially a dark, damp basement; they dread going down there, so it adversely impacts their joy, not to mention their productivity.

A while back, I interviewed Sheryll Hirschberger Reichwein, a feng shui expert and co-owner with her husband of the bed and breakfast The Beach Rose Inn on Cape Cod, to get some tips on how to leverage the power of space to enhance well-being, creativity, and innovation. Sheryll's theories are based in Taoism and a belief in the oneness of all things. Feng shui is about connecting with the natural world—hence the Five Elements—and enhancing thought and intention. In general, Sheryll says that there are very few set rules, but she offered some good suggestions to use as a guide for creative offices and studios:

1. Creative people are often high in either Fire or Water energy. People who are high in Fire energy like to be "on stage" and tend to express their creativity externally. They are highly energized, passionate people who can easily burn out, be undisciplined, and resist rules. To avoid the pitfalls of too much Fire, add grounding, soothing Earth energy to the environment by way of things made of stone, earth-tone colors, and square shapes. Water folks like to flow with their creativity in solitary ways and tend to express their creativity internally. They are intuitive, dreamy people who can find it hard to focus on completing tasks. To help support people with lots of Water energy, add containing, clarifying Metal energy expressed in things such as mirrors, the color white, and circular shapes.

2. If possible, keep a boundary between your work space and home space, even if it's just the use of a screen or an armoire to isolate a corner of a room. For creative people, there is great power in declaring both physical and psychic space for your creative efforts, and ideally, your creative space should be away from your bedroom, which is meant for rest. If you need to take over your guest room and use it 90 percent of the time as your art studio, do it. You can adjust when guests come, but give yourself priority.

3. Clear your workspace of images that are unappealing; incomplete or uninspiring projects; and anything that does not reflect your current self. You want to be nurtured by the lighting, the furniture, the colors, and special objects.

4. Keep one or two objects in your space that represent your talents and prosperity, like a framed picture of your first royalty check, or a letter from a fan of your work, or your best painting on the wall.

5. Have your desk or work table facing the door to welcome positive energy into the room.

To learn more about feng shui so that you can select the principles that resonate personally for you, Sheryll has authored *The Feng Shui Deck: 50 Ways to Create a Healthy and Harmonious Home,* in collaboration with Olivia Miller.

Shift your workspace so that you love to be there and feel nurtured. I have a whole wall of built-in bookcases, a window seat where I keep my decks of affirmation cards, hydrangea wallpaper, and a lavender rug. In fact, my office was once photographed by *The Boston Globe* as a creative space.

Ali Brown loves to work at her home on the beach in California. While her company has an office, she never goes there, and her team is virtual. She does meet with clients and staff at her home, but sets very careful boundaries with her time and space. Ali says: "To be creative, I need open time, and open time for me is non-scheduled time. I actually think two things, there's time and there's environment. And the first is time and I remember working with a mentor once who, when I was asking her about time management, said, 'You should schedule every five minutes of your day.' And I thought I was going to vomit. That's maybe the most unnatural, non-intuitive way to work. You have to have scheduled things, but creativity comes from space and a lot of women don't give themselves enough space in their day. So I need time to just kind of putter or sometimes I need to sit and read or get out of the office and take a walk on the beach. I got a great idea once by watching a fashion show on Bravo. You never know where your next idea is going to come from. As women, it's really important that we have an environment that stimulates us or is beautiful. You won't be able to have a great idea or focus on something that's important to you if your desk is a mess and there's a pile of laundry next to your fax machine. It's very important that women start paying attention to their environment. Whatever your budget is or whatever your situation is—you may be in the corner of the kitchen with your business—make it the best you can for what you're doing."

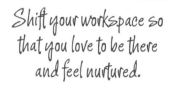

Shift your workspace so that you love to be there and feel nurtured.

But some people cannot write in their home or office, like Victoria Moran. She has a different routine: "I go to a place to write. I either write in a library or in a Starbucks. People say, 'How can you do that? There's all that noise, all those people.' Well, that noise and those people are what I translate into the words. It's my raw material. I need it. So once I'm there, it's almost like the muse gets the call. When I try to write from my regular office where I do all the coaching, marketing, and the clerical stuff, she wants nothing to do with me. So the best way for me to tap into my creativity is to go where I create and my brain and my psyche know at that moment that that's what they're supposed to be doing."

One time Victoria told me that she was going to take a thirty-hour train ride back to New York from a speaking gig so that all she could do was write. She got some work done, but not as much as she had hoped. I asked her if leaving town worked for her and she said: "I have gone away a couple of times. I went to Saratoga Springs to the national park there, this wonderful kind of faded-glory Victorian hotel, and finished up my proposal for *Younger by the Day.* And I went to a bed and breakfast in Ocean City, New Jersey, to finish writing *Fat, Broke & Lonely No More.* But the only thing I really need to get away from is the email and, to a lesser extent, the phone. But now there's WiFi everywhere and we all have cell phones and most of those get email. There's no escape! It used to be writers could just go away. I have a wonderful writing mentor, Jerrold Mundis. He tells the writers he helps: 'In the morning, you can meditate if you do that, and if you're somebody who gets hungry in the morning, you can eat, but other than that, you don't do anything. You just write because that's when you're freshest; that's when you're closest to the source of creativity. There was a time when that was so simple. I just got up early and I had my typewriter or my word processor and that was my work; what else was there to do? Now, it just feels like there's work to do—all the email and various requests from people—before I'm allowed to work. And, of course, if I do the email before I write, it expands to fill the day and the writing is left behind. I'm learning to escape ever earlier in the morning before anybody expects anything!"

Many of the women I talked to mentioned the need to put time limits on emails and social media so that they could focus on their key projects. I even have a sign on my laptop now that says, "Write—don't check email." I am trying to set specific times a day to check in and that's it.

As you know, the art of creativity is not just for artists. We are all creative beings, as we are always reinventing ourselves and making or inventing things that are new, whether it's designing a new program for our clients or introducing a new product internationally or inventing a robot that will clean your house. Creativity gives you the extra edge in today's marketplace. Making a commitment to our inner muse and cultivating our creativity and our uniqueness helps us to be successful and to stand out from the crowd. But we need to focus our creativity and embrace it wholeheartedly for it to result in success. Remember, there are thousands of ways to express yourself creatively. It helps to have a written Muse Contract that answers the following questions.

> The art of creativity is not just for artists.

Exercise: *Your Contract with Your Muse*

The goal of this exercise is to help you develop a communication and a contract with your muse, similar to a personal mission statement or an artist's statement. Using these questions as a guide, you can then write a paragraph or a one-page statement that reflects your creative purpose and goals for this year.

- What creative ideas are calling to you right now?

- What is your vision for how you want these ideas to take form?

- Which idea do you want to explore first? What are the first three steps in that exploration?

- What do you predict will be easy for you, and what will be the most challenging?

- What promises will you make to yourself to keep you connected to your process? How will you reward yourself?

Success comes from tuning into our creative ideas and leveraging them to build a heartfelt business or career and a fulfilled life. Read your Muse Contract daily—it will change your life. By the end of this book, you will have a myriad of ideas for action steps, based on your inspirations, talents, and loves.

AVOIDANCE GAMES

The progressive realization of worthy goals propels you toward your vision of prosperity. The addition of positive choices every day improves the quality of your journey. So, why not get started? In case you're a procrastinator, here are eight tips to help you begin:

1. Acknowledge that avoidance creates needless stress for you. By procrastinating, you put yourself under an energy-draining emotional strain. Procrastination is the opposite of success. If your procrastination represents indecision, then identify what information you need to make that decision and get moving.

2. Break down overwhelming tasks into small ones. You want to write a two hundred-page book? Write a page a day and you'll be done in seven months.

3. Do a start-up task to break the stalemate. If your goal is to find like-minded joint venture partners, start with your stack of business cards and then move to the Internet to give you some initial prospects.

4. Work on your goal for ten minutes. Denise hates filing, but if she sets a timer for ten minutes and puts on her favorite CD, it gets done.

5. Use your moods to your advantage. Recently, Judy had a big marketing proposal to write which could earn her a coveted promotion, but the words eluded her. Feeling social, she called several contacts in her marketing association and brainstormed more ideas for her proposal. These conversations illuminated why she had writer's block and the next day, the proposal flowed.

6. Procrastination can also mask ambivalence. If you're still doubtful about your goal, list the pros and cons of accomplishing it. If the advantages don't outweigh the disadvantages, then the task isn't worth it.

7. Make a contract with a friend or a colleague that you'll meet your goal by a specific date. If nothing else, fear of embarrassment will motivate you. This is why job hunting groups, leads groups, small business planning groups, mastermind groups, and support relationships, like mentoring and coaching, work. Use the advantage!

8. Lastly, reward yourself for meeting your goals beginning with your first steps. Latoya loves inexpensive costume earrings and treats herself to a pair whenever she crosses off an action step.

Avoidance rates as a prime time waster. Make sure that you stay in charge of it! Whenever you find yourself falling into the procrastination rabbit hole, whip out your journal, and write about what is stopping you. The truth will become clear to you.

Remember—every day is an opportunity for you to gain headway toward your life of positive choices. All these exercises will increase your proficiency and increase your likelihood of a fortunate outcome. Act today!

SOLITUDE

In talking with women all over the world in my teaching and coaching work, I hear a consistent theme. Women are all saying the same thing: "I need quiet. I need to be able to be still and alone so that I can hear my inner voice."

Getting that solitude means being intentional and setting a firm boundary around ourselves in order to revel in silence. Many spiritual traditions have retreats and rituals centered around being silent. Retreat centers all over the world are hopping with business as women and men are booking quiet time. Solitude allows us to unplug from the overstimulation of today's world and tune into our inner world. My good friend Marilyn Veltrop, cofounder at PathFinders in California, practices a morning of silence each week and faithfully goes to a retreat center once every month or two. Another Cape Cod friend and my favorite novelist, Ann LeClaire, wrote a great book on silence called *Listening Below the Noise* and has practiced full days of silence each month for over a decade. She also goes to writer's retreat centers for periods of time to work on her novels. She leaves her family temporarily so that she can immerse herself in her plot and her characters.

In order to be successful and capture our power of innovation and competence, we have to be dedicated and take time to be alone with our thoughts, away from the stress of our everyday lives. So often, this is when the gold shows up. Then we can decide when and with whom to share our discoveries and discern what kind of input, brainstorming, critiquing, or feedback we want. Then we can launch our product or service into the real world. The life partners or significant others, friends, and family who love us will help us take the time we need to find the answers we are looking for. As for those who try to sabotage our plans, we have to decide whether or not we want to be in relationship with them and, if so, on what terms.

In addition to silence, we need to spend time with other women in order to stay strong. Research shows that women desperately need their friends and peers. In this computer age of workaholism, many women have abandoned their friends except for an occasional email. We need to make time with other women a priority—we need to play with the women we know and love, and we also need to venture out to conferences, spas, and other places of nurture and learning to connect with an even greater circle of women. As Western women, we need to use our individual power as well as the power of sisterhood to transform the lack of humanity and love in today's world. Successful women are tuned into the potential that we all have to do good and to give back. Pick a cause and stand behind it. I know mine is to support PBS; this support is in black and white in my will. We need this balance of time alone to percolate, and we need time with women (and men) to consciously make the world a better place.

Lastly, as successful women, we have the opportunity to become external muses to other women. We can take young women and our peers and pull them up to new self-confidence and give them the lessons we have learned on our own paths. Mentoring, teaching, and coaching others is sacred work, and ensures that each generation of women becomes stronger and more daring. We need to help other women take calculated and positive risks so that they can grow to their highest potential.

Secret Seven

Crafting a Business Plan That Helps You to Grow Personally, Generates Prosperity, and Enhances Your Lifestyle

MONEY CONFUSION

Money has always been a hot potato for women. We get a lot of messages to be "nice" and to do things for free or give people things on the cheap. No wonder the "fear of success" dynamic is still so prevalent. We fear that if we are successful, we may become a different person and get attacked by men, as well as by other women. The truth is that the more visible we become, the more we are a target for people's jealousy or projections. This forces us to let go of the fantasy that everyone will always like and approve of us—an impossible dream. Some women donned the feminine version of the suit and little scarf tie and acted like men and made it. Other women have worked themselves to the bone to benefit someone else and paid the price in terms of their health and self-esteem. I had a client last year who made $5 million for her last company because she was a whiz at sales relationships. But her boss started to hide profits from her and worked her into a health crisis. She is a superstar, but she can't own it yet.

And then there is the "greed is good" lingo and the messages about corporate profits at any cost. The Wall Street crash and the credit default swap debacle sends chills through those of us who trusted the system to safeguard our IRA money. Money is simply energy, but what we project onto it is amazing. Many women are "unconscious" about money and misuse it by not adding up their numbers, not balancing their checkbook, not saving, and so on. America as a nation got hooked on credit card spending, equity loans, and "having it now," even if we couldn't afford "it."

All the women in this book, myself included, feel strongly about being of service in the world. We are all connected to some kind of purpose and the value of what we bring to the culture. Integrity and authenticity are important, and many of us mentor men and women to grow personally, professionally, and spiritually. We do "good work;" some of us are multimillionaires with thriving businesses, some of us are solo entrepreneurs who make enough to suit our lifestyle and protect our health, and some of us are affiliated with organizations for which we can focus on our creativity with the support of a system that takes care of the other business elements. Many of us are on the path to grow ourselves and our businesses to achieve greater wealth and personal freedom and to help more people. As women, we are seeking to balance our personal lives and our commitment to family and relationships with work that expresses our creativity and our values and contributes to the financial well-being and lifestyle of ourselves and our loved ones. Too many women are trying to do it all themselves; they are staying up late doing housework on speed or battling constant fatigue or burnout, which we will discuss in detail later in this book.

We are living in a profit oriented world, which is fine—except that it has gotten off track. As Brenda Michels says, "When it's all about profit, it takes us away from who we are and why we are truly here. Our obsession with bigger, better, faster, more turns businesses into predators, and people into competitors, competing against one another instead of cooperating with one another. Middle America is being decimated in this country. People are fighting one another. Big banks and multi-national corporations have only one way of doing business—making a profit at the expense of people, animals, and the planet. When it's all about the bottom line, the heart and soul of who we are is discarded, and we become empty inside. This can lead to greed and the hoarding of our resources in order to fill us up. And this, in my opinion, is not so much a social or political problem as it is a spiritual problem, because we will never be able to fill the empty void until we turn inward and spiritually connect to the God in us. "

> When it's all about the bottom line, the heart and soul of who we are is discarded, and we become empty inside.

How many times a week do we hear about companies that continued to keep drugs on the market even though they were killing people, or manufacturers, like car companies, that kept vehicles on the road when they knew they had faulty brakes or some other malfunction, or companies that know that the foods they produce are filled with chemicals and hormones that are making us sick? What kind of culture allows that to happen? The women in this book are going against that grain of profit just for profit's sake or promoting products or services that harm people. That is part of the new success for women. They are starting businesses in droves so that they can have control of their time and their work quality, and they are speaking up about human values in their organizations and in their joint ventures with other people-focused business owners.

A NEW CONSCIOUSNESS

There is a revolution going on to create conscious businesses, ones that care about people and the planet. Patricia Aburdene, who is an expert on conscious capitalism and future trends, sees business undergoing a metamorphosis. Patricia says that "Business as usual or traditional capitalism (which is a sort of unconscious capitalism) is dying and there is a bottom-up grassroots megatrend of conscious capitalism, which is a self-organizing trend of visionary CEOs in conjunction with values-driven customers and socially responsible investors. Investors certainly want a good return on their investment, but they want it to be through a business that's doing something that contributes to the world in some way. And I think that really good conscious capitalistic companies live by two rules. They have a purpose that is greater than making money, even though they want to make money, and they honor the stakeholder model of capitalism. To succeed today, you've got to do business with an ecosystem that's complete and whole, one that involves the customers, the employees, the suppliers, the investors, and the community that you do business with, and ultimately the planet itself, especially in an environmental sustainability context."

Patricia acknowledges that too many companies "cook the books" in a way that is just as far as you can go without being completely illegal. She likens it to an eating disorder where someone might engage in all kinds of strange behaviors just to get the number on the scale lower. In the case of business, however, it probably also includes lying and cheating. She does remind us that all of us as investors have to take responsibility for market crashes, too, because we participated in the system. We put our resources at risk because we believed we had to in order to make more money. As Patricia says, "I would call it a cultural virus to believe that you must make more and more money because that's the smart thing to do. And that's very similar to the Wall Street mentality—you have to kill the numbers because that's what smart people do, and you have to take little risks if you want to be successful." And so we go into denial and stop tapping into our intuition and doing what feels right to us—instead doing what the business and investing so-called authorities tell us to do. That's why many people are out of the market now or learning to invest differently or pursuing socially responsible stocks and funds.

CREATING PROFITABLE AND POSITIVE CAREERS AND BUSINESSES

There is nothing wrong with wanting to be successful and accumulate wealth, as long as what we do is in harmony with our values and does not harm other people. Some of us are natural empire builders and some of us want a simpler life with a business that does not overwhelm us. As Ali Brown says, "Money only makes you more of who you are. You get busier and you have nicer stuff, but it only makes you more of who you were in the first place. So that's why women shouldn't be scared of becoming wealthy. In fact, you can help a lot more people. I love writing checks to charity. I love showing up at events and hearing how it's changed people's lives. Speaking of charity, Ali will be featured on ABC's *Secret Millionaire.* Ali told me that this was a life changing experience for her.

"Some people say money doesn't matter— I don't need those things. That's fine. But I wanted a beautiful home, I wanted everything, I wanted a hot car and I love beautiful clothes. For me, I had to give myself permission to do all those things, because when you don't have money, you pretend you don't care. You tell yourself, 'I don't need that. I'm fine with this.' And then when you start making money, you realize how much fun it can be to have beautiful things, great experiences, to travel, and all this great stuff, so you give yourself permission to enjoy it. I do have a certain percentage that I put away. It may not be as much as some people would advise, but I know that when my father passed two years ago, it shifted my perspective in a huge way. I thought, what if I got hit by a bus tomorrow and I've squirreled away all this money in the bank and I never really had fun? I know on my eulogy I want them to look at everything and say, "My God, that girl had a blast. She loved life. She helped a lot of people and she had great shoes." And Ali does wear great shoes.

Baeth Davis's business has mushroomed into the millions of dollars over the past five years. Her big goal is to "reach hundreds of millions of people and help them discover their life purpose and to make the language about purpose commonplace in the world dialogue. I hope that families will wonder, 'What's my child's life purpose?' so that they can nurture and support that child in truly actualizing what they've come here to do." Her philosophy of money is that it is a "neutral energy that allows us to create and have experiences." She has a very pragmatic view of money; she sees it as "a very good reflection of how I am giving value out in the world." She thinks that most of the world is struggling with money because people are not in their right work. But for her, "if there is a blip in the money, I'm either not delivering enough or I'm not shipping enough, I'm hiding out, and I need to get the next project out or I'm somehow not aligned with what I'm doing. So money is a wonderful way to measure how much you are hiding out. Most people are struggling because they are hiding out."

Sheri McConnell is an advocate for women owning their own businesses that make a profit for them and for their families. As she says, "Because entrepreneurship involves money, it seems to offer some real accountability to learn at a faster pace . . . because there are risks to be taken. I've always found that entrepreneurship really helps women grow in all kinds of different ways, fast. Once I figured out how to be profitable and successful, I could stay in business and do all these creative, fun things that I love." One of the things that Sheri teaches women is to tune into the "why" or the purpose of their business and what they feel passionate about; this helps them to discover what to play with creatively. Sheri's new book has a great subtitle: *Smart Women Know Their Why: The Guide for Discovering Your Life Purpose While Owning A Business So You Can Create Positive Change In the World and . . . Make Big Profits.* In this inspiring book, Sheri candidly tells her personal story of an abusive childhood and how with the support of teachers and therapy and sheer will, she decided to end her relationship with her destructive mother and create a positive life for herself and her family. She is now happily married with four children and a business that she loves. She is known for expanding on the Dali Lama quote that Western women will save the world by adding that the Western women *entrepreneurs* will save the world. She is rallying women around her and teaching them to be smart about how they run their businesses by teaching business models, such as forming an association, and balancing that with a family.

Shama Kabani is growing her business carefully. As Shama says, "My clients are really, really nice, but I have never been afraid of saying "no" to people who want to become our clients. We've actually turned away more people than we have taken on as clients because so much of our energy goes into working with people. If we don't absolutely enjoy our work, then it's not going to be fruitful in the long term. You can't do someone's marketing if you don't believe in them." Shama did a lot of traveling this year to promote her book. She has slowed that down, though, because as she says, "I wish I was totally comfortable jetsetting, but the truth is that I'm much more comfortable at my house in my pajamas than I am on an airplane." I asked her if she planned to write another book, and her answer was very practical—it depends on the financial return on investment (ROI).

MERGING THE LEFT AND RIGHT BRAIN SKILLS

This brings me to a very important challenge for many women—learning to access both the right brain and the left brain. As I detailed in my first book on creative women, women are holistic thinkers and men are often better with focused attention. For so many of us who are driven by our ideas, our passions, our quests to change and improve people's lives in some way, we often dismiss and ignore the importance of math, metrics, accounting, etcetera. Many very successful women have taken business courses, have MBAs or sales and marketing backgrounds, or have someone in their lives that plays the role of analytical advisor. Lisa Sasevich considers herself a great businesswoman; she was trained in corporate America and sees herself as "very feet on the ground with real tactics and real-world business strategies." Lisa's business combines real-world business practices with a spiritual element and empowers heart-centered entrepreneurs to go out in the world and share their blessings. Lisa also joyfully tithes regularly.

Other women in the book have an organization to provide the left-brain structure, or husbands/boyfriends who advise them in the ways of business and keep them grounded. We need to have colleagues who run the numbers for us and who can give us tools for measuring that ROI to help us make decisions about what is working and what we need to let go of. We also need to have a business model that leverages our strengths and targets a market that wants and can afford our products or services. For those of us who never went to business school and are not strong in accounting or certain types of analytical thinking, we need mentors and continual development to put the people and systems that can support us in place.

Access both sides of your brain.

When I asked Chellie Campbell if she planned to write another book, she said that it was a huge amount of work and she wasn't sure about the payoff. Chellie has a background as a bookkeeper and ran a small business with employees for years before she developed her Financial Stress Reduction Workshop™, so she has her own ideas about how she wants her business and her life to work. Interestingly enough, Chellie loves to play poker as a hobby, and wants time to enjoy that as well as spend time with her family. She is very pragmatic: "The whole question is: What is enough for you? At the top of my game, when I am doing my workshops and filling them up, I work with a hundred people a year. That suits me really well. There is all this moaning and groaning that women aren't on the boards of the Fortune 500 companies, and that not many women are the presidents of Fortune 500 companies, and I just laugh and say, 'That's because women are smart enough not to want that gig. Who wants it? Sure, you make a lot of money, but you don't have any time to spend it.'"

Chellie is also a frequent guest on television, and people keep telling her that she ought to have her own show. To that she remarks, "I don't want my own TV show. I want to be on somebody else's TV show, show up one time and be fun and funny and have people buy my books, take my workshop . . . and then I live my life. I've been in show business and I've done fourteen-hour days on the set, and I don't want to do that. I thought Dr. Phil had the best gig, he showed up on *Oprah* once a week, or once every two months or whatever it was, and you looked forward to him coming on, but he didn't have to do the fourteen hours a day like Oprah did. Now he's working too hard too—that's the male testosterone thing—he wanted to have his own show and make a lot of money and have more attention. I think I've matured—I just don't need that much attention. But I do want your attention when you are in my class and I'm trying to help you." It's all about choices.

Elizabeth Stewart moved herself and her family to Minnesota from Boston to take advantage of a better opportunity for her work on fibroids. She is currently working toward an integrated approach with doctors at the Mayo Clinics in Florida and Arizona, as well as her own in Minnesota, to set up a multi-site clinical trial network so that they can carry out research and clinical protocols across sites, which makes research much more efficient. She talked about the discrimination against women that she experienced in medical school, and when I asked her about her ideas on the best strategy for women to get paid what they are worth, she said, "That's where you have to look at other opportunities. If you are not willing to move to other opportunities, then you are sometimes taken advantage of. Women are often more reluctant to move, especially two-career families or families with children. I think there are some institutions that will value you monetarily, even if they know that you have no serious intention of leaving. But I think in most situations there is complacency where they say that we don't have to offer you more or compensate you more."

She goes on to say, "Money is important and, I think, particularly for women. Even though you may value the flexibility of your work or the environment more than the money, you become undervalued if you don't put that as a priority or you're not paid what you are worth. I see women trainees being hesitant to ask for money. They ask for what they think they can get and they tend to undervalue the importance of money as a symbol of your worth. I also think the flexibility that savings provide is important. Again, for me, having more money to spend is not so much a priority as having enough to be able to say if someone in my family is ill that I want to be able to take an unpaid leave of absence, and I can afford to do that. Or if I reach a point in time where my job is intolerable, I want the freedom to walk away and not have to stay until I find something else." Elizabeth talked about a time when a family member was ill and she wasn't as available as she wanted to be, and she wants to be sure that does not happen again. For women, relationships are so often the top priority.

Family has always been top priority for Mary Hayden, who has raised three great kids whom I have known since they were youngsters. Yet Mary has had to learn how to play politics and negotiate for funds for her projects. As she says, "I travel and give talks. I had to give a briefing to the Senate last year about vector-borne diseases. I make sure that when we have workshops that we invite the right people from NSF or NASA so that they can see what we are doing, and I keep them updated all the time. But you can't really reap special favors necessarily with them as the process is fairly objective. We have to write the grants ourselves because they have to be scientifically sound. I collaborate with many scientific specialists in writing these proposals and then we weave them into a story. It's not a one person kind of thing anymore—we're really multidisciplinary or transdisciplinary even." Mary feels that she is a good negotiator and relies on administrative staff to keep track of how much money she has spent and what she has available. This allows her to focus on her research.

When Cindy Morrison got laid off, her best choice was to start her own business. I asked Cindy if she was feeling successful now, and she said, "When I spoke at Tory Johnson's event and had other speaking gigs, I felt successful in that I wasn't still on the unemployment line and I wasn't beaten by last year. But I wasn't necessarily successful financially. So I am learning to come up with various revenue streams and collaborate with other women to make money and to look at making money not as a bad thing. For twenty years, I had always gotten a paycheck. So for me to suddenly turn around and charge people for things I used to do for free, as part of my obligation as a journalist in my community, I really struggled with that. Now I need to make sure my paycheck equals my passion, and I have turned my business around financially, and I feel these two things are in line." Cindy has one book out already, lots of speaking engagements lined up, a spokesperson contract, and is in talks with a mainstream publisher for more books. She has made her transition.

Lesley Bohm loves doing her photography, but had to learn to value her services enough to expand the vision for her business. She creates a whole experience for people with makeup and clothes, with help from expert stylist Tamara Gold, and zeros in on the person to help them send out the best business or personal message they can. It was someone in a workshop who finally said to Lesley the words that squared her away about money. This woman told her: "Lesley, if you don't start charging more, people won't think you are worth it. Money in this world is a gauge of value, and people think if they're going to pay a hundred dollars for something you're not worth it, even though you could be the most spectacular photographer in the world. If people pay three thousand dollars for it, they will think you are amazing." Lesley said this comment caused her to shift her prices, and it did work. She raised her rates and is now moving into teaching workshops. She just put together a beautiful new book of her photos, which are stunning.

BEGIN WITH GRATITUDE

One of the best exercises to increase our prosperity consciousness is the gratitude exercise where we write down a list of all the things we are grateful for and then continue to write down three new things each day. It keeps us focused on the riches we have. That doesn't mean that we don't want more abundance or more reach with our message, but it is important to experience fulfillment with where we are at right now. Lynn Robinson regularly stays connected with her abundance. As Lynn puts it, "Would I like to make more money? Yes, I would love for there to be more than enough and I'd love to be more generous with others and with other charities, etcetera. That would be really fun. But I've always found that my business provides enough and sometimes the thing that I want doesn't always come in the form of money. For example, I was thinking for a while that it would be nice to have X dollars more a year so that I can do more international travel. Well, the X dollars didn't come, but an opportunity to speak in Japan came." As it turns out, she has spent time in Japan twice now, and has many new clients as a result.

> *It's important to experience fulfillment with where you are right now.*

Lynn calculates that, between her books, her intuitive readings, and her speeches over the past twenty years, she has helped tens of thousands of people, and she feels incredibly grateful for that and for the continual flow of people who need her services.

SHARING YOUR GIFTS REQUIRES SELLING

I am always telling my clients that artists can be successful, but they need to learn marketing skills. Jeanne Carbonetti is such a successful artist. When I asked her if she was a good businesswoman, she said, "Yes." She went on to say, "I am a good businesswoman in that I really respect the art of business, and that art is a business as well. Happily, I learned that lesson early on when I had my first part-time job in a gallery here. The gallery director would often have me go around and talk about the paintings because I knew a lot about art, but she knew how to sell. So I began to pay attention to the art of selling and recognized the power of advertising as well. I have learned over the years that there are so many wonderful artists out there that could make a living if they were willing to go into the logical mind world a little bit more. They need to put on their own logical mind hats and spend a little time having that kind of a goal." Once again, that left-brain logical mind can train us to think differently about selling and making money.

Victoria Moran, too, has a lot of gratitude, but sometimes struggles with business demands. She has written two books on "charmed" living. She says, "I look around my life and I think, ' I'm a lucky lady.' And I think the most important thing is to keep that overall sense and not let what goes on at any particular time shake that. So often everything is going along and then maybe there's a disappointment or something's rejected or something doesn't work out that was supposed to work out, and all of a sudden it's so easy to go into woe-is-me. But regardless of whether this thing works out or that thing works out, the overall picture is: I am a successful woman and I am very grateful."

In our talk about how the writing world is in the midst of change, she said, "It's a very strange thing, because I'm not a businessperson and I'm not an entrepreneur. I have fallen into some of these things. Some people fall into them and find that they're extremely good at them. I'm not. I'm an artist, a performer and a philosopher, and I really need to be clear about what I am good at and what I'm colossally *not* good at and see what can be eliminated and what can be delegated. I guess something else I wish I had known is that money is really important. I was of the generation where money was considered to be the establishment, and you really weren't supposed to think too much about that. You were supposed to be more interested in art and social welfare. Well, art and social welfare are great, but if you don't save your money, and you're not a great success with your art, then you will need social welfare. So it's very, very important to take care of yourself. I think about that when all the fairy tales say 'and then the young man went out into the world to seek his fortune.' Well, today it's the young man and the young woman—and as a woman, you need to take that seriously. You go out into the world and seek your fortune and you can do whatever you want once you have it."

It is interesting to note that Victoria's mother was a stellar saleswoman. Victoria says, "For years I refused to sell anything because that sales energy was already 'taken' by my mom. Now that she has passed, I call on her for energetic helping in that part of life in which she was so gifted and I am not." Yet Victoria can rise to the occasion when she wants to. As she says, "I love spokesperson work; that's one of the favorite things that I do—talking up a product I believe in, in the context of an interview. And I love performing, I love radio and I like TV. TV is a little more daunting, but I think I've learned to do it fairly well, and so if something like that opened up, I'm there."

Many women are squeamish about seeing themselves as businesswomen; one well-known woman declined to be interviewed for this book because she didn't see herself as having a business, which she does. Other women, like JJ Virgin, grow into the role of businesswoman. She likes to say that as a celebrity nutritionist she made tons of money, but she never kept any of it. She says about money, "I disrespected it. And I decided to start paying attention to money and to pay attention to what I spend and what I make, and pay attention to our investment margins, and it has shifted everything for me. I have an assistant, but I look at my bank account, I look at my sales reports and my shopping cart numbers, I look at everything. I know where every dime is going now." She mentioned that she gets sent products seeking her endorsement all the time, but that she is not going to align herself with food products that she thinks are unhealthy. That seems very clear to her. Now she is making more money and keeping it, and still standing by her principles as she becomes more famous.

One of the most interesting stories about business and money came from Pele Rouge. She told me: "My father was not only an amazing farmer, he was also a banker. I'm fifth-generation farm family. I grew up in the Midwest and my family helped form a bank in 1913. My grandfather sold part of our farm during the Depression to keep the bank from going under and to keep the community from going under. So the dance between business, relationship, community, and family is part of my cellular structure; the notion of business as responsibility to a world that's larger than just the self. I remember my father telling my nephew (with whom my brother is still farming, so it's my brother's son), that it doesn't do any good to get the best deal with your neighbor if getting that better deal puts your neighbor out of business. So for me, the business world has never been about just the bottom line. But I know I'm a businesswoman—I manage the money in our family. I was a certified financial planner for about eight years in my life. I love helping people get a handle on their finances and building a roadmap to get them where they want to go through the lens of money. My whole position about money has shifted in the last thirty or forty years. I was with a man in my thirties and I was really concerned about money and he looked at me and said, 'Okay, how much money would it take for you to feel safe?' I told him with a straight face, I said two billion dollars. And I wasn't kidding. But in the ten years that I was with my teachers, I experienced a totally different way of being with money. For instance, if you had more than someone else and someone else needed something that you had, you gave it to them. And you trusted that it is an abundant universe and that life would provide, and it did and it does. So my experience now is that, in doing what I am supposed to do, I am provided for and money comes to me in totally unexpected ways, in strange ways, it just shows up. Is my Iowa farm girl gene comfortable with that? Well, she's more comfortable than she was thirty years ago, but it's still a stretch to live with finances that operate that way."

My intent here has been to share with you a variety of stories and philosophies and styles of businesses. Our beliefs about money impact how much money we make and keep, and our inner desires about how much we want to work and play impact what we are willing to do and not do. This is your life and you are the architect. So take out your journal, find a quiet place, and answer the following coaching questions:

1. What are my real feelings, pro and con, about making money? What do I want to do with my money after I make it?

2. Is the business I am in now operating with integrity and consciousness? Am I doing the work that I want to be doing?

3. How do I feel about being a businesswoman (yes, even if you are an artist or work in nonprofits) and how well do I manage my money?

4. What are my greatest strengths and weaknesses that I need to build on or deal with in my business and in my life?

5. Am I mostly right-brained or left-brained, or am I in balance? What skills do I need to develop on either side of the brain to make me more successful, as I envision success? How am I going to accomplish that?

6. Is my business model giving me the money and the lifestyle I want? If not, what am I missing? What's the vision of how I would like my time and my days to look? How can I make that happen?

7. If I am not making the money that I deserve, why not? What needs to change internally and externally? What kind of help do I need to create what I want?

8. Who are the people "on my team" now? Who do I need to invite onto my team to help me to get my business and life to the place that I want it?

9. What are the top three things that I need to learn and who can teach me?

Write down a learning plan for yourself for the next twelve months with specific steps and deadlines.

Take your answers to these questions to at least one other person and brainstorm with them about the viability of your business model. Map out with them a list of the tasks that you need to do to make your business more fulfilling, more profitable, and more of a personal expression of what you value. It's time to grow to the next level of personal and heartfelt success, as *you* define it.

Secret Eight

Short Circuit Self-Sabotage, Obstacles, and Failures

"Some tension is necessary for the soul to grow, and we can put that tension
to good use. We can look for every opportunity to give and receive love, to
appreciate nature, to heal our wounds and the wounds of others, to forgive,
and to serve."
—Joan Borysenko

STAYING THE COURSE

Let me set the scene. The week had been taxing and traumatic. We had a family member in the hospital, our kitchen counters, sinks, and faucets were being replaced after months of indecision and confusion, and we had freezing cold temperatures and a snowstorm. This was on top of my having a full week of clients and marketing appointments. Thus, my morning routine had been disrupted, and it took me all week to settle down into my creative time. Now, on Saturday night, I am at my desk surrounded by lit candles, Seal is playing on CD player, papers and mini-paintings are in piles around me. I drew the Fertility Rune this morning. Starting something new is one of my favorite experiences, but it is also fraught with psychic dangers.

In fact, I just found out that my project called "Idea Hothouse" must shift because someone else is using that title. The word "greenhouse" doesn't really work either, because it gets too tangled up with gardening websites. Yikes. My Aries impatience kicks into gear and I catch myself resisting the flow. It's easy to "forget" how the creative process winds like a river with its own formations and pace, regardless of our wishes otherwise. Creative unfolding is a luxurious and rich process that takes us to magical places of discovery and invention. But it cannot be rushed—the process itself must be revered and nudged along so that it can follow its own natural plan.

Many of you have written to me about your intentions relating to your creative expression or some form of life change. So you, too, are beginning projects and processes. Starting a project has predictable pitfalls. To help to keep you fertile and faithful, beware of the following, so that you don't quit or get stuck:

1. Feeling lost

   If you don't push off from the dock of security, you will never enter the new worlds that you want to explore. Being lost and grappling for a roadmap or a familiar harbor all happen on the creative journey. Accept the fact that you feel insecure and hang onto your raft while it hits the rapids and whirlpools and gives you a wild ride. Relax and trust your inner wisdom as you play curious voyager.

2. Being frustrated with wrong turns, delays, and failures

   Every step and every clue along the way is progress, even if we end up feeling that we did not accomplish anything that day. Carefully considering each creative impulse is the passage to the truth. Often we must review and cover lots of topics and possibilities to achieve clarity. Throwing out many ideas actually gets us closer to the best idea.

3. Fearing that your idea is not original

   This is your internal saboteur taunting you to stop now and discount your creative impulses. We are all creative conduits with unique perspectives, capable of innovation. Tune into your own personal life story, feelings, challenges, and insights and you will find your own distinguishing slant on the material or medium. Express yourself fully.

4. Doing it solo

   What are the best supports for your creative process? Do you need to call in your spiritual advisors, do a visualization, make a timeline, go out and buy the best materials, or talk to people about your project? In order to stay focused and persevere during times when our ideas are tested or elusive, we need to honor our own creative style and leverage its idiosyncrasies. Use props, rituals, or retreats—whatever it takes to help you commune with your fascinations.

5. Forcing results prematurely

    Creativity takes time. I just watched a video by Jeanne Carbonetti in which she reminds us that 90 percent of all paintings are rejects. But we need to paint them in order to get to the 10 percent that are wonderful. Creativity is a dance between you and your medium, and it has its own rhythms. The secret is to stay with your project daily, even for five minutes, and to not get intimidated by the dead ends and experiments that don't work at first.

6. Forgetting the joy of it

    Creativity is life-affirming and is your gift to yourself and to others. How marvelous that you have creative power to make or invent something new and meaningful to you. Your talents and passions are among your top possessions. Cherish them, and nurture them to the fullest. Feed your creative spirit with new learnings, and listen carefully to what it truly needs to blossom.

As Baeth Davis says, "When people decide to change, very soon into that process they become panicked and freaked out. The breakthrough in life is to be able to feel the panic and move through it. As Seth Godin writes in his book, *The Dip*, most people quit in the face of short-term pain because they are not able to visualize long-term gain. The dip is where you have an initial idea for a project, you head into it, and then you reach the dip—that's where persistence is required. What happens is that every time people hit that dip and quit, they feel like a failure and then they just amass a stack of failures. It's when the going gets tough that the tough get going. I don't know if people in our culture think it should be easy or that they are entitled to have something for nothing or not work."

When Peggy Whitson was nine years old, astronauts were walking on the moon. Then, when she graduated from high school, they selected the first female astronaut. So at the time she thought that if that first woman could be an astronaut, then she could too, but she had no idea how hard it would be. As Peggy says, "I started applying to become an astronaut as soon as I got my PhD and I applied for over ten years and didn't get an interview. But during that time I became the project lead for the US/Russian program of doing the science together, and it gave me the opportunity to be a leader and manage a small group in an unknown environment. I was basically starting from scratch and trying to pull something together with almost nothing. The failure to become an astronaut when I thought I was ready turned out to be my best asset for actually being an astronaut, having that experience base, working with a team, working in that environment, and overcoming the obstacles we did. I look back and it's one of the most valuable experiences of my life."

But now with the space shuttle flights coming to an end and a change in the administration in Washington, Peggy says she has one of her most challenging mental situations right now, as chief of her office. While she has an incredibly talented group of people working for her, it is not clear exactly where to steer the ship. As she says, "With the new administration we've had changes in the overall space program, and it has been very challenging in my role as leader to keep morale up during all of these changes. With so much unknown, so much uncertainty, it's a really huge challenge for me to keep everybody motivated, focused on tasks, and getting the job done as we should be getting it done. We're still going to be flying people in space. We're going to continue to keep people living onboard the space station full-time every day of the year, but the uncertainties are somewhat frightening in the sense that I don't know how best to lead, as I don't have all the answers I would like to have."

Yet Peggy is committed and she will figure it out. One of her favorite things is to go out and talk to young people, share her story, and hopefully allow them to dream and live their dream too. Her favorite age group to work with is fourth graders, who are at the same age that she was when she decided that she wanted to become an astronaut.

Learning to say "no" is a huge challenge for most women.

When we are stretching and trying to explore and master something we care about, of course it will get hard, and we may want to quit. That's when you can pull out one of my Creativity Courage Cards, read the affirmation and tune into the photo, take a deep breath, and keep going.

FEAR OF CHANGE

Are you feeling stuck or afraid to tackle a challenge that you know you must? Change is a certainty and a constant in life, but it's also unnerving and frightening, and we often resist it vehemently. What helps is to identify the specific barrier you need to dynamite through. Here are some common barriers that block our ability to make life changes that we know we need to make, such as networking with new people so that we can increase our referral sources, or learning a new skill. Check to see if any of the following barriers are detouring you from the path to success:

1. Not eliminating unrealistic options and therefore staying overwhelmed.

    Learning to say "no" is a huge challenge for most women. As Victoria Moran says, "I sometimes labor under the misconception that I can do it all, and I can't. I have this misconception that if the event is far enough away then I will have time for whatever I have committed to. If somebody says, 'Oh I need something tomorrow, can you help me?' and I look at the calendar and tomorrow is full, I am able to say, 'Oh gosh, I would love to help you, but I can't.' But if they say, 'Can you do it next week?' and my calendar next week doesn't look that full, I say 'sure.' But when next week comes, I wish I had said no."

2. Having standards so high that you can't move forward and experiment with ideas, including allowing yourself to make mistakes.

3. Continually procrastinating so that you never spend any time on your project.

4. Not being wholeheartedly committed to a goal that will make you happier and healthier.

5. Fear of rejection or of being misunderstood.

6. Being totally inflexible about how this challenge can be overcome.

7. Not being assertive with others about your goals or needs.

8. Not being willing to share your ups and downs with others and ask for support.

9. Forgetting to reward yourself when you accomplish a mini-goal.

Awareness is the first step toward change. Identify which of these barriers to change have a hold on your life and begin to dismantle them—one step at a time.

DARE TO BREAK A BAD HABIT

Recently many of my clients have been struggling with the tyranny of their bad habits and the need for them to devise strategies that really work to eliminate or transform them. That takes courage, which is why you have to dare your habit to a duel for empowerment. One client needs to commit to eating a healthy breakfast to control her blood sugar during the day; otherwise, she can't concentrate or get anything done. Another client needs to stop the negative self-talk about her leadership skills that paralyzes her ability to run a productive meeting. A third client needs to drop her habit of workaholism, learn to find joy in other parts of her life, and to rebuild her support system because she is so lonesome.

For years, Lesley Bohm had a steady stream of Hollywood actors and actresses to photograph in LA. People kept telling her to do a book and to market herself, but she admits that she gets too deep into her love of photographing people and doesn't always pay enough attention to the "back end" of her business. When the huge actors' strike happened two years ago, it shook her up—big time. As she says, "I wondered if I was still supposed to be a photographer. When the majority of your clients get their money taken away and then you don't make any money, the big question comes up—what am I doing? Am I any good? Do I go to Wal-Mart and take pictures of babies? So that was my failure—putting all my eggs in one basket. People always tell you to expand and do different things. Everything dried up all at once. That made me get down to writing the book, doing the seminars, and being open to trying new things."

Lisa Sasevich tries to remember to avoid getting off track by staying focused on her own ideas and on her mission. As she says, "A lot of people in business recommend that you keep your eye on the competition, but I actually find that doesn't work well for me. I start getting all distracted about other things that I should be doing or on what other people are doing. The truth for me is that when I just follow my own path and my own inspiration, that is when I am most successful and when I draw the most people to me. You are unique and you have a unique blessing; when I forget that and I start to think small, it does not bring out my highest self." They say that if we are truly on purpose and content with our lives, we have no real competition because we attract the right clients and the right customers to us.

Pele Rouge talked about needing to learn not to be judgmental, something that most of us struggle with. Many of us are too harsh on ourselves and often misunderstand other people. As Pele recounts, "Oh, you know humans are just such exquisite creatures. One of the issues that I had to deal with early on, that I still have to deal with, was judgment— judgment of myself and judgment of others. When I was with my teachers, that was when I was really working on the whole territory of "judgmentalness." One of them looked at me one day and said, 'You know, Pele, the opposite end of the spectrum of judgment is compassion. And anybody who has as much judgment as you do is also capable of an equal and opposite amount of compassion.' And when he told me that, I had this fear that I would never be able to let go of the kind of judgmentalness that I had been raised with or that I had within myself. But, somehow it began to dissolve, and the whole area of compassion for the human journey and compassion for myself began to grow and to blossom, so that now compassion is the first place that I go to with another human being, rather than judging. I think that this thing of being human is messy—it just is. We need to be kind with one another, and compassionate, as well as strict, when it's appropriate. But it all needs to be within this fierce ground of deep love and compassion for one another and for the journey—what it is to be a human being at this time on Mother Earth."

Excavating bad habits is hard work, and it takes time and tenacity. Here are some tips to help you make the changes necessary to meet your goals:

- Pick only one bad habit to start with and focus on it for one month.

- Make sure that you are tackling the right habit to resolve the real problem (for example, keep a log for a week and track your emotional responses to your habit to help you diagnose the underlying problem).

- Write out a statement of intention with action steps listing exactly what you will do and when to change this negative habit. Share this statement with one trusted soul who will lovingly keep you on track.

- Do a daily affirmation to support you in practicing your new positive habit that replaces the old destructive one.

- Evaluate your progress one day at a time. If you fall back one day, start fresh the next day. Change is a back and forth process. Keep telling yourself the truth about what is working and what is not, and change it. We discovered that my workaholic client needed to rebuild her self-confidence before she could start socializing again.

- Set up a reward system for yourself for each successful day. Make it a life-affirming healthy reward like meeting a special friend for lunch or going for a long walk or getting a manicure.

- Lastly, acknowledge the fear that comes up when we let go of a part of ourselves that has served a purpose, even a negative one. Grieving is part of the package as we lose an old part of ourselves.

I wish you much success and a renewal of your self-esteem.

REJECTION AS GROWTH

Mary Hayden is used to rejection at work, because scientific grants get rejected all the time. If that happens, she reads the reviews and hopes that the reviewers will provide some insight into how she can write a better grant. She says, "We'll take the critiques we get, incorporate those into the next edition, and submit it someplace else. It's important to have people who are completely objective about it, who can step aside and say, 'Well, you could have done this a little bit better.' Because you know how it is when you write something and are so embroiled in it, it's really hard sometimes to be objective about it. I think it's good to get those critiques and decide which advice to act on." When I asked her how she handles it emotionally, Mary says rejection can trip her insecurity about thinking she's not quite good enough or smart enough. Let's face it; any kind of rejection can sting a bit for all of us.

But she has a counterstrategy. In addition to redoing the grant, Mary says, "What I have found works well is to focus on some articles that I am writing for a project and to get those published, which is a kind of peer affirmation that everything is okay. I try to squelch that insecure feeling, which comes to the surface, not often, but it's there. I go back and work on something that's productive as opposed to just dwelling on that." The best defense is a good offense. Mary is a brave soul who frequently goes to Africa, where there are very poisonous snakes around. She asked to take anti-venom with her, but was told that she wouldn't be able to keep it cold since there is no electricity. I asked her what would happen if she or a member of her team got bit by one of these snakes, and Mary said, "Good-bye." Yikes, that sure puts fear of grant rejection into perspective!

Cindy Morrison's rejection from television catapulted her into a major growth cycle with a number of big crises along the way. Cindy tells the tale of what happened to her:

"Two weeks after I found out that my job would go away, I was diagnosed with a grapefruit-sized tumor. Two weeks after that I was on top of an ovarian surgeon's table. It turned out that it was benign, which was a huge relief. My grandmother had died of ovarian cancer, so it was a scary time. I spent a week in the hospital, came home, and the next day our house was struck by lightning. It was literally and figuratively that my career, health, and home were all struck. All I had left was my family and friends, and that's when I started writing *Girlfriends 2.0*. Even though it was not a business book, it was the book I was destined to write, explaining to women how the people you surround yourself with are so important." Cindy has now slogged through starting her own business, and is teaching women about how our connections can make us successful—personally and professionally.

Lisa Sasevich also had a heartbreaking layoff from a personal seminar development company. She recalls, "After six years of devoted service, the owner decided it was time to part ways with me, and I wasn't ready for that. I thought I was going to be there forever. So it felt like a failure. It definitely rattled my cage. But I will tell you now, I thank that experience every day, because it forced me to find my personal blessing. Look at the difference I make now in the world, doing my own work."

THE REAL TRUTH ABOUT THE TIME IN YOUR LIFE

We are all busy. Some people stay on target with their life and creative goals, and some people do not, even though we all have the same amount of time. In the process of designing a workshop called "The Creative Time Catcher Program," I created an exercise called "75 Excuses for Not Moving Forward in Your Life" which helps you to tune in to your individual dance with time and the dangerous perception of not having enough time to do what you want.

Here are a few common excuses:

- I fear I'm not talented enough.

- I can't do anything if it doesn't pay off right away.

- If I spend time on myself and my passions, I am being selfish.

- I can't decide what I want.

- The people in my life are unsupportive and will criticize my efforts.

- I'm too old.

- Even though I hate my life, it is secure (probably a fantasy).

- I don't have the energy because I am so tired from taking care of others in my family and/or servicing my clients and customers.

- We have a recession or there is too much competition in my field, so there are no new opportunities.

- I should just learn to like things the way they are.

If none of these excuses resonate for you, I bet you have a long list of your own. I challenge you to make that list and see what beliefs or saboteurs are blocking you from having the life that you intend to. Claim what you want for your life, write it down, and get busy making it happen.

LOST IN THE CREATIVE DESERT

Is your creative output at a standstill? Have you lost your way? Are you stuck in the void of emptiness? You are in the Creative Desert. All around you, the land seems barren and absent of life, mirroring what is inside your head. You are in the cycle of the Desert where the new growth is invisible to you; it's buried deep in the sand. It's not a comfortable place to be. It is painful, unnerving, and it creates a lot of self doubt and a lack of faith in the regeneration of your creative ideas and originality. It can be brought on by burnout, illness, fatigue, too many rejections, experiencing a plateau in your business, and a host of other factors. I am hearing from many of you that you are walking in circles in that desert, trying to find a spark of inspiration.

CHALLENGE

Ask yourself a series of questions:

1. Am I lost or procrastinating? If you are procrastinating, decide if you are going to do "the thing" you have been avoiding or not. If not, throw everything related to it out. If you are going ahead, set a timer for thirty minutes and begin. You are not lost, you are stuck, and your commitment to doing "the thing" step-by-step will get you results.

2. Am I healthy enough to do this task right now? If you are ill or have been ill, it may not be the right time to push yourself to go through the experimental process of finding a new path and embarking on it. We need energy and clarity to find the signposts to get us out of the Creative Desert. When we are ill or

undergoing treatments that make our minds fuzzy, we can't always trust that our process is "clean" and accurate.

When I was under the spell of CFS, my body, mind, and spirit were taken up with dealing with my symptoms, which included brain fog and dizziness. I was not grounded enough to be following my fascinations and making decisions. I had to wait. My Trusted Source was already on overload helping me to get well.

At some point in a healing cycle, there will be a window of light that appears along with a message from your inner voice with important clues for you. These clues can be about very important life changes that will actually facilitate your healing. Back in the mid-1980s when I first got CFS, I was lost in the Creative Desert. First of all, CFS was still not seen as real, so I had to find the right doctors who would take me seriously and help me. I had to be very tuned in to my intuition for that to work, but I found my healing team and avoided other doctors who had been recommended when their energy didn't feel right.

One of those doctors, who was quite famous, got busted for dosing women with the drug ecstasy and doing vaginal rolfing on them when they were under the influence. He had been recommended to me by a very famous doctor whose name you would recognize. Miraculously, I saw this abusive doctor at the Interface Conference Center event I went to in Boston two weeks before my scheduled appointment with him. I walked into the meeting room and saw a man with a dark cloud over his head. I asked my husband if he saw a dark cloud over this man's head, and he looked at me rather strangely, and said "No." I then asked someone else at the meeting who the man was, as I had never met or seen a picture of him. When I heard his name, I knew at that moment that this doctor was not to be trusted and cancelled my appointment as soon as I could. He was arrested two weeks later, to the shock of the New Age community. When the windows of light show up, even in the midst of the Desert, pay attention.

When the body is challenged by a virus or cancer or any other disease, our minds go back to basics instead of trying to create peak experiences and progress toward our goals. Questions like, "Am I strong enough to go to the grocery store?" or "Can I get into a suit and go to a business meeting?" signify that we are still lost and need time to get strong again. When our inspirations finally start showing up, it is a glorious moment indeed.

continued on the next page

Short Circuit Self-Sabotage, Obstacles, and Failures

continued from the previous page

3. Can I make time to rest or to slow down? We seem to have this anti-rest trend going on, and many people are exhausted and overwhelmed. This is not what was predicted twenty years ago. Back in the 1980s, my husband got a master's degree from Boston University in Movement, Health, and Leisure, with the plan of doing recreational therapy, leisure counseling, and so on. I typed many term papers for him, so I was up on the research. The prediction by many esteemed authors was that by the year 2000, we would have such advanced technologies that the average person would only have to work part-time. We would have all this newfound leisure time on our hands, and we would need help deciding how to utilize it. This is when a leisure counselor would show up to help people discover or rediscover their interests, talents, and the things that they enjoyed doing.

What happened? We now have the 24/7 lifestyle. People are plugged into something all day and all night, vacations are getting shorter, people are working at a furious clip (partly due to the layoffs of their coworkers), and are not getting enough sleep to restore their energy each night. Where is all this predicted leisure time?

The truth is that we desperately need that time. The word recreation, broken down, means "re-creation." We need to rest in order to recover from what we have been doing—to gather up the stamina to step into our next level of growth. In the research I did for my first book, *The 12 Secrets of Highly Creative Women,* all of the women knew the importance of restoration of the body, mind, and spirit. In the cycles of nature, there is a winter, a fallow period in which the ground rests and builds up new nutrients for future growth. If you over-farm one area, the plants will stop growing into healthy specimens.

You need rest too, just like the soil. It is a necessary part of the creative process.

Being in the void, wandering around the Desert, or simply staying put are all fine. Periods of rest can lead to great fertility and can allow brilliant new ideas to develop. Successful people take their vacations, seek balance in their lives, and embrace rest as necessary. Many people struggle to give themselves permission to stop and regroup. I have two clients right now who are so exhausted from work that they hate to wake up in the morning on a work day. This is serious—this is a fire alarm. Yet both of them learned in their families not to "stop" at any cost, and they have to learn to love themselves enough to let go, rest, and then find new reasonable, meaningful work. One of them just gave her notice at work; the other one is at least looking to see what other jobs are out there.

When we are in pain, we need to give ourselves permission to put our health—physical and mental—first. These are folks with multiple degrees who can afford to take a private sabbatical, but they have to release fear, old beliefs, and underlying insecurities first. I am visualizing them sleeping, reading, being with loved ones, eating good food, having massages . . . and tapping into a new lifestyle that will have them jumping out of bed in the morning.

4. Do I need a guide to get out of the Desert? Am I ready for one? There is an old axiom that says that when the student is ready, the teacher appears. So readiness to get out of the Desert is key, but often we have to go through an assessment process to figure out what kind of guide we want to partner with. What skill set does he or she need to have? What kind of temperament? What kind of teaching style? Do we need a one-time experience or an ongoing one? Do their values mesh with ours? When we have been lost, we often need a sign to help us find the right direction to go. It may be an astrology reading, a workshop, a conference, a mentor, or a coach, but we need to select carefully and reach out our hand.

For Gillian Drake, it was reading Marianne Williamson's *A Return to Love* every night for three years so that it really got into her system during a time of huge upheaval in her life. Now she feels like she is living the life of her dreams. But fifteen years ago, her life fell apart and she had to start over. As Gillian says, "When my third marriage ended and I lost my home, my livelihood, my savings, had serious surgery, and then one of my parents died, all within a few months, I saw it not so much as a disaster, but as a rare opportunity to build my life the way I wanted it to be. Thanks to Al-Anon, I saw that my life wasn't working and that I had to do it differently. I was consciously aware that every single decision, from what I ate to what business to start, could be made with the help of Spirit, and be right for me. It was a scary, intense, exhilarating time, and I was so glad that I was aware of what I was going through, because it was, in fact, one of the best times of my life. My daughter, who was eleven at the time, also remembers it that way—she saw me pick myself up, dust myself off, and start all over again, and she developed such respect for me. She didn't see me as a victim. It was a great lesson for her. I had lost all my real estate, so we moved into a rented waterfront condo in Provincetown, but we had to move out every August because the owners came for that month."

Now Gillian owns and has renovated two amazing homes and rental properties and has been a successful serial and creative entrepreneur for many years. Her

continued on the next page

Short Circuit Self-Sabotage, Obstacles, and Failures   135

continued from the previous page

daughter, Tesa, just graduated from college and is a bright young woman full of optimism and a love of learning and adventure—just like her mother. Gillian grew up in the British upper-middle class, where the boys went to college and the girls didn't. There was no expectation that you would have to support yourself with a serious career, so learning to type was considered a career track for women. Gillian's vast knowledge and wisdom have been garnered on her own.

CREATIVE ROLLERCOASTERS

Two summers ago, it rained for almost the entire month of June. I was at the Cape, where my favorite beach beckoned, but I only got there for one cold hour that whole month. Despite the grayness, I was especially happy during that time.

For several years, I had this vision to create a new product about creative courage. I did a survey of my newsletter audience, and they were interested in the product. In my mind, it has had several incarnations and formats. At first, it was an actual card deck, then it was a tool kit of sorts, but then it became a beautiful e-book called *Creativity Courage Cards* as well as a large deck of affirmation cards.

I wanted to use my original quotes and photographs by my husband and put them together to create an engaging and inspirational guide to help you to stay brave during the creative or change process, despite all obstacles. I was entranced as I wrote and rewrote, resized photos, and moved pages around so they flowed. After each edit or change, I kept getting clarity about what I wanted you, the reader, to experience. It was an exciting and magical series of moments.

Every time my virtual assistant sent me an updated version, I couldn't wait to open the file and print it out and see the results. We finally got it to the place of perfection. My virtual assistant and my husband both contributed ideas for changes, but I was committed to a particular look and feel, and I kept redoing the file until I achieved exactly what I wanted. While this took many hours and lots of paper, I thoroughly enjoyed the time and effort that it took. It was joyful and fulfilling. It reminded me of the creation of all my books and products and how absorbing they become while you are immersed in bringing vision to reality. When you are passionate about what you are doing, you can be so focused.

In fact, I ended up creating another e-book called *The Path to Creative Success* at the same time. I found the best photo for the cover and put together some of my favorite tips for building a life of creativity and fulfillment. Working on both of these at the same time made every day an adventure. Did it take courage? Yes, as it kept changing, but I honored my own words and pushed through the chatter of doubt.

Then we hit a snag. When all the files were combined, the sizing changed and we were all getting different sizes on our computers. We were stuck, and we had to call in the gurus to take a look and figure it all out. It was hard for me, frustrating for my assistant, and my husband consulted with two photo buddies for additional ideas. In addition, our original printer who was supposed to be great with artwork could not give us the high quality color we wanted. Happily, we ended up with friends of mine who are outstanding printers. So that was a gift.

As of this writing, we have redesigned the printed cards several more times with new affirmations, photographs, and a beautifully designed box. This is such a reminder that the creative process has its own time-table and generally does not evolve seamlessly.

> The creative process has its own timetable.

This is where many creative people lose their nerve. They get one rejection and quit, or one person criticizes their work and they cower, or they get stuck in a plot that makes no sense. These wild rides are usually inevitable, and they require determination and a creative problem-solving spirit to resolve, despite the uncomfortable feelings. But going ahead and doing it right until you know in your heart it is complete is the way to go.

Our lives, like our projects, are a creative process too. We can fall into the darkness and have to revive ourselves. That's what Madeleine Randall had to do after overwork and stress brought her down. As Madeleine says, "I basically fell apart. A "medicine person" takes themselves apart into teeny little pieces and then puts themselves back together; it's like the creation of a rainbow. That is what I did, and I also became a cancer survivor during that period. Then I was offered a prestigious position as the Executive Director of Rancho La Puerta." But she only stayed a few years because she felt a calling to go elsewhere.

As Madeleine says, "I was being called back to California, back to the people there. At the Ranch, I was teaching, but I felt that I should teach and also minister. I use the word minister—for to me medicine is holy work. I am more than a doctor—I'm a teacher, and I minister to the body, mind, and soul. That is my calling, and I was missing part of that. I also think that my people, my tribe, my patients were calling me back and I know that to be true, because once I returned, I didn't advertise or anything and soon had a full practice. When you are walking your path, sometimes you need to go various places to gather new knowledge so that you can bring more to the people you are working with and healing. . There's a difference between knowledge and wisdom. A great, great medicine man, who I was very fortunate to know before he passed away, who was considered to be one of the greatest medicine men alive or in his day, is Frank Fools Crow. He said, 'Wisdom before power.' And what he meant by that is that you gather knowledge, you gather life, and then you allow that wisdom to come from yourself and interact with what I would call the divine, and that is what really, truly makes you powerful. That is power in the true sense of the word, not power like 'I'm going to squish all you guys' or 'I'm going to shoot you up or burn you up.' It is wisdom and compassion that is real power." Madeleine has clients internationally and is often sought out by people desperate for a diagnosis and treatment that no one else has been able to come up with. As for wisdom, she has gone back to school and become educated in Functional Medicine.

Debora George Tsakoumakis grew her cake business by continually shifting her business and solving problems one-by-one. She started with a list from *USA Today* of the top forty cities in the United States and researched bakers in those cities to build a network. Slowly she began to get corporate orders for her cakes, and then put up a website, and business was good. In 2003, she made $250,000. Then, the economy slowed down and her corporate business dropped off. Consumer orders went down too and many bakers went out of business, delivery costs increased, and she had a few snags with her bakers. So she consolidated everything and made a contract with a local baker in California to handle all of her orders. She persevered and in 2008, Debora sent some test cakes to some marines and they were a success. So she then began shipping cakes overseas to the service men and women stationed in Iraq and Afghanistan, as an expansion of her business. With this new focus, her business went up 80 percent from 2008 to 2009 and she began doing lots of public relations and the business kept growing. I first read about her in a magazine. When I asked Debora what the secret was to her success, she said, "The real secret? I'm a good business woman because I listen and I am open to suggestions." She listened to her bakers who wanted an 800 fax line and got one. Her military families were requesting that she send paper plates, forks, knives, and napkins with her cakes, and now she does. Then they asked for candles and she added them too, although she can't send matches to a war zone. Now she's got new packaging and has printers that run edible food ink which gets projected onto frosting sheets to decorate her cakes. Her flexibility and patience have paid off. Now she and her cakes are stars of social media.

Lynn Robinson has authored a number of wonderful books, but her masterpiece is her first book, *Divine Intuition,* which was published about ten years ago. The book is a work of art with gorgeous graphics and Lynn's wise words, and it has sold internationally to rave reviews. A few months ago, Lynn got the word that Amazon and other retailers could not get copies from the publisher. Lo and behold, after getting on the phone, Lynn discovered that the publisher had let her book go out of print. Lynn had just redesigned her new website and, of course, that book was featured on the home page. So she had her agent, John, look into it since he was not informed by the publisher either. As Lynn laments, "They definitely decided to take it out of print. My understanding is that sometime by the beginning of next year, I will have the rights revert back to me. John is trying to find another publisher for it because this is the book's tenth anniversary and it would be great to re-release it. I still think the book has such a valid message. I'm just surrendering it. I was making myself really nutty for a while and I finally said, you know, this thing is making me too crazy to try to navigate the whole thing and to push people to do things. It just doesn't feel right, so I am surrendering it, because that's what I would say in the book." Lynn is an active and dynamo marketer who knows how to hustle, but as she says, sometimes you have to step back, hold your intention, let things play out, and trust the process. Then you know when to make the right move. She is in talks with other publishers already since this conversation.

WHEN THINGS AREN'T WORKING OUT

What do you do when you feel like you have tried everything and are still not getting the results that you have envisioned and set as your intentions? How do you maintain your hope and faith in the midst of adversity? Where do you find a reservoir of patience while you wait for new clues and the manifestation of your goals?

Basically, what do you do when an illness doesn't heal, a house you are done with doesn't sell, or you can't find a publisher for your book proposal? Hanging in there during those times often calls upon all of our inner strength and perseverance. We try and try to follow our intuition and take the "right" action steps and think positively, but when the struggle goes on too long, we can lose our belief in our goal and feel very stuck and discouraged. It's times like these when we need our support systems and some kind of spiritual or humanitarian axiom to rely on.

One of the things I teach people about stress is that with every stressor you have three choices: you can avoid it, modify it, or accept that you can't change it and deal with it. Sometimes avoiding or quitting is a really healthy choice. Pat

Schroeder stayed in Congress a long time and accomplished a lot, and she broke new ground for women, children, and families. But around 1994 through 1996 when Newt Gingrich took over, things shifted for Pat. She had always believed that if she fought hard enough, she was going to make it. But, she says, "Suddenly, I began to feel like I was in a middle school lunchroom all day and all we did was food fight. And you would go home at the end of the day, clean up, come back, and start all over the next day. That didn't seem like the way I wanted to spend my time. I also felt that the Democrats just plain didn't get it and that they were not out there pushing back. There was a hardcore group of us who started meeting every day and trying to get a message together, but we couldn't rally the support. People thought it would change, but it lasted twelve years. Finally, I decided I didn't need this. We're not going to get anything done except throw bullets at each other or throw epithets or name-call each other. That's when I decided to retire." Sometimes we need to lay down our hammer and move onto our next step in life. Pat fought valiantly for twenty-four years.

CHALLENGE

Try the following strategies for dealing with a creative challenge:

1. Surrender to the fact that you are up against an inordinate challenge. Stop struggling with the fact that you are in this pickle and accept it on some level as part of your path.

2. Step back from the current situation and look into your life history for similar situations and times when you handled this kind of challenge well. Also, look for a pattern that keeps repeating itself, like not negotiating contracts well or hiring the wrong people, and know that it might be time to change.

3. Do some soul searching to see if there are hidden fears about achieving your goal. If your product gets noticed, it could be criticized, for example. Be sure to deal with any fears you uncover.

4. Get the best advice you can from professionals, preferably more than one. Have people review your situation and give you their opinions and recommendations.

5. Visualize daily the results that you desire, but be open to the prospect of a different formula emerging for you.

6. **Above all, be kind to yourself.** Know that you are doing the very best you can to get your challenge resolved and acknowledge all you have done so far and are still doing.

7. **Keep an active communication with your inner guidance and intuition** to help you to glean the truth and choose the right action steps.

PROTECTING YOUR PRECIOUS IDEAS

For the past few years, I have heard heart-wrenching stories of a novel disappearing on a computer, a fire destroying a lifetime of photographs, paintings that got moldy in a basement, and work that had not been copyrighted showing up in the wrong place. Is your work protected? Are you backing up your computer, making slides, or legally registering your work? Make this a year of self-protection. Your creative ideas are valuable and part of your legacy as well as your business. Don't put this off!

For starters:

1. Face the truth about your situation. Do you really back up your computer regularly or do you need a new plan? Either buy an automatic back-up service or an external hard drive to store your files. I keep an extra set of files on a CD in a fireproof safe and, when I am writing a book, I keep another duplicate CD in my car, updated daily. If you have art or photography, get it photographed or scanned, and keep duplicates in two places. Do it this month.

2. Register your business. If you are selling creative work, register your business name with your town and look into declaring yourself as a DBA, an LLC, or an Inc., depending on your needs. Set up a business bank account and track all of your expenses and deductions. You may want to consult a business attorney or the SBA for guidance on the options in your state.

3. Invest in your creative potential. Give yourself a budget for your creative projects and business. Make your creative work a priority, fund your business account each year, and develop a strategic marketing plan. You must invest in new materials, updated equipment, and the right advisors in order to be successful. Take yourself seriously and honor your creations.

4. Know what you are both earning and spending each quarter so you can make solid financial decisions. Are you making enough money? Where is new business coming from? What expenses are really paying off and which ones are duds? Has your target market changed? Which services or products are selling well? For many of us creative souls, we have to learn to collect and pay attention to the data in our business.

WHICH IDEAS DO WE NEED TO PROTECT, AND HOW?

To help us with these decisions, I interviewed intellectual property and business lawyer Jean Sifleet of Clinton, Massachusetts, author of *Advantage IP: Profit from Your Great Ideas* (Infinity 2005). Jean and I met years ago at a business conference. Here are some of Jean's guidelines:

1. Intellectual property pertains to creative work and bringing something new into being. Trademarks protect the brand name. Jean suggests carefully selecting a distinctive, memorable brand name, like Lexus, for example, then securing the domain name and legally registering it. First, do a Google search to make sure that someone else is not already using a similar name to yours. If someone else is already using your name or a similar name, it may not be worth a legal battle and you may want to select another name.

2. If you write a song or a poem, make it tangible—put it on a CD or on paper. As the creator, you automatically own the copyright, but it's a good idea to put the copyright notice on your work. If you ever need to enforce your rights, then your work must be legally registered with your copyright. She recommends that it is a good business practice to copyright all material that you value. It's an easy and inexpensive process.

3. Be cautious when you give away rights or license your material. Don't sign contracts without understanding the terms. You can do short-term rights or licensing until you see how a product sells. Reserve the right to reuse your work in another format in the future as well.

4. Choose your deals carefully and don't agree to anything that does not feel right. Decide carefully about the use of nondisclosure agreements, as ideas differ from implementation.

I recommend Jean's book as an essential guide to empowering yourself in this complex arena. Her book is fascinating as well as practical, and uses easy-to-understand charts and lists to simplify the whole process for you. Above all, Jean and I agree that you need to follow your intuition and stay away from negative business partners.

Sheri McConnell loves to create products and programs with novel ideas and great visuals. One of my favorite products of hers is *The Smart Woman's Business and Marketing Planner: A Daily Companion for the Female Entrepreneur,* which helps me keep all my book, product, and marketing ideas in one place. Thank you, Sheri. She is a powerhouse with several books published under her own imprint, and she is constantly developing up-to-date learning experiences for her members. She is passionate about being by herself and inventing things. When I asked her about what she considered to be her point of vulnerability as a business owner, she was very clear and candid. She said, "It would

Invest in your creative potential.

definitely be around managing people. I just don't like it at all. I want to delegate it and I don't know that you ever get to delegate those meaningful things when it's your own business, because I want to hire skilled people. You hire for skill and dependability. I've had the hardest time letting them go, but I've gotten better about that in the past few years, letting them go in the middle of Christmas and all of that and having everybody be mad at me for it and all that fun stuff. I've gotten smarter about it, but I don't think women ever deal with it as well as men do. I always become very close to the people around me and so that's the other key. I've been told that you can't be friends with the people who work for you and I'm not sure I'm ready to accept that yet. My problem with the employee stuff is because I am so open, I have trouble not being completely honest."

Sheri is hinting about semi-retirement already, so I know she will make a solid plan to deal with this issue. In my projects as an HR consultant, I have coached many women to become assertive, compassionate leaders with the skills to coach employees through development issues, including termination. Sometimes companies will let me try to move someone around in the organization first if we can find a job that matches their skills and interests in order to avoid a layoff. Many people who love inventing or making deals want the freedom to just do it; they feel bogged down by people management issues. We have a choice. We can get support to hire and manage a very independent, competent team of folks who need minimal supervision and are self-motivated. Or we can design our company or our job so that we have a manager who handles most of the people issues for us.

Knowing ourselves and making the right plan is key to preserving the part of us that wants to keep generating those precious ideas.

FORWARDING THE ACTION

Life is a series of opportunities and new commitments. Have you stopped selling or sculpting or exploring the results that you pledged to yourself for this year? If you gave up, now can be a new chance to forge ahead. Quitting permanently is always dangerous to our self-regard.

Chellie Campbell is in the business of helping people get financially stable and reduce their stress. But when the recession hit, people who had taken her program didn't pay her. So Chellie personally went through a tough time. As she says, "I'll admit to being really disappointed when the recession hit. It was so hard, and I was mad at the universe. This was not in my game plan. I got to be depressed for a while, and then I just had to say, you know what? What's so is so. You weren't in charge of that, but you are in charge of a response and now you have to get with the program. Then I picked myself up and started doing the teleclasses that everyone had been telling me to do. That's what I wanted to tell you, that is my big failing. The downside of Chellie is that I have the 'yeah but' disease. Yeah, but I don't want to do that because . . . ' I've practically been dragged kicking and screaming into doing everything that I do. People told me for years before I wrote a book, to write a book, and I said I don't want to do a book, thank you very much, it's too much work, and I'm not interested. Until the day I had this conversation with a woman in my class. She said, 'You changed my life but what are you going to do for my girlfriend in Arizona and my mother-in-law in New York? They can't come to your program live for eight weeks.' That's when I said maybe I should write a book and give people who can't come here the tools. I said no to teleclass ideas for the longest time because I did one once that was a big turnoff and I didn't enjoy it. I like interaction, like you and I are having. During the first teleclass I ever did, the female hostess introduced me and said, 'Well, I'm going to go away and I'll come back to close out the end of the hour.' I was left to talk non-stop for an hour, which I did, but it wasn't fun." Now Chellie is happily running teleclasses and has written two books. It's working, and she loves having international clients in her circle now. She is licensing other trainers, which has had a slow start, but she is hopeful that people will take advantage of this new opportunity as the economy recovers.

Marilyn Tam's first book is inspiring and wonderful, but her book agent turned down a deal with HarperCollins for her books and told her to instead go with a small publisher because he said that they would be more dedicated to the book. She agreed to the small publisher's low advance with their promise of stronger and more extensive marketing. It didn't turn out well. As Marilyn says, "They weren't ethical people and I had a three-book contract with them. I ended up buying my rights back and getting out all together because they made so many horrible mistakes. But the good news is that I'm now in the middle of negotiating with great publishers on my next book, and I have some wonderful choices." Some people stay stuck when their first book experience is negative. But Marilyn took it in stride and is creating new opportunities. That's what successful women do—they get over it and begin again. She claimed her power when she bought back the rights to her book. She is a wonderful writer and I look forward to reading many more of her books.

Jeanne Carbonetti is a prolific painter, author, and teacher with a lifestyle that promotes her inspiration and serenity. She is entranced with the art of watercolor painting and builds her life around it. But she has an obstacle—rheumatoid arthritis. While she has tried all kind of remedies, it is an issue to grapple with. As Jeanne says, "You will notice when you see me that my hands actually have deformity, even in my DVDs. I have worked over the years to try to hide it a bit. That's when I finally accepted actual, real, big-time medicine. For years I had tried not to, and I read everything I could and did everything holistically, which I must say has helped me a great deal. But the deformity was still there and was continuing, so at that point I decided that I would get infusions. Now I get an infusion of medication every seven weeks." Jeanne confronted her limitation head on and followed a healing journey until she decided what was best for her. Successful women do what they can to be proactive and take care of themselves, their businesses, and their families. When you meet Jeanne and see her stunning work, you don't even notice her hands, because her passion, talent, and her creations are so overpowering.

CHALLENGE

I offer the following initiatives for you to try:

1. **Face your failures.** Write down what didn't work and why. Did you set the wrong goal or create an unrealistic scenario for yourself? Failure is part of the journey, so leverage the learning and make a new plan.

continued on the next page

continued from the previous page

2. Reconnect with the payoffs for your passion. Are you still excited about your project or goal? If so, how can you add play or deepen your connection to the meaningfulness of what you are doing? How is your work spiritually inspired or of benefit to others? If you are not passionate about what you are doing, you need to make a new decision.

3. Experiment. Play around with possibilities until you find a formula that suits your work and your personal style. Creativity is about new linkages and experimentation is part of the challenge. If you work best in large chunks of time, for example, make it happen. You can, you know.

4. Subtract creative barriers. Release limiting beliefs, outmoded ways of working, and anything or anyone else that eclipses your personal zest. Learning to set the boundaries that we need for protection is a daily challenge. Keeping on track with our goals is life-changing and self-loving, not selfish.

5. Fortify yourself with soul mates, mastermind groups, affirmations, classes, music, special materials, project software, etcetera to keep you confident and in action mode. Avoid people who cannot genuinely tune into your true self.

6. Celebrate what you have done right so far this year. Acknowledge all the baby steps or giant steps on your path of progress. Do something that nurtures your craft and your spirit, or throw a party for your support team to celebrate intentions fulfilled. If you have done nothing, and I doubt that, honor your humanness, and begin again. Every day is a creative possibility.

GRATITUDE AND GRIT

Right now is a good time to take a moment and to give thanks for all the things in your life that you take for granted—your heartbeats, your one good friend you can always count on, or your creative interests that inspire you. Especially now, in this era of financial defaults, disillusionment with government, and a climate of fear, we need to be grateful for what we have. I've been thinking a lot lately about the people in California and Colorado who lost everything they owned in those relentless wildfires. Yet, we spend a lot of time thinking about what we don't have yet. All of us are dealing with some area of our lives where we are waiting for manifestation or results, and we are impatient. This patience takes grit. People struggle with questions like: Why don't I heal faster? Why is my soul mate not showing up? Or why isn't my business growing as fast as I would like it to? I talked to a client the other day who was totally panicked that she had not accomplished all of her goals this year and there was only one month to go.

For most of us, the areas in our life where we struggle the most can be mysteriously slow. I often ask people to make sure they have the right goals and that this is what they truly want. If they have the right goals, are they taking the right actions to make them happen? If you want to grow your business, you may need to create a joint venture or send out a press release or network more.

We need to be proactive, but we also need to realize that achieving the results we want often takes time, so we need to be tough enough to wait it out. It's like trying to pull up roots in the garden before they have flowers on them—things have their own timetable. Yes, it was important that we planted the seedlings correctly and gave them water, sun, and fertilizer, but then sometimes all we can do is continue to water and weed them and wait.

Waiting can be hard, and it requires inner strength. When we have done all that we can, we need to let go and trust that results will come in their right time. It's important that we don't blame ourselves or feel like victims. Each of us has a cross to bear and we need to learn to bear it with grace after we have set our plans in motion. So, each day, be glad for all of your gifts in life, acknowledge the challenges you face, and make peace with both of them.

CHALLENGE

Try the following strategies to move you forward:

1. Review your own financial situation and take action as needed. Consult with your financial planner, if you have one; talk to your broker or your bank about how to protect yourself or if you need to pay off debt or move money around in some way. Do what you can.

2. Do an assessment of your job or business. Are you at risk of a lay-off? Do you have fewer clients or customers right now? You may need to start networking again for jobs or instigate an innovative marketing plan for your business. It's time to be proactive with your life.

3. Pull out the Treasure Map that you made and make sure that you post it where you can see it and meditate on it daily.

4. Use your personal prosperity affirmations daily to focus on all you have to be grateful for and to reinforce your vision of abundance.

5. Gather people around you who have a similar quest for prosperity consciousness and avoid people who just want to dwell on the negative.

6. Tune into your beliefs about faith and adversity, and use them to keep you moving forward.

Secret Nine

Learn to Let Go and Leap—Embrace Transition and Being Unnerved

"Just go out there and do what you have to do."
—*Martina Navratilova*

MOVING UP TO THE NEXT LEVEL

Feeling that you have hit a plateau in your business or career is a predictable dilemma. Successful people understand that they need to continue learning, trying out new strategies, and changing with the marketplace. Because you continue to evolve and change, you also need to become very clear about how your business needs to transform to reflect any shifts in your priorities and interests. The belief that one focus will work for a lifetime is usually not correct. To move up a level, we must invest in ourselves and do a complete self-analysis. Then we need to do a career or business assessment and create or expand our plan of action.

This past year, I have invested thousands of dollars in training to upgrade my business and resolve some chronic issues. These changes will bring me to a whole new business model and streamline my operations. I can now share this wealth of knowledge with my clients and colleagues. In addition, I have enrolled in an intense training program for 2011. Taking risks and learning advanced skills helps you maximize results and develop new possibilities. Advancing your career or growing your business is a powerful creative process. You need to tap into what truly grabs you and dig into it deeply, so that you can discover your own version of it.

CHALLENGE

Here are some tips to guide you as you strive to climb higher toward the model you really want:

1. Go back and review why you chose to start your business or master your career, and remember what you most loved about it. Is that still true today? If so, harness that passion. If not, it's time to rediscover what you do like about what you're doing, or to change direction.

2. Take a look at your lifestyle. Are you happy with how you are using your time? Are you having enough adventures? Do you get to rest and rejuvenate? Are you spending time with people you care about? Are you having fun? Are you taking care of your health? Our career and business paths don't always jibe with our desired lifestyle. Change is in your hands.

3. How is your creativity calling to you? Are you ready to make or invent new products, services, or initiatives to satisfy your creative interests? Get your creative projects on your current "to-do" list and focus on them. Your business and career both depend on it.

4. I always ask people this question about work: "Who do you want to talk to all day, and what do you want to talk about?" Write down the current answers for yourself. Make sure that you shift things if you have to so that these people and topics are part of your day.

5. What do you need help learning now? In order to move up to the next level, do you need a coach, a mentor, a class, a conference, or an educational product (or a series of products) to encourage you to think about your career or business in innovative ways and to strive to make a bigger vision for yourself? First, you have to visualize it, then you need to write it down and get excited about it!

6. What do you want to improve about your health, your personal relationships, your living situation, your special interests, and so on? Choose one project at a time, develop a plan to achieve the result you envision, then enlist a support system and go for it!

Secret Nine

PERSONAL AND PROFESSIONAL LEAPS

A few years ago, I wrote an article called the "Out on a Limb Club" about what it takes to dare to go after what you want. I even ran women's groups with that focus for a few years. All successful women, and all of the women in this book, have made leaps of faith. We have felt both unnerved and scared as the moment came to leave the safety of the familiar. Leaping is a key strategy for getting what we want. Often, though, we don't have support for what we are doing because it scares or threatens people in our lives, even the people who love us.

> *Successful people understand that they need to continue learning.*

Patricia Aburdene knew in her twenties that she wanted to be a writer, even though she says that everyone thought she was nuts. She invested a good five years learning how to write, rather than playing it safe and getting a "real" job. Working for *Forbes* magazine was the culmination—her first writing job. As Patricia told me, "I majored in philosophy and got a degree in library science after graduation. But the only reason I became a librarian was because I thought it would give me the credentials to write book reviews, and at least they would get published. Thank God I didn't think to myself that I should get a degree in journalism, because that would have ruined me as a writer. I took writing courses, even one journalism course, here and there, and I wrote articles on spec and I tried to get them published. I found a boyfriend (who was otherwise not a very good boyfriend!), but he was a good writer, and he taught me a lot. I completely bootstrapped it. My first publication was a book review when I was about twenty-four or twenty-five, which I shopped around as part of my portfolio. By the time I got the job at *Forbes,* I was twenty-nine, and I had a big portfolio of things that I had somehow managed to get published. I learned so much on that job, and the best thing I learned was fact-checking. I learned how to do that very well, so that when the *Megatrends* book came along, I made sure that every single fact was properly fact-checked and footnoted. It's an interesting combination of skills, because I am a very expressive person. Being on stage speaking allows me to express that part of myself, but deep down inside, I'm a nerdy little Virgo librarian. I'm actually an introvert, even though I am a pretty good speaker."

Patricia also told me a story of a personal, physical challenge that stretched her nerve and her courage. Patricia says "At the age of forty-five, I learned how to row a single scull on the Charles River in Boston, which is the hardest thing I have ever done physically. It was unbelievable, and so hard that it took me two years until it became a relatively enjoyable experience. At that point I was a decent advanced beginner. Each time I went out in that scull, even though I had a coach along in a motor boat, I thought I was going to die. In fact, I did capsize a few times and then I really thought I was going to die. It was absolutely terrifying." Successful women often find that mastering physical challenges fortifies them to go further out on a limb in their lives as a whole, because it gives them a huge dose of bravado.

Brenda Michels survived her close encounter with cancer many years ago, even though she was only given a year to live by her doctors. This event prompted her to become a licensed minister, so she could do emotional and spiritual counseling with people who are not only ill, but for those that are emotionally and spiritually wounded. Her husband is a graduate of the Stillpoint Institute and together they make a powerful healing team. Brenda was previously in television, and living a lifestyle where she was smoking and drinking and not eating right. She was involved in toxic relationships and she was holding onto hurt, anger, and bitterness from the past.

When she was diagnosed with cancer for the third time, , she intuitively felt that taking chemotherapy treatments was not the answer for her, and she went inward and asked for another way to be shown to her. As Brenda says, "I did an alternative program with Dr. Nicholas Gonzalez, who is an MD of immunology in New York and has an entire treatment program based on metabolic ecology, which supports the body to do what the body does best—heal itself through nutrition, cleanses, and supplements. I had experienced a real breakdown, and not only in my body. At the time, I was a newlywed, with no savings in the bank, and no health insurance. We sold several things to get enough money to put me on Dr. Gonzalez's program, and I remained in it for four and a half years. Through the inner work I did on my own, I developed the faith and belief that my body had the ability to heal itself if I was willing to give it the proper environment. I believe that all illness and disease starts in the spiritual body, moves through the emotional body, and then into the physical body. So, for me, finding out the real cause of the disease that was present in my body was a huge risk. Along the way, I read incredible, inspirational books, and I discovered that Marianne Williamson, the highly respected spiritual teacher, was speaking a block away from where I lived. So every Tuesday night, I glued myself to one of the seats in the front row and listened with an open mind and heart. I vigilantly took notes, and started reading *A Course in Miracles.* Thank goodness there was a part of me that was aware that I needed to heal my destructive, unconscious patterns in order for me to make permanent changes that supported a higher level of health and well-being in my life." With her new book coming out soon, Brenda is gearing up to bring her message of healing to her readers, It takes a lot of courage to buck the system and design your own path to healing.

Olga Aura has already told us about two of the miracles in her life: her spiritual breakthrough from the Ego death experience, and the step-by-step map to freeing her mind handed to her at Naropa. But there is one more. As Olga tells us, "I had been on a student visa this entire time, and as long as I was paying tuition to a university, I was fine." But after Naropa, she wasn't sure if she wanted to go to graduate school. She went to see an immigration attorney, who told her that she could get a green card if she got a job at a corporation or if she got married. Olga says, "I looked at my options. Road number one was a problem, because corporations were not hiring spiritual mentors at that time. And the second road was very scary, because I had never been in love. I had three months until my student visa expired. The tough immigration system in this country was my biggest challenge/teacher/blessing/whatever you want to call it. It said to me, Olga, if you want to stay here, you are going to have to crack your heart open and allow your soul mate to come and love you, just the way you are." And so began "the Summer of Love."

Olga had a dream about Arnold Schwarzenegger waving at her, and she knew that she was supposed to go to California, because that's where her soulmate was. She traveled up and down the West Coast, meeting people and, as she calls it, "kissing many frogs." Her three months ran out, and she hadn't met "the one" yet.

She went to San Francisco and won a part in a cutting-edge theater production. But she didn't know anyone there, and she didn't have a job, a home, or a car. But then, Olga says, "It was a full moon at midnight, and I was walking around downtown San Francisco. I wandered through Union Square, and as I was staring at a beautiful window display of Turkish rugs and fabrics (which had this mystical, romantic feeling to them), I turned around and there was a tall, dark, handsome prince standing right there, quietly admiring me. He greeted me in Russian and my jaw dropped. We grabbed each other's hands and started spinning around like children, right there in Union Square, looking up at the stars and the full moon, overwhelmed by joy."

Olga talks about going for what you truly want and letting your intuition guide you step-by-step. We must pay attention to the clues that keep showing up along our path and take action. This is how you become master of your destiny.

Pele Rouge also took a major risk by saying yes to love. As she says, "When I realized that I loved FireHawk, he was married, and in my divorce there had been another woman. I had promised myself that I would never be the other woman. When FireHawk and I realized that we loved each other, it wasn't like we ever fell in love; it was more like realizing that we had never *not* loved one another." They tried to be just friends, but it soon became clear to Pele that she couldn't do it—it was too painful. She said that they either had to get married or be apart. She says, "So saying yes and trusting that this love was different was the biggest risk that I've ever taken." She and FireHawk married, and together they are co-creators of their family, many ceremonies, and leadership training.

Several women said that their big leap was quitting their jobs to start a business.

Victoria Moran told me, "Quitting my last day job twenty years ago, and going freelance, let me work at home, homeschool my daughter, and have the amazing life I've had all these years, with the books, the talks, TV, radio, and meeting and working with wonderful people. I've loved being on my own for these two decades. I don't know what will happen in the future, but if I had stayed at that job writing about weddings and other people's parties for a society magazine in Kansas City, I would have a very different life today."

The big leap for Chellie Campbell was letting go of her bookkeeping business and trusting that she could support herself doing workshops. She had already survived bankruptcy and foreclosure when a big client didn't pay her, and her heart was no longer in the business. So she made a plan with projections for shifting into the workshop business—she did not want to get a "real" job. Once again, a dream held an important message. Chellie recalls, "I had a nightmare that I had to go get a job, and that I was hired to work for my attorney as her secretary, and that I was getting her coffee all day long. That was the nightmare, and I will tell you, I woke up sweating. I said 'I don't care how many networking meetings I have to go to, or how many people I have to call, I will do whatever it takes to make this workshop business work.' But that was the risk and that was the fear. The fear made me pick up the phone when I didn't feel like picking up the phone. The fear got me to the networking group when I didn't feel like going to the networking group. People have often asked me, 'What kept you going?' And I say, 'Fear.' I was terrified that it wasn't going to work." Chellie has created her own term for making sales calls. She calls the process "sending out ships" and she encourages her clients to keep a "ship's log" to keep track of their calls. As we have talked about before, many businesses go under as they do not send out "enough ships" and increase their client/customer base and make sales.

For Kathleen Dudzinski, it took moving all over to accomplish what she wanted. Kathleen says, "I've looked at everything I've done as opportunities. It didn't seem like a risk to me. I moved from Connecticut to Texas to do my PhD, which worked out well. Then I moved by myself to Japan for two years to do my post-doctorate work, and I didn't speak Japanese at that time. In 2003, my husband and I packed up and moved from California to Connecticut, which many people said was moving the wrong way. Yes, it is colder here. I don't ever look at things in my life as obstacles. I say, okay, you put that box in my path. Should I go around to the right? Or around it to the left? Or should I go over it? The only person who can tell me what I can or cannot do something is me."

For Lynn Robinson, an article written about her in *The Boston Globe* really jumpstarted her intuitive reading business. Lynn was in a secure job as an operations manager of a software company, with benefits and growth opportunities. She started doing her intuitive readings at night, on weekends, and during her vacations, and she finally decided that she couldn't do both jobs at the same time. So she asked for a dream. Lynn says, "One of my favorite techniques when I am confused about something is to ask for a dream. I write down a few paragraphs on what I am confused about, and then I try to summarize it as a question. My question at that time was, 'Can I keep both jobs?' I had a funny dream where I was out on a lake in canoes. I had one foot in one canoe, and the other foot in the other canoe. If I didn't make a choice, I was going to fall in the water and maybe drown. So I gave my notice that day to the software folks and I have never looked back." As Lynn reminds us, "To recreate our lives, we have to be willing to let go of the trapeze swing, because nothing is certain. You need to focus instead on what is possible."

The biggest leap for Baeth Davis was starting her business as well, but for a different reason. Baeth says, "It wasn't leaving my job; that wasn't a risk. It was starting the business, and having months where I made nothing and lived off my credit cards. That freaked me out. Eventually, I was forty grand in debt, which makes me smile, because that is often our monthly American Express bill now. But at the time, it took me years to pay off the debt, and I was proud to pay it off. The freakiest thing for me was incurring debt, as I never been in real debt before. Once I was able to see it as an investment in my education, I stopped worrying about it, and that's when things really started to turn around. That, and delivering my first info product, were both big breakthroughs."

Mary Hayden went back to school to get her PhD in her forties, with three kids, a husband, a dog, and guinea pigs at home. She says, "I think that was a pretty big risk in the sense that I wasn't sure that I was going to be able to manage my time well enough to do it. That's where, of course, John had to step up to the plate too, in the sense that he had to fill in for everything that I wasn't able to do. That's when I first learned to effectively multitask, and I was super organized during that time."

Caroll Michels has taken a fascinating and unconventional route to get to where she is today as a career coach, artist advocate, and author. She eloped at eighteen, and her parents were furious. This was the beginning of her journey. Caroll says, "Then, to punish me, my parents pulled me out of college, so I worked for the American Automobile Association as a clerk typist in their editorial department. I was around writers all day, and I thought 'I can do that!' because as a teenager I had written some articles for a newspaper. My boss said I could write some articles, but he would not give me a raise. But I acquired a byline, and a portfolio of articles, and I got a job at *US News & World Report* in the art department without a college degree. I was selecting photographs and illustrations to accompany articles and writing captions. Then my first husband and I moved to Oxford, England. It was impossible to get a job, the pay was very low, and I had to support my husband. So I lied to get a job in the editorial department of a publishing company, assuming correctly that the British were not going to check to see if I had a degree. My husband was in school, and when we moved back to the states, he finished his education at Yale. I got a job in the public relations department of Southern New England Telephone Company, writing articles for their various magazines and with all my editorial experience behind me by the time I was twenty-two, a college degree was not a concern. After my husband graduated, I went into sculpture."

Destiny had another shift in store for her: "I stopped working as an artist for many reasons. My second marriage ended, and I decided that I just wanted to make a lot of money. I went to work as a media buyer for a large European ad agency in NYC. Then my boss asked me to produce a television spot for a tire company. I had never produced a commercial, and I did it really well. But then out of the blue my boss asked me to hand-deliver a television spot to Los Angeles, one that he produced for our client, the Robert Stigwood Organization, the management company for the Bee Gees, for airing on *Saturday Night Live*. I didn't understand why a courier couldn't run the errand! I had just fallen in love with Dennis, the beginning of a twenty-five year relationship, and I didn't want to go to Los Angeles. I got fired for not cooperating, despite having done some great projects for the agency. I had never before been fired, but it turned out to be a very fortuitous event that led me into career coaching. I was determined never to work for anyone else again."

So, quite magically, this consulting business lead to her writing her classic book, *How to Survive and Prosper as an Artist.* In doing research for her clients, Caroll realized that there was a need for a book like that, and she connected with a literary agent in London who sold the idea in six weeks.

Marilyn Tam speaks and consults with many groups in large corporations, and has noticed that often people who are here in America from other countries are afraid to take business leaps. She has also noticed that almost everybody is afraid to take large risks, for fear of dire consequences. So when Marilyn presents, particularly to diversity groups, she will ask, "How many of you are first-generation immigrants? And how many of you are second generation?" She tells them to think back or imagine when they or their parents made that first step to pack up their lives and move here from wherever they came from. "That was the biggest step you or your parents can take, because you broke the ties in a very physical way to everything known before, to land in another place far away to start all over again. That dwarfs everything else, and if you or your parents can do that, nothing else is a greater risk. The biggest risk has already been taken. I left home in my mid-teens and did not even finish high school. I came to this country by myself, to go to college midway through high school, which I guess was a huge risk. But at the time, I honestly didn't think of it as a risk, it just felt like the next logical step. I already knew my life purpose, which is to make a positive difference and give back to the planet; so coming to America for education as soon as I could was what I needed to do to fulfill my mission. Nothing is too big a risk if you know why you are doing it. As you know, that is one of the four principles in my book; you need to dare to potentially "Make Big Mistakes."

Many women in this book have been part of potent mastermind groups which they credit with being a turning point in their businesses and in their lives. Mastermind groups have been around for centuries. Napoleon Hill, in his classic book *Think and Grow Rich,* defined a mastermind group as "the coordination of knowledge and effort of two or more people who work toward a definite purpose in the spirit of harmony. No two minds ever come together without thereby creating an third invisible intangible force which may be likened to a third mind (the mastermind.) As Sheri McConnell says, "Putting six figures down for a mastermind group, and then coming home and telling your husband that you did that, was a risk. But I realized that if I converted ten people into my program, I would get my investment back. Seven weeks into the program, I had my investment back. I experienced a 398 percent growth in my business that year, because I stepped up and said 'Okay, we're going to the next level with my business.'" Sheri began to move herself more into the limelight, and she started doing her own events, where she provided three days of content. She admits to being nervous, but one day, just before one of her events, she had headphones on and was reading her slides and got a flash of inspiration. "It said, 'This is what I was meant to do.' And it was like this pure joy went through me, and I felt ready for this. I couldn't believe that I hadn't been doing this a lot more until then."

As we are making big leaps, we have to accept that a high percentage of them will not pan out, especially in the beginning of new chapters of life or business.

To help you deal with some of the specific challenges that are urging you to take a leap and grow, we will look at some very common ones in more detail.

CAREER CHECK-UP

In this time of high unemployment and financial swings, it's prudent to do a work check up. Don't get caught up in the "doom and gloom" of it. Instead, look for new venues, and be proactive. For example, if your company is not doing well, you need to be networking and looking at other options. If you are in financial services and they are laying people off (I just got several new clients from this industry), you need to assess your value to the company. Perhaps you should talk with your boss about your prospects. If you own your own business, you need to talk with your audience to understand their pain and develop solutions to help them. Worrying will get you nowhere, and it will just stress your body, mind, and spirit. Do some assessment and take actions. If you don't know what to do, get some advice.

CHALLENGE

If a transition is in order, ask yourself some key questions:

1. How do I want to contribute to the world at this point in my life? What creative aspirations can I express now?

2. What are my best talents, and which are the ones I most enjoy using?

3. By what criteria will I judge my success in life?

4. What kind of work environments stimulate my best work?

5. What kinds of people do I want to engage with on a regular basis?

By answering these questions, you can begin to see a new path. Many people know that they need to make a change, and they may even know where they want to go, but they need a guide to help them find the courage and the best strategies to get on the right track. Investing in your future is a wise move in times like these, and it will pay off in terms of your happiness and in monetary gain for years to come.

DEALING WITH LAYOFFS OR REDUCED BUSINESS

One of the many hats I wear is that of a human resources consultant. I work with HR directors and help them tune into the needs of their executives and employees. Then I develop programs to honor and remedy those needs. One of the pieces of work I do is individual inplacement or outplacement. With inplacement, I coach an executive or employee to uncover their true talents, and to hopefully find a new spot for them in the organization. I love doing that, and it's a win-win for everyone.

However, in these tough economic times, I am again being called on to provide outplacement services for laid off executives and employees. People turn to me because I offer all the basics, like resume writing, interview coaching, career testing, and so on. The HR people and the newly unemployed choose me because I customize a program for each person, and I inspire people to work toward doing work they truly resonate with—work that uses their uniqueness and their creative spark. Our work may result in a career change, a move within an industry, or the starting of a new business.

I also work with entrepreneurs to help them grow their business, and I teach marketing to creativity coaches in particular. The lagging economy has created more challenges, but there are also opportunities for new products and services, joint ventures, and innovation.

I want to offer some quick tips for dealing with layoffs or reduced business.

If You Have Been Laid Off

1. Get a career assessment of your skills and interests so that you can decide on the right career direction for you and don't waste time.

2. Network with other people who have been laid off, and support each other through the job-hunting process.

3. Create a professional workspace in your home where you can receive phone calls/email/visitors in a quiet, organized place.

4. Connect with the leaders in your field, either personally or through their books, blogs, social media, or websites, so that you are up-to-date on trends.

5. Target companies that you want to work for and apply directly to them along with trying to network your way in.

If Your Business is Down

1. Research what your competition is doing—meet with people, check out websites and blogs, do a Google search for recent articles, etc.

2. Listen to what your clients or customers are telling you that they want, and create new products or services to meet those requests. You might want to do an email survey, a focus group, or an interview with selected clients or customers for ideas.

3. Think about teaming up with a colleague in a related field and doing joint marketing together, such as giving a series of teleclasses or staging an event.

4. Join a professional networking group, or actively use the new social media, such as Facebook, Twitter, and LinkedIn to meet new people and exchange business ideas.

5. Ask yourself what creative project you've been thinking about doing to advance your business, and start it now. When business is slow, it can be a great time to create something new.

Most importantly, in either situation, you need to take good care of your body, mind, and spirit. Get out and exercise, meet supportive friends for coffee, pursue your creative interests, develop a spiritual/philosophical practice like journaling or meditation, and keep paying daily attention to what you want to manifest. Take some risks, try a part-time job that will give you some new skills, or volunteer your time so that you feel connected somewhere. Work transitions can be difficult, but they also present a "stop in the action" for you to retool and refuel.

WORKING ON YOUR OWN

Recently, *Boston* magazine did a whole segment called "Change Your Life." I was quoted in the section called "Be the Boss" with advice for striking out on your own. I was asked to come up with three questions that all potential business owners should ask themselves:

1. Are you honestly passionate about the business?

2. Are you self-motivated enough to work without direction?

3. What's it really going to cost?

Whether you have owned a business for a while, are just starting out, or are retooling mid-stream, working on your own is a challenge. Yet asking yourself these questions on an ongoing basis is a key success strategy.

As my colleague Cliff Hakim says, "We are all self-employed" and we need to operate from that mindset. Even if we love our business, we can get burned out, our referral sources can shift, and the marketplace can make new demands for skills and expertise we don't have and need to get. Change is constant, and it can be invigorating or threatening. We must learn to expect and embrace it in order to thrive. So I want to add three more questions for you to ponder:

1. What are the key trends in your industry that you need to pay attention to?

2. What does your creative soul need to stay interested and inspired right now?

3. What kind of connections and support do you need in order to be more productive and efficient?

Get a notebook, find a mastermind buddy, or take two days off and muse, and see what you discover. Working on your own requires your continual input and self-assessment.

Knowing how to communicate your plan and negotiate on your own behalf are critical skills.

NEGOTIATING YOUR BEST DEAL

What I love about coaching and consulting with clients is the privilege of helping people discover and achieve what they truly want. Getting the vision together is the first step, but knowing how to communicate your plan and negotiate on your own behalf is another critical skill set needed to design a life of positive choices. Too often, we are afraid to ask for more, fearing rejection or conflict, and do not resolve our "deal-making" with comfort and contentment. For many creative types and small business owners, not creating a sound business for yourself undermines the possibilities for your work. If you are employed or job-hunting, selling yourself short or not pushing for a promotion keeps you "underemployed."

CHALLENGE

To avoid common mistakes, try the following preparation tasks:

1. Don't make a move until you thoroughly research all aspects of the deal. Talk to colleagues who have done these kinds of deals before, talk with your lawyer, scan the Internet, ask for help on LinkedIn, but protect the identities involved. Look at what your product or service is selling for in the marketplace, so that you have a way to compute margins. Then write down your exact goals for this negotiation and three possible situations that you would consider. Also, you need to know what breaking points will make the deal a bad choice for you.

2. Make sure that you have gotten all the necessary details from the person/organization that you are looking to partner with. Sometimes overlooking one detail turns that target person/organization into a candidate that is not viable. Keep meticulous notes after each call or contact. Make sure your sales presentation covers all the points necessary to make your case.

3. Above all, trust your intuition. If even the slightest hint of a red flag goes up, write down what is happening so that you can see it in black and white, and deal with it as opposed to denying it. Remember, hungry people make poor shoppers. Don't ever do anything out of desperation—it will most likely backfire.

4. Pick one issue that needs to be resolved this month to negotiate with your boss, your spouse, your friend, your neighbor, your colleague, or anyone else with whom you need to work something out.

5. Write down clearly what you want and detail all the components that you desire. Anticipate the other person's possible objections and plan your responses.

6. Write out a script, and then find a convenient time for both of you to discuss the matter, calmly and clearly. Try to keep the discussion logical and nonemotional so that you can achieve resolution. Do not attack, name call, or blame—simply keep repeating what you are asking for and stay on message. If the encounter blows up, end it and try again later, or request the help of a third party.

CHOOSING THE BEST PEOPLE TO AFFILIATE WITH

Selecting the right colleagues and affiliates is a key ingredient for success. Whether you work for an organization or have created your own, the people with whom you partner impact your results as well as your fulfillment and reputation.

Creativity also thrives in relationships with complementary skills nurtured by mutual respect. Successful partnerships and alliances depend on complete honesty, self-assessment and awareness, open communication, and a dedication to resolve conflicts on the part of all participants.

Over the course of my years as a multifaceted coach, I have cautioned many clients against taking jobs ill-suited for them or joining forces with partners where there might be a mismatch. I have seen a pattern with many female entrepreneurs where two insecure women team up together with the same weaknesses and a shaky business plan. Disaster usually strikes, and it may even end in the courtroom.

If you are considering doing contract work or becoming an employee of an organization, do your research. If the company jerks you around in the hiring process or your intuition tells you that it's all too "perfect," beware. You want to be connected to the best people, products, and services. Desperation and the impulse "to just get it done" both create dangerous liaisons. As a business owner, there are huge differences between collaborations and official partnerships. You can fulfill your needs for collaboration with a variety of networks, team projects, peer groups, and other modalities. You don't have to make an alliance official unless you have road-tested it and know that it makes sense legally and professionally.

Do your research and shop around.

CHALLENGE

So if you have the "urge to merge," ask yourself these key questions:

1. Are you an introvert or an extrovert? How much alone time versus group time suits you?

2. What is your relationship pattern? Do you have a string of collisions in your past or a steady track record of positive connections?

3. Of the collisions you have had, what part did you play in the process? Pay attention to your vulnerability pitfalls.

4. What can a potential partner or employer do for you? What are your real fantasies and hopes for this alliance? Is it something you could or ought to be doing yourself?

5. Are you confident that you can negotiate well on your own behalf? If not, what data/skills/knowledge do you need to acquire so that you can advocate for yourself?

6. What kind of collaborations sound like FUN to you?

7. In what circumstances do you love to be in control, and when do you long for company and input?

- Before you seek alliances, write a mock ad about what you are seeking in another person or organization. Include all the necessary details, such as integrity, availability, essential skills, personal style, and so on that are critical for a positive outcome.

- SHOP AROUND. Be picky and value yourself enough to take your time. Know what you want and write down every discrepancy you uncover. As with any relationship, readiness is key. Both parties must be on the same wavelength at the same time.

- Set up an experiment with one project before you decide about a long-term affiliation. Trust is earned! Face up to the truth, whatever happens. You can find the right people and the ideal model for you, but be sure to subtract the colleagues and organizations that fail your test!

- Do a 360 feedback exercise on yourself and ask your friends, coworkers, peers, or associates how you excel as a person and a professional and where you have let yourself and others down.

Then visualize attracting the right circle of influence for your needs.

SELF-MARKETING IS A MUST

You must always strategize about your target market and then connect with it directly, whether you need more clients for your business, are looking for a job, or are seeking sponsors for a nonprofit organization. In order to achieve your personal and heartfelt success, you have to decide:

1. What do I have to offer?

2. Who wants it?

3. What's it worth to them?

Self-marketing is about leveraging assertive communication skills and overcoming the gremlins of insecurity. If you don't feel confident and centered in yourself, you won't be able to convince anyone else to partner with you. I have had the privilege of working with many bright professionals who have trouble speaking up about who they are and the benefits of their expertise. I teach them to use clear and succinct language, laced with meaningful success stories, so that they can meet their goals. Self-marketing has many dimensions, since every interaction we have with people telegraphs our personality, compassion, competence, and values. Learning to self-market is not optional; it is a skill that we all must master.

CHALLENGE

1. What are your best talents and greatest liabilities as a person and a professional? Which liabilities are you motivated to remedy, and which ones do you choose to accept and get someone else to do for you?

2. What is unique and original about your ideas?

continued on the next page

continued from the previous page

3. Who are you trying to connect with or serve?

4. What is your most natural self-marketing style, and where do you need to stretch?

5. Set quarterly goals and put together an accountability/support system to help you meet them.

Success begins and endures with an honest assessment and a written marketing plan.

TIPS FOR GREAT PUBLICITY

I have been blessed over the past ten years with a lot of publicity. I've been quoted in the Sunday *New York Times*, *Redbook* (4 times), *Self*, *Woman's Day*, *Shape*, *Woman's World*, *The Boston Globe* (twice), *Boston* magazine, *The Improper Bostonian*, *Investor's Business Daily* (twice), and the list goes on.

I've also done a lot of radio and some TV, and I have several radio clips posted in the pressroom of my website right now. I want to share with you some key strategies that have worked for me so that you can develop a PR campaign for yourself or your business right now.

1. Send out regular press releases about something new that you or your business is doing. Let them know about new groups, e-books, media appearances, new products or services, awards, memberships, etc. Use the Vocus Directory as a resource, and check with your library to see if you can access it online. Check out the wire services for their best deal to mail out releases for you.

2. Your local media is always looking for good stories. Check to see if your local media will do a story about you and your business, and watch your local cable TV station to see what show might be appropriate for you to be a guest on. I was once the co-host of a show called "Professionals in Transition" and all four hosts got great exposure and TV reels.

3. Decide what social media you want to frequent, and post helpful information regularly. Publicize your events, appearances, new blog posts or articles, research in your field, etc. Again, try to form relationships

with people that are mutual and collaborative. Don't post constantly with nonsense—be thoughtful.

4. Direct mail still works. Try mailing postcards about your business (I use *www.modernpostcard.com*) and mail them out to your target market, and pass them out to people you meet. Collect snail mail addresses when people go to your website or when you speak to a group, and mail cards to friends and colleagues as well so that they know what you are up to.

5. As you read magazines, newspapers, blogs, etc., identify key press people in your niche market and begin to email them regularly or post on their blogs. Invite local press people to your events, and always ask how you can be helpful to them as a resource.

6. If you enjoy writing, start a clever blog or newsletter, write a column for a magazine, or post articles on your website. This will give you credibility, and it will create ongoing new material to use. Try to get your articles posted on other websites like *www.ezinearticles.com.*

7. If you want to do public speaking and are a novice, check out Toastmasters, Speaking Circles, a speaking class, or get a coach. Put together a press kit and a workshop/seminar flyer, and send it to adult education centers, workshop centers like Omega in NY, networking groups, local Chambers of Commerce, conference planners, etc. Make a DVD of you speaking as part of your press kit.

These are just a few of the many ideas about generating publicity. I always advise people to do things that interest them and to showcase their best talents. You won't be consistent if you don't enjoy what you are doing.

THE NEW SCOOP ON PR

I did a wonderful interview recently with Jennifer Robenalt, owner of Robin Hill Media in Austin, Texas. Jennifer is a PR whiz and has some invaluable information for you on how to navigate today's new media options. She has an engaging radio show called "Soul Lab," on which I was a guest. Jennifer is passionate about her business and about helping people to communicate authentically.

To Jennifer, PR is building a platform for your business using both online and offline media. It is all about building a solid relationship with your audience. She is an advocate of blogging as a way of getting noted as an expert. For too many creative people, she says, PR is an afterthought. As soon as you have the go-ahead on a project, she advises, you should start the PR process. She suggests that it is worthwhile to get a one- to two-hour consultation with a PR professional to help you develop some action steps and avoid common mistakes.

If you decide to go it alone, you need to build a custom media list. You can use the new Cision resource (which used to be Bacon's). It can be accessed at the library, or you could purchase it with some colleagues. In addition, Jennifer says, you can do a Google News Alert search on people who are in a similar business to yours, and look at the journalists that have been covering those folks.

> *Use social media networks to reach out to potential employers and customers.*

You can check out blogs that are in your field by using Goggle Blog or Technorati. Start to read them and comment on them. Also, note the blogs they are linked to. All of these resources will help you identify journalists and develop relationships with them. As you interact with the media, be sure to focus on a simple message, with no more than three core points that emphasize solutions and benefits for the audience. It's not just about you—it's about serving real people.

Social media allows you to reach out to your audience directly. Don't make every post to Facebook, Twitter, or LinkedIn a promotion. People want to get to know who you are, what you are working on, what you believe, etcetera. Give people something of value, and engage in genuine communication.

Be thoughtful as you comment on other people's blogs and share their information with others. Jennifer suggests you be sure to include tags on your blog posts, and to update your blog roll as well—it's your neighborhood. In addition, plug in to the natural news cycle, and give people and journalists unique content for their readers/viewers.

Jennifer is also a big proponent of video, because people like to absorb information visually. I asked her if she thought people need to get a professional video or if they could use a flip video camera. Her preference is for people to get a short video done by a professional, who can add graphics and music, unless you are good at staging your own with a flip camera. A key point is that people want to do business with and have relationships with people they like, and videos can facilitate that. Jennifer loves the idea that her Soul Lab shows can be archived so that many people can access them on their own timetables. Blogtalkradio is exciting for Jennifer, because it gives people a chance to share their passions and their voice with people all over the world.

Lastly, Jennifer says that she is heartened by the number of entrepreneurs she talks to now who are living in integrity. She sees business transforming from the themes of competition and fear to an era of opportunity, partnership, and responsibility. What a hopeful message!

This chapter has been arranged to inspire you, but also to give you specific action steps to take in the process of redesigning your career, your business, and your life. If you honestly answer all the questions in this chapter and follow the guidelines, you will have the data you need to begin to take one well-thought-out leap. And then another one . . . and it goes on. Hiding out is no longer an option.

Secret Ten

Avoid the Female Burnout Traps

"The most common way people give up their power is by thinking
they don't have any."
—*Alice Walker*

Too many women try to do too much—myself included—and we can overwork
and get burned out. We can also suffer from the "Type E Woman Syndrome,"
which means doing everything for everyone else first. Type E women try to take
care of everyone and everything before themselves. In order to be successful and
healthy, we need to get a grip on those old female paradigms and live in the land
of equality. It is essential to our success.

Recently, a *Women's Health* Study funded by the National Institutes of Health
and authored by Brigham and Women's Hospital cardiologist and assistant professor at Harvard Medical School Michelle A. Alpert, MD, MPH, was published.
This is a startling new study that proves that for women, a lack of creativity and
not enough decision-making power in their work puts them at risk for suffering
a heart attack or heart disease. Having a stressful job is even more stressful than
losing a job, according to the study. Women who report high job strain and active
job strain have a 40 to 56 percent increased risk of cardiovascular disease, including heart attacks and the need for invasive heart procedures, compared to women
with low job strain. Heart problems were not the kind of workplace equality with
men that we wanted.

According to *Women's Health* in September 2007, 77 percent of women feel
burned out in their job. The magazine also noted that women work an average of

ninety-four hours per week as working moms, between time spent at the office and time spent caring for children. According to CareerBuilder's annual Mother's Day survey conducted in 2009, one-third of working moms reported feeling burned out. A Harris study in 2008 concluded that three-quarters of all American workers feel burned out. One of the reasons that we have women starting businesses at rapid rates is so that they can spend more time with their families or themselves, have control over their time, and do meaningful, creative work. My client list is full of these women.

According to the Center for Women's Business Research, there are about eight million women-owned businesses in the United States alone. These generate $3 trillion and create or maintain twenty-three million jobs (or 16 percent of all US employment). According to a new report by the Guardian Life Small Business Research Institute, women are, or soon will be, responsible for creating one-third of all new US jobs—5.5 million of them by 2018. On a global level, women own or operate 25 to 33 percent of all private businesses. Using the Guardian report research, *Forbes* reports that women will transform the workplace from a male-dominated environment to one with "characteristics such as a positive working environment and opportunities for all involved in the business, better pay and health care, better customer service and customer loyalty, a smarter focus on ideal clients, better collaboration and communications, and better long-term planning, including a succession plan and a solid retirement plan not only for owners, but for their employees." (*Forbes.com* "Women-Owned Business: America's New Job Creation," 1/12/2010).

Women are at great risk for stress overload and burnout, as we are still doing 60 percent of the work at home and we make up half of the workforce. We are also the ones who stay tuned into daily things like, "We need a present for Susie's birthday party next week; your mother needs more physical therapy so that she can walk better; Bob needs a new tent for camp, and the dog needs her shots." Hence the label multitasker—we are focused on multiple levels of needs at work and at home, and we are hopefully focused on ourselves, too. We grew up with enormous pressure to be "good," which means being polite, cooperative, nonassertive, helpful to others, and the quintessential caretaker. We are under pressure to have prestigious, high-paying jobs or successful businesses; to have well-behaved children and an immaculate home; to look great all the time; and to have everyone like us. Who can do all that, do it well, and stay healthy? All of us are anxious or insecure about some aspect of our lives that is less than glorious.

Combine all of those pressures with the common characteristics of women who burn out, and you'll see we face some serious challenges. Burnout is stress overload, and it creates both mental and physical exhaustion and a dimmer view of life. It can cause you to question the meaning of your life and your work. When you are burned out, your body and your psyche are sounding an alarm that you need to drastically change your life. Who is most likely to burn out? Women who are conscientious with high and/or unrealistic expectations of themselves are very vulnerable. They set the bar too high on their own and/or may work or live with people who also set the bar too high. These women tend to be perfectionists, and to fear criticism from others. I always tell women who have a tendency to be workaholics to be sure not to work for a workaholic boss or in a workaholic company, even their own. These women are superachievers, and they need to learn how to set boundaries and renegotiate impossible expectations.

The second candidate for burnout is the woman who is overscheduled. She is on too many committees, has her kids enrolled in too many activities, volunteers for too many organizations, takes on too much responsibility at work (often without compensation), and has a very difficult time saying the word "No." When I ask a woman like this to keep a written log for a week listing everything that she does, the log is pages and pages long, and she will usually also attach a sheet of things that she didn't get to. Her original to-do list was meant for herself and three clones. In order to recover from burnout, she has to start subtracting unfulfilling tasks from her life.

A third pitfall for women is the attitude that we have to do everything ourselves, and therefore we do not delegate. We are certain that no one can do "it" as well as we can, so we are reluctant to let go of tasks, even if we hate them. These women need to learn how to hire the right people and to train them well, and they need to get their family members to share in the household duties. We need to remember that as CEO of our job or business, we need to focus on activities we are passionate about and/or that generate income.

> *Learn how to set boundaries and renegotiate impossible expectations.*

Another group of vulnerable souls are the women who expect to be liked all the time. This is impossible to achieve. So many of us are afraid of being disliked that we don't voice our opinions, we overlook things when we should not, and we are afraid to ask for what we want. As we become more successful, even if we are wonderful, caring people, we will attract more people who do not like us. A perfect example of this is the woman who wrote an Amazon review saying that one of my books should be thrown in the trash. I know many authors who have had the same experience with their books. Some people have nothing better to do than to throw daggers at other women—especially at those of us who are actually doing things.

Women often struggle with what I call the caretaker versus creator paradigm. We want to be there and be responsive to our friends, family, coworkers, neighbors, and all the other people who we care about. Yet we also need to have a life of self-focus where we can take care of ourselves, explore our creativity and the things that we love to do, rest and dream, and do the things on our own personal "bucket list." Many women who burn out try to do too much, often in both categories. There are clearly times in our lives when things will be out of balance, such as when we are caring for a small child, elderly parents, or a sick spouse. But we need to keep track, so that we know when one side of the seesaw is too high or too low. On the creator side, sometimes we have so many ideas (especially those of us with ideaphoria), that we get overwhelmed by our own curiosity and enthusiasm. We either get too passionately immersed in what we are doing, or we jump from project to project, or we disengage from other people and other things in our lives. But sometimes actual solitude is exactly what we need and, if we honor that, we can often prevent the stronghold of burnout. Own the truth about what works for you. Being in balance most of the time is important. Our health depends on it.

I have dealt with burnout a number of times in my life, and so have the women in this book. We all need to face the truth about our seduction points and develop counter-strategies to protect ourselves. There are different kinds of burnout, as you will learn from the women in this book.

As I write this, Marilyn Tam is negotiating with publishers to write a new book on life balance, focused on helping women who feel torn and worn out trying to do it all—to live up to the twenty-first century dauntingly formidable image of all that a woman is expected to be—accomplished professionally, beautiful, physically fit, knowledgeable, good friend, wife, mother, self-actualized and active in the community. Marilyn has accomplished amazing things in her life, earned a lot of money, and has helped people worldwide, but she has kept some balance in her life as well. After a very successful corporate and entrepreneurial career, she created her nonprofit, the Us Foundation, and then invested in and ran HealthWalk, an integrative healthcare company. Marilyn is refreshingly candid, and tells about her own need to be reminded about life balance. "If we forget about ourselves, we're not doing anybody any good. And I know that I've said this many times to many people and I practice it most of the time. But because the rewards of this last venture, HealthWalk, were so exciting. When you see people become able to walk again or go from stage four cancer to being in remission and running a marathon again, it's a real high. But, after three-plus years managing the clinic, I realized I had lost my own life. I had to stop and say, 'Wait, I'm not living the very life that I'm telling my people that they should be doing.'

"I think I'm actually embarrassed about it, because I just couldn't believe that I got to that point again. For me to fall into that trap again after all that I've learned; it is a good reminder how when a person is passionate about something, it is easy for that passion to take over one's life. With HealthWalk, I said, 'All right, it's time for me to shift again.' We hired a director of operations who also did the marketing. I stepped back about a year and a half ago and am now engaged in a more balanced way."

Marilyn's other love is her foundation. "Us Foundation is active in helping the people of Haiti recover from their earthquake. In conjunction with other organizations we've sent about 600 medical volunteers so far, over eighty geodesic domes for medical facilities, orphanages, and other things that need quick setups. I've continued to work with Vitamin Angels, giving anti-parasitics and vitamin A to nutritionally deficient children around the world. This year we're going to reach over twenty-two million children. So, I am active, but I have stepped back from HealthWalk so that I can be a little more involved with these other projects."

After her battle with cancer, Brenda Michels had to deal with the burnout that can come from making such major life changes. Brenda says, "Oh yes, I felt burned out after I went through my healing process, mainly because it was an intense program that demanded all of me to participate. I actually needed to take a vacation from all that and do what I call 'lighten up.' It was during this lightening up period that I began to learn about balancing life outside of my healing process. I was committed to getting healthy, and once I was on my feet again, I knew it was important to practice living this new, healthy lifestyle as best I could." Brenda needed to learn flexibility and make sure that she maintained a strong spiritual connection as she continued her journey.

Shama Kabani happily works about twelve hours a day, but she does get burned out too. As Shama says, "I get burned out all the time because I go at such a high speed; I can get burned out every two weeks. My husband forces me to take vacations, so that helps. But because I work at such a fast pace and my life in general is very fast, I also recover quickly. So I don't have career burnout, I have more of "I can't look at the computer any longer" burnout. Luckily, there are lots of cures for that. I love what I do, and because my work is so multifaceted, I never do the same thing two days in a row. One day I'm talking to clients, another day I'm creating a strategy, another day I'm hiring new team members. The way my work is structured is very different, and when I set my mind to something, I'm like a little bulldog—I don't give up. For example, my goal in 2011 is to double our company revenue. Because we're a private company, we don't reveal our revenues but, essentially to meet our goal, it will put us in the top 4 percent of the companies in the world. So having a long-term goal, pacing yourself, and taking breaks in the middle certainly help with burnout." Shama also mentions that watching movies, reading historical fiction and getting lost in other people's stories for a bit, and eating great food are also antidotes to stress. I should mention that Shama and her husband live with their extended family and do not have children, so Shama is mostly exempt from household responsibilities. She acknowledges that this makes a big difference in allowing her to pursue her goals more fully.

Peggy Whitson actually had an experience with burnout before she became an astronaut. She said, "I saw that one of your questions was 'have you ever been burned out?' And the answer is yes. Prior to that point in my life, I would have said, 'Oh man, you're just a wimp, that burnout stuff is a state of mind.' I found out the hard way that that's not necessarily the case. It happened when I was working in Russia about 50 or 60 percent of the time. I was in charge of the science program that we were doing jointly with the Russians, and we were training crew members in Russia. We had to do preparations for crew training, baseline data collection, and preparations for in-orbit procedures and timelines. It was an extremely stressful time, with a ton of travel involved. I found out that I could get burned out. It was interesting; because it was shortly after that that I was selected to be an astronaut. That was great for me, because it was a huge break in my life where I could just focus on one thing, which was to train. It was perfect timing in my life because I had really burned myself out in the sense that there wasn't much left. As timing worked out, a change in direction is what ended up being my recovery time. That helped me let go of some of the things that I was overstressing about and overloading myself with physically. But it was a good experience to have pushed myself that hard and to realize that there is a limit. Now I can see it, and I know that I need to just step back, take a break, and hand this off, so that I don't do the same thing again."

> Set a long-term goal and pace yourself.

Changing circumstances is a proactive strategy to prevent or remedy burnout. As Madeleine Randall says, women get burned out because they don't change. That's what Mary Hayden does. As she says, "Honestly, I guess I've never really thought of it as being burned out because I've changed jobs when I've had enough. Before I get burned out, I tend to shift gears. Of course, everyone has day-to-day frustrations in their job, when you're totally exhausted and you think, 'Oh my God, where's my bed?' But burned out so that I didn't want to do it anymore? No. Maybe when I was younger, but since I've been in Colorado, I've liked all of the jobs that I've had."

Burnout in the medical field, as in most helping professions, is an occupational hazard. Elizabeth Stewart takes an analytical approach. She says, "I think there are a couple of creative ways to deal with whatever is burning me out. First of all, if it's stress at work, I need to ask myself, 'What about this situation can I change? How can I change it to suit me better? If I can't change it, how do I work around it to make sure that I can deal with the stress?' Secondly, it's spending more time on the things that I do find rewarding, apart from whatever is causing the stress. I think that's a good part of the reason that I did change jobs. I wanted to be in a different environment, and I think the Mayo Clinic model has suited me very well. There may come a time when that isn't the optimal model for me, but when it was clear that I should be looking for other opportunities, I sat down and made a list of what I was looking for, what I needed, and what I wanted. For me, it turned out that the Mayo Clinic embodied more of that than other places where I was looking."

Variety can help diminish the stronghold of obsessing over one project too much. Kathleen Dudzinski works three-quarter time with Geo-Marine, runs her nonprofit on dolphin communication doing both research and educational programs for children, and is the managing editor for an international peer review journal called *Aquatic Mammals Journal*. As she says, "I'm lucky, because the three major things that I do overlap, so I can shift between them and not get burned out on any one thing too often. I have hit burnout before. I do have times when I get overwhelmed; when I just need to step back from it, and put it on the shelf, so to speak. When that happens, I take a day or an afternoon off and do something completely unrelated. If it's in the wintertime, I might sit down and watch some stupid TV or a movie, or read a book completely unrelated to science, maybe a detective series or whatever. Or I'll go and spend some time with family, with my nieces and my nephews, or have a sleepover and have them come over. That takes me out of my routine, out of my normal day. I haven't felt burnout as much because I make the time for myself now. Early on, when we first moved back to Connecticut, I was working eighty hours a week, and I wasn't really taking time for myself. I've learned that I can take time. I can take a day off a week and not look at email or respond to it, or I can take our beagle for a long walk, or go for a swim or a bike ride with my husband, things like that. We're doing a lot of different house projects and doing some yard work, so I've learned that it's okay to step away from what everybody else calls work. But I don't really define it as work because it's sort of what I do, if that makes sense."

Cindy Morrison was forced into changing careers, but it has given her more control over her time and her well-being. As Cindy says, "I got really burned out a lot more often when I worked in TV then I do now because, in television, I always had to work those forty to fifty hours plus I had appearances on nights and weekends, so I was constantly going. Unless I had a sick day or a vacation day, there was no stopping. Now I'm smart enough to say, you know what, today I'm exhausted. Mandi, my assistant, and I have learned that when I travel to a convention, I need a rest day when I get back. I need to be able to unpack my bags, sleep, kiss my kids, read a book, and recuperate. That kind of recovery is so vital to your physical and mental well-being. I don't think corporate America sees that. Some corporate jobs do get it, and allow women to work nontraditional hours; do job sharing, or take naps. But I think that's the exception, not the rule."

Baeth Davis is a dynamo. If you take a workshop with her, be prepared for long hours, because she gets energized by the material and the group and she wants to give you more and more information and more learning. She is on a mission to be a powerful spiritual teacher with a message for the masses, as her hand print indicates. When I asked her about getting burned out, Baeth said, "Oh yeah, I take on too much and then I get overwhelmed. And then I have to take a break and then I get behind and then I get more overwhelmed and it's sort of this crazy cycle. But, I have moments now, longer and longer stretches, where I'm actually on top of everything and breathing easy. So that's one of the things I have to watch out for. I just get so excited, which is the other thing I have to watch out for, my enthusiasm. One of the things I've finally discovered is that people misinterpret my enthusiasm as a 'yes.' To me, it's not a 'yes,' it's just 'hey this is really cool, sounds great!' Now I've learned to say to people, 'Look, I get really enthusiastic about things, but until I sign on the dotted line and hand you a check, it's not a yes.' I tell all my friends, don't get your hopes up until I've shown you my flight information. And that's been really helpful, to know my shortcomings. I tell my team 'Don't let me take on another project until I finish this one.' And now they don't. They give me the old smack upside the head and say, 'Baeth, rein it in.' I've probably upset friends the most because I want to disappointment them the least and then I end up disappointing them. That's been the hardest thing for me. Now I'm trying to be conscious and train my friends to say to me, 'Yeah, Baeth, I know you're saying yes, but take a moment, is this really a good time?' And then they give me an out. Then I'll admit that it's not and that I need six weeks' notice. I think that if we are conscious of our liabilities, people are much more forgiving to us when we can own up to them. I mean, I'm not perfect."

While these women may burn out, it is important to note that they fix the problem and it doesn't bring them down. They have the self-regard to take the necessary steps to restore themselves to their personal power. Successful women don't give up—they cut their losses and move on, or they change their behavior based on self-awareness and good communication with others. They keep moving forward with a commitment to their life purpose and with faith in themselves and the universe.

I have written a lot in my other books about the power of making positive life choices that support your body, mind, and spirit and that make you want to greet each new day as a gift. But most of us, at times, fall into a ditch, and we have to claw our way out. As we subtract negative people, bad jobs, lousy clients, and other stressors from our lives, we are not as stressed, and we are less vulnerable to burning out and losing ourselves. We have to value ourselves enough to push back and take control of the things that we can and to learn to live in peace with the things that we can't change, as the Serenity Prayer teaches us.

For each of us, something within us needs to heal so that we can put our own needs first. Just like they tell you on an airplane, you must put your own oxygen mask on first, so that then you can help others. What are some of the blocks that you must dynamite through before you can get a handle on the negative stress in your life? Here's a list:

BARRIERS TO SUCCESSFUL STRESS MANAGEMENT

1. A lack of understanding of the specific causes (stressors) of the problem.

2. Procrastination—not doing what you know you must do.

3. An unwillingness to take responsibility for the problems in your life and your health.

4. Feeling overwhelmed by the solutions available to you.

5. Giving up after one coping plan has failed, instead of acknowledging the problems in Plan One and then designing Plan Two, then making a Plan Three, if needed.

6. Not making stress management a daily priority.

7. Not being willing to share your problems with others or to ask for help with solutions and ideas.

8. A lack of assertiveness in asking for and getting what you want.

9. Having unrealistic expectations of yourself and the time it takes to change many things and resolve them. You must be committed and patient.

10. Not rewarding yourself for your efforts and for each victorious step along the way!

Here are some very specific strategies that you can do yourself or share with your employees and colleagues. Keep them in mind as you craft wellness policies for your own organization, or when you need to rally support from others to make changes in the company that you work for or with. You can get a handle on burnout and stop its devastating effects on you, your friends, and your coworkers.

STRESS RESOLUTION STRATEGIES

Burnout and low employee morale leave in their wake individual casualties, loss of productivity, high absenteeism, chemical dependency, strained family relationships, and broken dreams.

How do you recognize burnout in yourself or an employee? Warning signals may include the following signs if they occur on a regular basis:

1. Difficulty getting up in the morning

2. Frequently being late for work

3. Skipping work

4. Irritability and quickness to anger

5. Forgetfulness

6. Frequent illnesses

7. Inflexibility and resistance to change

8. Boredom

9. Frustration

10. Fatigue

11. Feeling unappreciated

12. Hopelessness and detachment

13. Tension

14. Accidents, either on or off the job

15. Procrastination

16. Increased alcohol or drug consumption

Learning to manage stress means taking care of yourself by taking responsibility for your well-being and making positive life choices. Managers and organizations can help their employees by analyzing their corporate culture and instituting positive changes.

The following is a list of powerful steps that you and your company can implement to halt the downward spiral of burnout and low employee morale:

For Yourself

- Take a personal stress inventory and make decisions to avoid, alleviate, or adapt to whatever causes stress for you.

- Make plans to identify and actively pursue your personal and work goals.

- Do work that you love, work that matches your personality and your lifestyle, and that challenges you creatively.

- Build up your stress resistance with a healthy lifestyle.

- Learn relaxation techniques and use them daily, even for just five minutes.

- View yourself, your job, or your business realistically, and identify potential pitfalls ahead of time.

- Develop strong personal relationships with your managers and coworkers.

- Limit your overtime hours and take your vacations.

- Learn to say "No" and to actively negotiate to prevent your workload from becoming overwhelming.

- Keep your life balanced with satisfying personal relationships, recreation, and creative pursuits.

If You Manage Others

- Model the stress reduction strategies listed above to your employees.

- Watch for the early signs of burnout in your employees.

- Meet regularly with your staff to review job responsibilities, company objectives, and employee career development goals.

- Regularly give earned positive recognition to employees.

- Don't overload your best employees with too much responsibility.

- Limit employee work hours and set realistic expectations.

- Encourage employee participation in decisions whenever possible.

- Ensure that your employees have proper training, resources, and support to do their jobs well.

- Encourage your employees to follow their creative ideas in order to bring innovation to their work and to the organization.

For Your Organization

- Announce an organizational commitment to stress-reduction, and identify key problems and solutions.

- Provide stress management information to all employees.

- Train your managers in effective coaching and people skills to utilize with their employees.

- Offer company benefits, such as health club memberships, smoking cessation groups, yoga, and healthy lunches to support their well-being.

- Review departmental job descriptions and expectations to develop new and innovative models of efficiency and job satisfaction.

- Communicate organizational goals and initiatives to employees so they feel like a significant part of the team.

- Be certain that all policies and procedures are up-to-date and equitable.

- Provide ongoing coaching, professional development programs, and technical training for all employees.

- Arrange for employee assistance counseling or coaching for employees dealing with burnout.

If you empower yourself and your organization and do your personal self-development work to release low self-esteem, traumas from the past and present, outdated belief systems, and impossible expectations for yourself as a woman, you can prevent and/or recover from burnout. You can get a grip on the stressors in your life and avoid them, modify them, or get the support you need to cope with them and shift your attitude about them. Here are some additional strategies to help you to take care of yourself.

RESTORE INNER BALANCE

Ah, the fantasy of time off and lots of leisurely thoughts and activities. Yet research shows that in this 24/7 world, people are taking shorter vacations, staying wired up to work, and not relaxing. Too much stress is a creativity choker. Your inner peace and connection with your internal whims and spontaneity allow you to recreate the landscape of your mind and invent the new. Here are some tips to cultivate your tranquility and make your creativity a priority:

- Actively clear time on your calendar for the very best creativity enriching experience you can imagine. Do you need a weekend alone, or an interactive workshop with diverse people, or simply time to play with your creative projects?

- Do a stress inventory for a week and see what is draining your psychic energy, and try my three-part Positive Choices model of proactively trying to avoid, modify, or learn to cope with whatever stressor is stealing your serenity. Resolving the issues will set you free.

- As a child, most of us loved the summer for the freedom we had to have adventures and commune with Mother Nature, the arts, sports, or family. What does your heart long to have the pleasure of this season? Make it happen.

- Set aside some time for silence—quiet time to listen to your own thoughts and firewall you from the outside world. My clients are all telling me that they long for inner peace and an escape from all the external noise and information that descends upon us daily. Give yourself that essential restoration time on a regular basis.

- Review your life path at the moment. Are you heading in the direction that you desire or are you lost on a side trail? Recommit to the path you want to be on and fight your way back to it. I have one current client who wants to start a design business, and another client who hates having her own landscape business and wants to get a job. Tell the truth about what you want now. Change is scary, but it's ever-present and beckons us to heed its callings.

SLOW DOWN

My clients always complain about how much they have to do when school's in session (even if they don't have kids or aren't taking classes themselves). I call it the Labor Day launch syndrome, and it can actually happen any time of the year. People let go of the leisurely state of mind of the summer. They launch into initiatives for all kinds of projects, from learning to license their art work to adding programs to their business to cleaning out junk. Then they start getting colds or complaining of fatigue.

It's time to stop and reevaluate. Are you having fun? Do you look forward to what you are doing? If so, that's great. If not, what's wrong? This week, run away to a coffee shop or a park for an hour and do some journaling about how your launch period is going so far. If you are already frantic or tired, figure out why. Too often, we add too many activities, social events, work projects, committees, and so on so that we can capture all of the opportunities out there. Now, we need to review and most likely subtract something (or a few somethings) from this manic schedule. If we run ourselves ragged, there will be consequences, and we will miss all the enjoyment of the things we love. Write your ideas down so that you don't lose them, but get them out of your mind for now.

Write a prescription for yourself about how you need to slow down. Give yourself the psychic space so that you can capture special moments and stay connected to your creative thoughts and dreams.

THE ENERGY BOOSTS OF ADVENTURE AND REST

There are two kinds of vacations: adventure vacations and rest vacations, and we need both. While traversing around six countries on my Mediterranean cruise, I was stimulated and pulsating with creative energy. My desire was to experience an overview of lots of different cultures and scenes quickly. The excitement of immersing myself in the Mediterranean seaside and revisiting my love of art history and mythology was just glorious. Barbara Sher once told my photographer husband that he "lives to travel," so adventure vacations are a priority for both of us. And, as many of you know, I have a fascination with islands, especially warm ones.

Which brings me to the second kind of vacation: rest vacations. A rest vacation is one where you stay put and meander through your day. No schedules, no deadlines, and no long list of sights to see. Many people are heading for the woods for silent retreats—no conversation, no stress—just peace and quiet to illuminate their own thoughts. Spas are very popular as they offer pampering and soothing treatments in a serene setting. A while back, I was ready for one of these vacations myself, and so I flew off to Rancho La Puerta in Mexico for a week. Except for co-presenting a workshop with my friend Alice, I spent my time lounging, reading, and communing with pools and mountains.

Of course, there are hybrids of the adventure and rest vacations—a varied menu that suits a mixed venue. My husband and I often try to do a combination so that he can go up in airplanes to photograph scenes and I can lie in the sun on the beach or have a healing massage. Tune in to what you're craving for yourself. Even if it's not a year for a luxury trip, make a list or a collage of what you need to experience this year to recharge your intellect or your inner artist, or to mellow your body, mind, and spirit. As I wrote in all of my books, time off and time away are powerful creative catalysts. You have to make a space in your life for inspirations to appear and communicate with you. Change houses with someone, go camping, take a workshop, stay in a hotel overnight alone, or hit a day spa—but do something novel and rejuvenating that clicks for your original self and appeases the vacation gods of both adventure and rest. Bon Voyage.

THE BENEFITS OF RESTORATION
"A rested mind is a receptive mind."

As I said, I loved my week in Mexico at the spa Rancho La Puerta. I fell in love with Nia and doing water aerobics outside. Nia is a sensory-based movement practice that draws from the martial arts, the dance arts, and the healing arts and promotes health, wellness, and fitness. It's great fun! The Ranch looked like the Garden of Eden, with beautiful statues and lovely flowers in bloom everywhere. The food was gourmet vegetarian from their own organic farm, which I hiked two miles up and down to visit. I also toured the Ranch's Foundation, which has educational programs for children and families with a park for community gatherings. The whole week was truly a peak experience.

The week I returned, however, my beloved laptop turned into an alien. I was right in the midst of my website launch and my major plans for catch-up work. My plan had been to replace the laptop in the fall and go through a lengthy process of researching models, comparing buying versus leasing, etcetera. But my laptop had another agenda—no more disk space, regardless of what I deleted. Thanks to my husband's initiative to just go to Costco and "get it done," I got a new laptop that day and I stayed amazingly calm. I was at peace with this chaos because I was rested and had stored up extra reserves to call upon in a time of stress. Had this happened in the midst of a period of relentless overworking, I might have dealt with this crisis with less grace. While I would never have chosen that week to dance with a new computer, I surrendered. Lack of time to restore yourself increases your vulnerability to dark days and high drama.

A second benefit of rest is idea generation. I get my best ideas when I am out in nature, in a novel environment, or on a vacation, as do many other creative women. Which I was at the Ranch, I had this powerful intuition to journal alone in this gorgeous circular building called the Oak Tree Pavilion. It was a stone building with luxurious pillows and couches facing a magnificent fireplace with circles of glass windows. Several times during the week, I hiked over with my writing journal, but there were always people there. Finally, I decided to go right before dinner and found it empty. I cuddled up with the pillows and wrote for over an hour. I wrote about my plans for additions and subtractions in my own life. I got laser clarity about next steps and priorities. It was a magical moment—sitting alone in Mexico in that lovely building, able to think clearly and in peace.

These were priceless insights, the kind that reveal themselves only when your mind is free.

A third benefit of rest and restoration is the energy for new commitments. When I got home, I noted how quickly I could potentially get overwhelmed by the details of life and work once again. This 24/7 world is a dangerous one, as we get overworked and under-actualized. It can eclipse our creativity and undermine our optimism. So I committed to honoring the spiritual practice of blocking off a sacred rest period every week. I want to preserve my stress resiliency, my soulful thoughts, and feel joyful every week. Rest is like an insurance policy for good health and an investment in our "becoming." I urge you to join me in carving out your own R & R time, beginning today.

CONTINUING GRATITUDE

In the season of Thanksgiving, we focus on the tradition of gratitude. It is a time to note and acknowledge the harvests of the past year and to give thanks for our family and friends, both living and passed on, and for the richness of life. A table filled with luscious food is a metaphor for nourishment and abundance. Gratitude is also the backbone ritual of prosperity consciousness, which is best practiced daily, not just once a year. In order to ask for "more," we must first give thanks for all that we already possess, both materially and spiritually. We need to practice gratitude on a regular basis with rituals, such as writing down three things you are grateful for each day.

I continue to be struck by the gremlin of "lack of belief in self" that eclipses the careers of so many talented creative men and women. Unfortunately, insecurity about our natural gifts and talents flourishes in a culture that worships celebrities (gifted or not) and material wealth (derived with integrity or not). We forget the value of doing work that expresses our creative impulses, reflects our strengths and passions, and is done with commitment and a value system based on contribution and service. So, on a regular basis, I urge you to enact the following:

1. Give personal thanks to all the meaningful people in your life and remind them of their special talents. Tell your accountant how much you appreciate his/her thoroughness and quick response to your questions. Recognize your local bookstore owner for his/her suggestions and knowledge of great writing that truly makes a difference in your literary adventures. Become an agent of acknowledgement to others. Send people cards or e-mail, or speak to them and let them know how they have made a difference in your life.

   I received a wonderful celebration card a few weeks ago from a cherished former client, thanking me for my support in her success. Her card arrived on a day when my desk was filled with piles of paperwork (not my favorite activity) and a list of problems to resolve. In that instant, her kind words reconnected me to the many blessings of the work I have done for the past three decades and why I was born to do exactly what I am doing in the world.

2. Celebrate yourself as well. Make a list or create a visual representation highlighting your special gifts and talents. Think of all the compliments and encouragements about your abilities that you have received in your life. Tune into your inner knowing about your own strengths. Acknowledge what you already do well, or that your new talents are unfolding. Post supportive letters, cards, gifts, etc. on a special wall, or in a scrapbook, or make an altar so that you have people's good wishes close by every day.

   I was talking with a poet this week who lamented that she wasn't a "great poet" yet. I reminded her that she was a "good poet" now and that if she continues to invest in her craft, she can, one day, be an even better poet. If she denies her talent and what she has achieved so far and quits, we all lose, especially her, since writing poetry brings her joyfulness and profound wisdom. She is now collecting compliments about her work to help spur her onward.

   Perfectionism, unrealistic standards, and the vile criticisms of our saboteurs have no place in this gratitude exercise. Send them away. Give thanks for the creative impulses and results you have brought forth until now. Can you improve your mastery? Of course you can. Do you have any weaknesses to overcome? I expect so. Do you have more to learn? There is always something new and exciting to explore. But for now, be grateful for your innate interests, current experiences, and your fascination with your art or business. Let what's already on your personal feasting table nourish and encourage you as you venture forward.

3. Make a commitment to mentor or support another creative soul or group this year in whatever way feels most natural to you. It could be writing a check to an arts organization, playing with a child and encouraging their creative expression without judgment, or sharing your own creative work with others in a new way. Enjoy your creative impulses, keep your commitments to yourself, and reap the bounty of an artful and satisfying life. Don't let stress and burnout hold you back. Your heart depends on it.

The Serenity Store

Leave your stress behind and enter the Serenity Store where you can fill up your shopping cart with Positive Choices for your life, and emerge feeling confident, successful, and serene

Start Here
If you are feeling:
↓

Disconnected
Tense
Unfulfilled
Unhealthy
Overwhelmed
Powerless
Frustrated
Exhausted
Unhappy
Burned out
Stressed

↓

Come and visit our Serenity Store, filled with wonderful options to soothe your body, mind, heart, and spirit. Take a look at all the selections in the store and fill up your shopping cart with all the Positive Choices that resonate for you right now. Highlight your selections.

↓

Store Selection of Positive Life Choices for You:

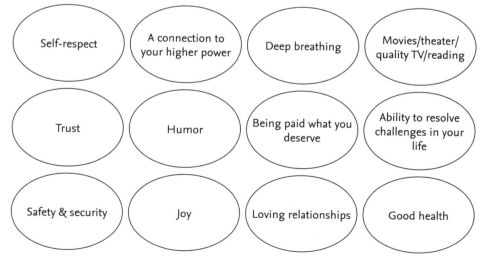

continued on the next page

continued from the previous page

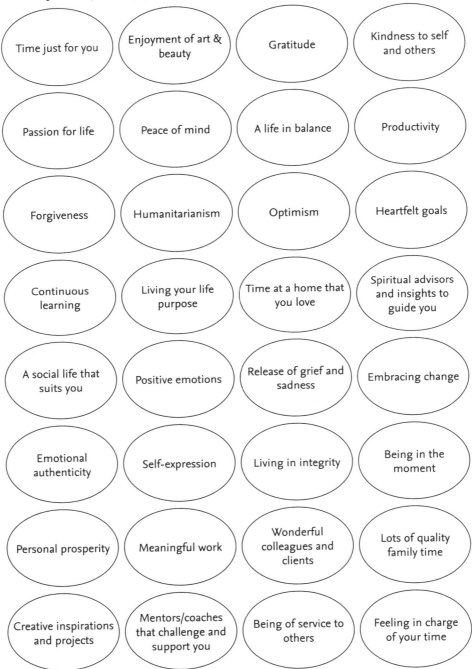

Time just for you

Enjoyment of art & beauty

Gratitude

Kindness to self and others

Passion for life

Peace of mind

A life in balance

Productivity

Forgiveness

Humanitarianism

Optimism

Heartfelt goals

Continuous learning

Living your life purpose

Time at a home that you love

Spiritual advisors and insights to guide you

A social life that suits you

Positive emotions

Release of grief and sadness

Embracing change

Emotional authenticity

Self-expression

Living in integrity

Being in the moment

Personal prosperity

Meaningful work

Wonderful colleagues and clients

Lots of quality family time

Creative inspirations and projects

Mentors/coaches that challenge and support you

Being of service to others

Feeling in charge of your time

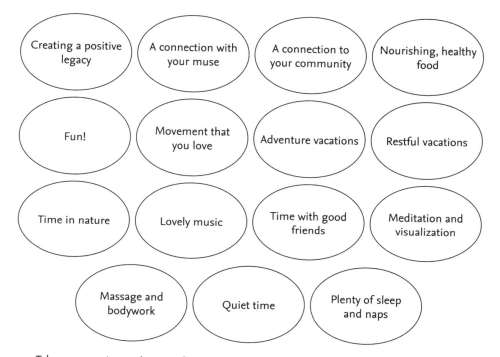

Creating a positive legacy

A connection with your muse

A connection to your community

Nourishing, healthy food

Fun!

Movement that you love

Adventure vacations

Restful vacations

Time in nature

Lovely music

Time with good friends

Meditation and visualization

Massage and bodywork

Quiet time

Plenty of sleep and naps

Take your precious selections from your shopping cart home with you and add them to your life, one circle at a time. Subtract your "serenity stealers," and you will find your personal serenity.

↓

After embracing your Serenity Store Circles, you now feel:

↓

Successful

Open

On purpose

Creative

Centered

Focused

Peaceful

Empowered

Fulfilled

Relaxed

Loving

Content

Calm

Happy

Secret Eleven

Build Effective Body/Mind/Heart/ Spirit Strategies to Nurture Your Success and Well-Being

"Life is not about waiting for the storms to pass . . . it's about learning to dance in the rain."
—*Vivian Greene*

TREAT YOUR BODY WITH DEVOTION

Women who maintain long-term success know that their physical body is an essential tool in their ability to be productive, sharp, and move quickly, both mentally and physically. If we don't take excellent care of ourselves, especially as we age, vulnerabilities, diseases, or illnesses may start showing up. Since stress, with its elevated cortisol and other dangerous physical changes, is such a threat to our well-being, keeping it in check is vital to our energy level and to our overall health.

Many of us can spend our days in our heads, oblivious to the needs of our bodies until they start screaming at us to pay attention. How many times have you gone all day without eating, or getting enough sleep, or not getting to the bathroom enough? There can be a tendency to just push yourself a little longer, a little further, until you get it all done. Well, you know—you never get it all done, never, because there is always more. But we can go numb to our body's needs and signals and wear down our immune system, feed ourselves toxic foods that upset our systems, and promise ourselves that we will get out for a walk tomorrow. We've all done it, but it's when we do it chronically that it can become a real problem. Our body is beautifully designed to signal us when it's in pain or discomfort, and our job is to honor the messages.

For example, if your back is killing you while sitting in your desk chair all day, you have the power to change that. In fact, it should be number one on your to-do list today. You deserve a new chair, if you need one, or ergonomic pillows, a foot rest, or a total rearrangement of your workspace so that you are not leaning the wrong way and aggravating your back any further. Your back is telling you that you need to make changes, so pay attention. Maybe you need to strengthen your core muscles with home exercises or the gym, maybe you have a herniated disc that needs treatment, or maybe you just lifted something heavy that you should not have. Play detective, follow the clues, and then solve the case and make the changes that you need to make so that you protect your back. We only get one back. I remember learning in anthropology that the back is very fragile, because man was never meant to walk on two legs—we were designed for four legs. So it's a vulnerable area to begin with.

With only a couple of exceptions, the forty-five women I interviewed for *The 12 Secrets of Highly Creative Women* exercised faithfully. The same was true for the women I interviewed for this book. This is no accident. Besides the usual health benefits and the benefit of preventing diseases by exercising, exercise and movement stimulate creative thinking and serve as an important stress reducer. If you are feeling stressed and you go outside for a walk in nature, you will probably return clear-headed and refreshed. Many of the women in this book get their best ideas when they are moving. It puts a kinesthetic element into the mix. As Gillian Drake says, "I do yoga and pilates every morning for ten minutes after I meditate, and go to yoga classes twice a week. I take my dog for long walks and often sprint or walk with her. And I bicycle in the summer, anything to keep me moving and be outdoors. Gardening is my favorite thing to do. All of these activities and being close to nature put me into right-brained mode so I can access my intuition, my inner dreams, goals, and desires. I solve all of my problems while I am gardening or walking." Debora George Tsakoumakis confirms this practice, and says, "I do walk every day, I either walk for thirty minutes or I go kickboarding in the pool for thirty minutes. That's my time to think. I usually do that by myself, and that's my regroup for the day, and I will debate what I am going to do about things. I'll come back and I'll tell my husband, 'I was thinking about something . . .' and he'll say, 'Oh, no,' because he's knows something is happening—there's some change coming. One example is that I got the idea about how to deal with our cake tins getting so expensive, and that was to take advantage of buying closeouts after the holidays so that we could get the discount. I am now using a new cake box made to our cake liner size, recommended by my baker, in an effort to keep costs down."

Lynn Robinson belongs to a health club, and she loves to do water aerobics and go swimming there. In addition, Lynn says, "The pool is on a hill and when you're there at night, you can watch the sun go down. I was there last night and it was just beautiful. The sky changed every five seconds and I felt like I was watching a movie. I remember stopping for a moment while my class was going on and thinking, 'God, this is so incredible, thank you. I am so grateful.'" Lynn's fantasy is to own, not rent, a house in Florida so that she can be in a warmer climate and outside more of the year, since, like me, she lives in wintery, cold Boston. I have a similar fantasy, which is just starting to come true, of spending time in warm places off and on during the year. Sheri McConnell is also soothed by nature. As she says, "I always say that we have to get out in nature every day to fuel our soul, and I get my creativity from that refueling. I love the ocean and I love hiking. I love, love, love, yoga. This year, I was finally able to make it a practice. I was always one of those people who loved yoga and bought lots of yoga clothes, but never consistently practiced it. I finally got a trainer and started doing it with the trainer and then I was able to do it consistently at home after that. It just changes your life. I'm also a religious bubble bath taker. I take one every day, and sometimes I'm in the tub for an hour and a half. I've dropped more than one book in there, and one of these days I'm going to drop my iPhone in there too." Sheri has four children between the ages of four and sixteen, yet she knows the importance of self-care for both her business and her family.

Shama Kabani admits that regular exercise has been a struggle for her because she doesn't really enjoy going to the gym. She says that she does love good food, and is careful to eat healthy food and not junk food. Shama says, "I am a big fan of treating my body with care. Coke, coffee, and caffeine—those are not for me. I will go out and order a lobster, and I don't care if it's not my anniversary. I really think about what I put into my body. But because I feel like I am behind in the exercise realm and I sit at my desk all day, I'm going to take pilates lessons from a personal trainer, because pilates is the only thing I ever enjoyed at the gym. I think that

Refuel with exercise.

having a personal trainer will make all the difference." Successful women acknowledge their weaknesses and ask for help. Having a trainer was a common practice among women in this group.

Caroll Michels is an avid dancer. She organizes her life around taking these dance classes every single week, and just revels in it. Her teachers keep her on the move and performing. Pele Rouge dances as well. She does a special Cherokee dance of alignment, balance, and prayer. Pele also pays close attention to what she eats and exercises regularly at the gym with weights, as she says that women in her lineage tend to have osteoporosis. She walks and hikes and has a daily practice of meditation and journaling as well.

JJ Virgin, being a wellness expert, says that hiring a coach is a great idea because there is so much misinformation out there and we need the right support. But she says, "You have to realize that incorporating good habits into your life happens over time, not overnight. One day of eating cake doesn't destroy your health. But eating cake every day does. The biggest keys to being healthy are to make sure that you get quality sleep and put some bliss into your life each day. That will do far more for you than taking your vitamins or eating your vegetables. You can't be miserable and be healthy. Have sex a couple of times a week with the partner you actually love. Eat well and exercise. Move. Start with the basics, just like building a business, and then continue to advance."

Peggy Whitson exercised even while she was in space. As Peggy says, "I'm a dedicated exerciser, for more reasons than just physical fitness, because it is also mental fitness for me. When I got bogged down or stressed out, even onboard the station, exercise was my escape mechanism for de-stressing."

When our body betrays us and we get ill, we may not be able to work, and we need to learn how to love ourselves in spite of our inability to "do." Instead, we must allow ourselves to just "be" so that we can get well. Brenda Michels has some wise words about how to do this. She advises, "When we get a disease, like cancer, there is a part of us that feels like a failure. We feel like we have become a burden—that we are burdening our husband, our wife, our family, our parents, or whomever and that can lead to a feeling that there is something wrong with us. So this is the point I'd like to . . . if you are ill, or have manifested a chronic disease, this is what's right for you at the moment.

> *The biggest keys to being healthy are to make sure that you get quality sleep and put some bliss into your life each day.*

"There is a gift in that and there's healing available. There is an amazing amount of gifts available in our willingness to have the courage to step forward and say, 'okay, I have this condition. Its not necessarily what I want, nor is it who I am. It is a part of my experience and a condition that my physical body is experiencing. What can I learn from this? What can I change about myself, about my life, about my lifestyle, about my beliefs, and how I think, and what I say that can make a difference in my life and in the lives of others?' When we take it to that level, we are now engaged in a healing process."

MANAGING OUR MINDS

"I am learning all the time. The tombstone will be my diploma."
—*Eartha Kitt*

Brenda illustrated how entwined our bodies are with heart, mind, and spirit. It is often difficult to separate one from the other. As Gillian Drake says, "I believe that we should strive to be the best we can, in body, mind, and spirit—always learning, growing, and evolving. I do not enjoy going to doctors and hospitals, so my goal is to stay healthy and out of the hospital. It's a great motivator. I weigh the same as I did when I was sixteen, and I feel great. I plan to live to be 100 and have just had my wisdom teeth crowned, because I figure I'm going to need them for a good while longer."

When we are growing and learning, things in our lives keep changing and expanding. Lisa Sasevich feels like she is living the life of her dreams with a lovely family, a supportive husband, a beautiful new home in La Jolla, California, and a business that empowers people. But that business growth presents challenges. As Lisa says, "With the rapid business growth that we are having, it's just a constant retooling of how to continue to free myself up to be the wizard in my company, to keep the creative ideas flowing, and to be able to have structures for implementing them. That is the hardest part because every time we get the systems down, the business grows, and what used to work doesn't work anymore, as far as structures or supports. It's kind of like parenting. You finally get a routine down with your children and then, of course, they change. So there's nothing missing, it's just a constant evolution out there."

Sheri McConnell is a working mom and had to make some tough decisions in her life to free her mind and energy to do the things she thinks are important, even if it meant rocking the boat. She had an extremely neglectful and abusive mother, and she ultimately decided not to have an ongoing relationship with her. Her first and now ex-husband was also abusive, and she left him to protect herself and her children. She is now happily remarried and running this mega-business, trying to juggle work and family. Ultimately, to make it all work, she had to subtract some Serenity Stealers. As Sheri says, "The women in the neighborhood don't understand why I say no to going out and hanging out with them. I used to be involved with the PTA and the school in the beginning because of guilt and then I was unhappy because I didn't have time for things that I treasured more. I finally made the decision that these activities that I didn't enjoy were taking me away from things I love, so who was suffering in the end? It was me, because I was spending a lot of time with my kids, but then I would have to be at the school too much or doing things that other people wanted me to do that I didn't want to do. So balance for me came from asking who and what do I love? Why am I doing this? Why am I not feeling good right now? I then started doing things that made me feel good and that work for me, my family, and my business."

Claiming our authentic self and telling the truth about what we want our life to be about allows us to make the hard choices that will ultimately bring us fulfillment and ease the stress of bouncing all around because of someone else's expectations. Successful women must have strong boundaries and must set them clearly to free up their mind and their energy for what they love.

It was Wayne Dyer who wrote the book *Excuses Begone,* and Baeth Davis operates from that philosophy. As she says, "It is up to me to show up and to be my best and that's why I get enough sleep, get a lot of body work, exercise a lot, and work with a nutritionist [JJ Virgin, who is also featured in this book] now to completely clean up my diet. I have big, big dreams and I know I can do it. I know if I can think of it, I can do it. I now have the resources to manifest some of the dreams that I have had for fifteen years. I never gave up on the dreams, but I had to find a way to achieve them. I take almost every weekend off unless I am holding a workshop and I plan nothing. I don't run errands, I don't clean the house, and the weekend for me is to chill out and to go and be in nature. You have to cut your losses and realize that everyone is not going to support you. Sometimes the people closest to you are not going to understand what you are doing and people may misinterpret your good intentions. They may try to sabotage your work or criticize you needlessly and you can't let any of that stop you. That's been my big a-ha, that no one has the power to interfere with my destiny, no one, because my destiny is mine." Successful women claim their independence from the other folks out there who are hiding out and not doing what it takes to reach their potential.

Many of the women in this book have group support for their stretching and learning via training programs, mentors, and/or mastermind groups. As Lynn Robinson said, "Successful people try to surround themselves with people who have a positive attitude because it feeds the process. Then you've got to have people to brainstorm with and to get some real valid support from as opposed to getting input from people who are being competitive or are too security-oriented. I have a mastermind group that I am part of [and, way back, Lynn and I used to be in a publishing mastermind group together] and I have found those to be helpful in a limited way, but often I plug into my informal network. For example, if I have an issue with a book, I might call you. There are different people in my life who have different sets of abilities or different skill sets to listen and then give me feedback that I really appreciate. It's also helpful to be involved with groups, and for me it is the National Speakers Association and the International Coach Federation."

As we grow and learn and interact with other people, our self-perceptions and personal strengths can change. Caroll Michels is happier now than she has ever been in her life, but it has been hard-won over time. Caroll says, "I know now that I've taken a lot of my talents, belief systems, and ways of looking at the world for granted. I wish I had realized at age eighteen that I am special and that I have a special way of looking at things. I always deferred to other people as being smarter, cleverer, or having the right answers, and I never quite fit. Even as a teenager, I was never really interested in the things that my friends were interested in, but I played along with it, thinking that maybe there was something wrong with me. So I wish I had the kind of chutzpah at eighteen that I have now and had been able to say no and know that my interests, my special way of looking at the world, were extremely valid." Now Caroll is radiant. She says that, "I have experienced happiness before, but never for such a long time on an ongoing basis. It's kind of amazing how happy I feel. But I took myself for granted for a long time and now I feel really good. Getting to that point has made me feel ever so grateful." This is a common issue for women—not acknowledging their unique gifts because those talents come so easily to them, or getting stuck trying to fit into the crowd instead of following their own path. Caroll has plans to move back to Europe one day, and she says that if she gets into a romantic relationship with a man again, she doesn't want to live with him—she wants to have her own space!

BEING HEART-CENTERED

"My whole heart for my whole life."
—A French saying used on poesy rings

Loving the people we keep in our lives is the essence of being rich with heart. Pele Rouge told me about a traditional Mayan phrase that describes this phenomenon beautifully. She told me, "The Mayan phrase is 'companions of destiny'. It comes from the belief that there are those people with whom each of us is meant to work with, to travel with, to journey with in this lifetime, and if we are lucky, we find them. It doesn't eliminate the need for each of us to follow our own path and to walk our own journey, but it does vastly enrich it. It's just so much more fun to do things together than it is to do them alone, and it's so much more powerful to do them in a relationship. And, from the perspective I hold, one of the things is that I think there is a foundational shift that's happening in the world. We are moving into the time of relatedness, of reclaiming our relationships with one another, our need for one another, and our joy in one another, as well as with the rest of life. We have pushed the paradigm of separateness, of aloneness, of give me land, lots of land, don't fence me in, I can do it all by myself as far as it can be pushed. In a sense, this is one facet of the Newtonian idea that the universe is made up of separate parts. The quantum physics perspective, as well as that of all indigenous peoples, is not that the fundamental nature is one of separateness, but that it is one of connectedness. Because we humans are a tribal people, in a very real sense, it's impossible to fulfill our destiny unless we are in deep relationship with other humans. So to find one's special companion of destiny is just such a gift and to find multiple companions of destiny enriches life." Many of the women in this book have found their companion or companions of destiny and have relished their support.

One example is Kathleen Dudzinski, who talks about how she and her husband collaborate together as a team on the Dolphin Communication Project (DCP). She is very appreciative of this collaboration, and says, "He's a documentary filmmaker and photographer. I met him on the first shoot for the dolphin film and I didn't actually start dating him until about a year later. He is my best friend, and I'm extremely proud of the work that he does. He also helps create videos for DCP, and when his schedule permits, he comes with me into the field and helps me do some documentation. He also documents me, because I'm the one behind the camera. I never had photos of me until the film came out, and then over the last ten years he's been with me in the field to document the programs that DCP does or the work that I do. He actually provided 90 percent of the photos for my book with Toni Frohoff as well. It was funny, because when he first started out working with me, he had this photography mentality of 'Let me get the glamorous, beautiful, Hollywood shot.' He always made them available to me. He said, 'Why aren't you using them?' And I said, 'Well, they're beautiful shots, but they don't really do what I need for the research. This is what I need for ID. This is what I need for behavior.' So I took his advice on making my shots look a little better, not just research-wise, and he took my advice on making them a little bit more useful to the research. Over the years, we have become a formidable team in the field. I also help him when I can with his projects and his production company. But he's definitely the camera person. He's my sounding board as well, on a lot of things."

Often in her newsletter Ali Brown will talk about her relationship with her mom—how she brings her on adventures with her and moved her to the desert after her father died. I told Ali that I loved reading about how she takes care of her mom and has strong connections to her brother and sister, too. Ali responded, "I'm going to cry right now, because I know if I lost everything that they're still there. I know that if I ever needed them, that my family is there. We weren't always close. There are years that we were bumping heads, but when my dad passed, the beautiful thing is that whenever there's a transition in the family, you all rediscover each other. We're closer now than we've ever been before."

One of Marilyn Tam's mentors and her friend for sixteen years was Robert Mueller, the former Assistant Secretary General of the United Nations and a prolific author. I remember reading his classic book, *Most of All They Taught Me Happiness,* many years ago, and marveling at Robert's charm and wisdom. When I spoke to Marilyn, he had just died two weeks earlier, and she had been to his small, intimate service. Marilyn says of Robert, "For me, it was his exuberance and optimism in life that inspired me. He said, 'I know some people think that I should be more serious because this is important work. But if you're not happy, why are you doing it?' He was always happy, and people would ask him, 'How can you be so happy when all these terrible things are happening?' And he said, 'But you can look for the positive side, because if you're miserable all the time, you cannot continue to do this work.' Once, at a huge, important gathering, Robert whipped out his harmonica and started playing it, and it just completely cracked everybody up. It was just so wonderful. Four years ago he taped an audio of himself playing his harmonica, and he said, 'I want this played at my service, as the celebration of life.' The piece that he's most known for is "Ode to Joy" by Beethoven, and every time I hear it, it brings that warm feeling in my heart, or up to my throat. He just taught me so much. As the Assistant Secretary General of the United Nations, you can imagine how many discouraging, horrible, horrific things that he's seen, people doing bad things to other people, but somehow he said, 'I am so committed to doing this and I can see . . .' and he cited good things that have happened and made a difference. If he could find hope and joy in the despairing, discouraging, and miserable news that he had to encounter all the time, how can I not? He was so fun and so encouraging."

We all hope to encounter people like Robert who care for us and touch our hearts.

For many women, it's their girlfriends who become their family. Cindy Morrison wrote a book about it, and Lesley Bohm talks about how her girlfriends have been a support for her, especially since her divorce. As Cindy says, "When you surround yourself with great girlfriends who are each a ten, when you trip and fall, they'll come, scoop you up, and help dust you off and get you right back to where you were or even better."

Lesley Bohm has also collected an amazing group of friends. But she says that in her divorce, she was the one who lost all the friends. She says, "The girlfriends that I call my support system are just there for me, even when I'm sobbing on the phone. Not that it happens often, but you know how it is. They also know about business, are creative, and they are coaches, so they understand this whole process. They're like my mentors and I'm theirs. I don't have a mentor per se right now. I've actually shifted my whole group of friends and, as it happens, when you go through a huge life shift, your friends shift. They say surround yourself with people who will take you to the next level and the new friends that came in to support me are just fantastic—they are my rock."

I asked Lesley if she belonged to any professional support groups, and she said that she belongs to the American Photographic Artists. She said that they assist photographers with insurance and legal protection if anyone uses one of their images inappropriately. Lesley says that she also does social media and she says, "There are groups for photographers on Facebook, and there are people that you hear about all the time, people that everyone knows, and I find that with Facebook and Twitter you can connect with those people on that level a lot more easily now. So that's actually a good thing."

Finding people who truly feel like soul mates, soul sisters, and soul brothers make life wonderful and help us not to feel so alone. We need to be in a "family" and to have those "companions of destiny" that Pele talks about.

CONNECTING TO SPIRIT, AS WE DEFINE IT

"Put your ear close to your soul and listen hard."
—Anne Sexton

Spirituality is living as though your life is being guided by a higher wisdom. It often has no ties to any religion, particularly in today's world, where many women are disenchanted with their lack of validation in traditional religions. But for both men and women, spirituality has an important place.

I have written before about my admiration for Dr. Wayne Dyer as a spiritual master and guide. I have been captivated by his new movie *The Shift*; I have watched it over and over. I finally sent it back to Netflix and got my own copy. In the film, Wayne talks about an amazing study called "The Moment That Turns Your Values Upside Down."

The film is about your shift from youth into what Carl Jung calls "the afternoon of our lives" and how our priorities and values shift. I found the study just fascinating, particularly the differences in the choices of men and women. Both Jung and Dyer talk about the shift as moving into the meaning phase of life with a transformation into being of service to others. So many us, my clients, colleagues, friends and myself, are dealing with these key issues. Here are the results of the study:

For Men

They begin their lives with these top priorities, in order:

1. The accumulation of wealth

2. A sense of adventure

3. Achievement

4. The pursuit of pleasure

5. To be respected

After the quantum shift into the meaning phase of life, the new priorities for men are dramatically different. Their new priorities in order are:

1. Spirituality—the connection to something greater than self

2. Personal peace (less stress and anxiety)

3. Family

4. A Sense of purpose

5. Honesty with their feelings as a man

For Women

They begin their lives with a unique perspective and hence have priorities that reflect our culture. The priorities for young women are, in order:

1. Family

2. A Sense of independence

3. Career

4. Fitting In—being like everyone else

5. Attractiveness

In the meaning phase of their lives, the focus changes to self, and then to spirituality, like the men. The new priorities become, in order:

1. Personal growth

2. A sense of self-esteem

3. Spirituality—the connection to something greater than self

4. Happiness

5. Forgiveness

This shift for men and women has major implications for coaching, marketing, product development, relationships, social policy, and more. Wayne talks about this transition from "what can I get" to "how can I serve?" Secondly, after the shift, he says you are more able to enjoy your life and to be at peace. It is intriguing to me, given what we have been talking about in this book, that women who have gone through the shift drop the priority of "fitting in—being like everyone else" and instead make personal growth and spirituality top priorities. That means that women are listening to their inner voices, not to the "shoulds" of our culture, and tapping into their authentic selves. Practicing forgiveness is also a spiritual practice with formulas such as writing "I forgive so and so for . . . " seventy times a day for seven days, which I have certainly done myself, and advise my clients to do the same as part of their healing process. Deciding to be happy involves gratitude and prosperity, which are also spiritual practices using affirmations, thankfulness, prayer, and a trust that we will be taken care of in the universe.

CHALLENGE

1 Where are you in your shift?

2. How does knowing your potential priorities in the future change how you plan ahead?

3. What does this information tell you about communicating with the people that you are in relationship with?

4. What can you do now to start living a life that has meaning for you?

For thousands of years, women have gathered together in spiritual circles to support one another, do crafts together, cook together, care for children together, and work together. When I hit menopause and began to wake up on the dot of 3 AM every day, a friend of mine told me that that was the time that women in the olden days woke up to gather together in their circles. When I asked other women about their experiences of waking up, we were all waking up around the same time, until we got on hormones so that we could get our much-needed sleep. But I thought how amazing it would be if we instead all got up out of our beds at 3 AM, left our houses, gathered together in circles all over the world, set our intentions for the day, and prayed for our family, friends, world peace, and harmony. The power in a daily ritual like that could potentially change the world.

> For thousands of years, women have gathered together in spiritual circles to support one another.

I have been in a number of spiritual circles, although they all met at a reasonable hour. They were indeed circles of love, caring, and creative expression as well as being grounded in an appreciation of the larger universe. While these circles all came to a natural end, their powerful memories still inspire me.

I urge you to read Jeanne Carbonetti's books and watch her DVD, because she has an amazing theory of her own about consciousness. I want to share one of her insights here, as I think it illuminates the connection between creativity and the divine. Jeanne tells us, "It happens in about the mid-cycle of creativity. Right at the stage of holding what we are doing is allowing ourselves to give it over to the universe, knowing that it's not just up to us. We don't make it happen. That's the challenge in the creative cycle, that when we move through the cycle, there are different challenges, and one of the challenges is not to try to make it happen so that it happens at the wrong time. You can't make it happen. There are certain qualities that the universe has to add to it so that it fits with the whole and it has to be good for the whole. *The Secret,* the little book and the film that are out now, is part one, in that you begin to recognize that you do have the power of thought to decide what it is that you want and to move in that direction. It leaves off at the place where you have to then let it go into the universe, and it's not up to you alone now. There is a moment when personal will must surrender to divine will. It's where you let the bigger rhythm of life, like a wave, take it and it's not exactly up to you where, when, and exactly how you allow it to happen, as it needs to happen. Probably a lot of people who are seeing *The Secret* have never really thought about the fact that if they actually really, consciously make decisions about what they want, they might be a little closer to getting what they want. I think it's a very good thing that we're now starting to take responsibility in a mass movement kind of way for what happens to us. The thing that we have to be careful of, just like in all New Age thinking, is that we can't stay only in the logical mind world because the logical mind world wants to do it with thinking alone and fixing alone and is not about letting it go. The letting go part is where you take it into heart mind and you allow it to incubate. Then you allow the body mind place to take it into an even larger place still. That's the next stage in the evolution of humanity's creative power."

I had a chance to meet John Asserof, one of the authors of *The Secret,* at a conference in California last summer. He told an amazing story of having made a vision board, many years ago, of all that he wanted to create in his life, which included a picture of the home he wanted. He went on to manifest many things, such as a family, a number of successful businesses, and research into brain science. A few years ago, John moved into a new house unpacked his years of vision boards that he had made from their boxes. His son picked up one of the vision boards and said, "Dad, here is a picture of our new house." John took a look and was stunned to discover that he had bought the house in the picture on his own vision board.

In DMA classes Robert Fritz talks about "structural tension"—the tension between where you are now and what you truly want. It's like a rubber band that we want to snap quickly, but we need to surrender and trust the timetable of the universe, which often takes a lot of faith in a higher power.

Jeanne told me, "That's why knowing yourself is so important and recognizing that the very way you are is the way that you are supposed to be and that's where your power is. The power of your statement is always what you do most naturally, and when you do that, then you start to trust yourself, and then I think it starts to roll. You allow yourself to hear those inner voices, and to trust the universe a little more. All creation is co-creation and so it's you and the universe. It's the particle and the wave always working together. I think of us as funnels and life is pouring through us and we are all distinctly designed to be different-shaped funnels for a reason. It's so that life can come through us *as* us. So we're supposed to be outrageously *us*, whatever that is, and accept all the parts that go with it, even the parts that don't feel so good. Because that's the thing in the creative cycle that I realize is so important. We need the energy of all the parts and as soon as we know and don't reject the parts that we think the public won't like, then we have that power to really create what I think the universe wants us to create. It's surrendering to that process as you, as only you can."

Many of the women in this book talked about their relationship with the universe, source, trusted source, spirit, God, or a higher power. They sought out its wisdom and their own inner stirrings. As Gillian Drake told me, "Now that I am in my sixties, my only strategy is to remain closely connected to Spirit, because that is what directs me. I meditate every morning, and I see a friend who is a psychic, so I can be sure of my direction. I have taken classes in metaphysical exploration, which has opened up a whole new world to me, literally, and has sent my life in a new direction. I also have wonderful friends who are very supportive. A very important thing that I learned from your book [*The Power of Positive Choices*] is to jettison people in my life who are not supportive of my goals and needs. Because of you, I ditched my 'best friend' in Paris ten years ago when I realized how abusive she was. It was difficult because she was also my daughter's godmother, but really, with friends like that, who needs enemies? Now I am very careful about who I associate with. Forging into the unknown with a new business or a creative project is hard enough without having naysayers or energy vampires in your life."

It's all connected—body, mind, heart, and spirit.

It's all connected—body, mind, heart, and spirit. When we allow ourselves to listen to our hearts and honor what our gut and our intuition know to be true, and we stay in close communication with our higher power, however we define it, we have a complete system for nurturing ourselves and then reaching out to our "companions of destiny," as Pele Rouge teaches us. In order to go out on a limb in our lives and our businesses, we need the support of self-knowledge (personal growth), high self-esteem, a connection to Spirit, the will to be happy, and then the courage to forgive ourselves and others. All of the women in this book have a passion to serve, and the body/mind/heart/spirit team needs to be stoked, so that it burns brightly and gives us the fuel and the energy to bring our magic to the world.

Secret Twelve

Initiate Transformation for You and Your Team

> "Every great dream begins with a dreamer. Always remember, you have within you the strength, the patience, and the passion to reach for the stars to change the world."
> —*Harriet Tubman*

Transformation is about changing potential into reality. It is about shifting the condition, nature, or function of our lives. Like the butterfly, in transformation, we change from a tiny cocoon into a glorious, colorful, flying creature that is independent and free to fulfill its destiny. We all want some part of our lives to be better. In the course of this book, we have looked at eleven secrets of successful women, and you have heard their stories and some of mine, too. If you have been doing the Challenges all along in your journal, you have lots of new self-awareness and many ideas for how to increase your happiness, make more money, grow your business, be in positive relationships, tune into your heart, and live your life purpose. Yet none of that matters unless you filter though the material, design a dream plan for yourself, and set it into motion. You have to decide that you want transformation with your whole being. Then you make a Treasure Map, write down precisely what you want, visualize it, meditate on it, say affirmations daily about it with feelings that touch your heart, rewire the old beliefs you have about not being able to have it, and associate with people who believe in you. Then you choose and write down specific daily action steps and execute them to create the change that you want to manifest.

There are lots of inner saboteurs such as fear, insecurity, ambivalence, lack of experience, not being fully committed to what you want or not willing to do what it takes, etcetera, lurking on this path of action toward having what we want and expressing our true self in the world. There are many demons in your mind and in the world-at-large. There are lots of people who will undermine and trample you as you grow bigger and more visible. So to be successful and manifest your personal, heartfelt kind of success, you must initiate your own choice points. It will be helpful to have books, mentors, coaches, peers, masterminds, trainings, support groups, and all of those wonderful catalysts to guide you along your path.

> *Transformation is about changing potential into reality. It is about shifting the condition, nature, or function of our lives.*

But ultimately, you must light the match for the fire that burns in your belly that will warm you and comfort you, as you take this journey to what you have claimed as yours.

LIFE SUCCESS CIRCLE TEST

First of all, let me give you an opportunity to tune into exactly what you want to change in order make your life fit your definition of success. You already have some ideas, but let's make a graphic of where you are now. The Life Success Circle Test looks at fourteen areas of your life so that you can rate them. You want to rate them on a scale from 1-10 points, with 10 meaning that you feel very successful in that area of your life and with 1 meaning that you feel very unsuccessful in that area of your life. If you rate an area as a 5, for example, you feel partly successful and partly unsuccessful. Be honest—this is your own private test or this can be a great exercise to do with a trusted, like-minded friend, your coach, or a mentor. Write your chosen rating number outside each slice of the circle. Think about your responses and take the test.

Rate on a scale from 1–10 points

____ Meaningful Work   ____ Creativity

____ Money   ____ Life Balance

____ Good Health & Well-being   ____ Love/Romance

____ Friends & Family   ____ Personal Development

____ Peace of Mind   ____ Fun & Leisure

____ Spirituality   ____ Where You Live

____ Emotional Fulfillment   ____ Connection to a Larger Purpose

Circle of Life Test

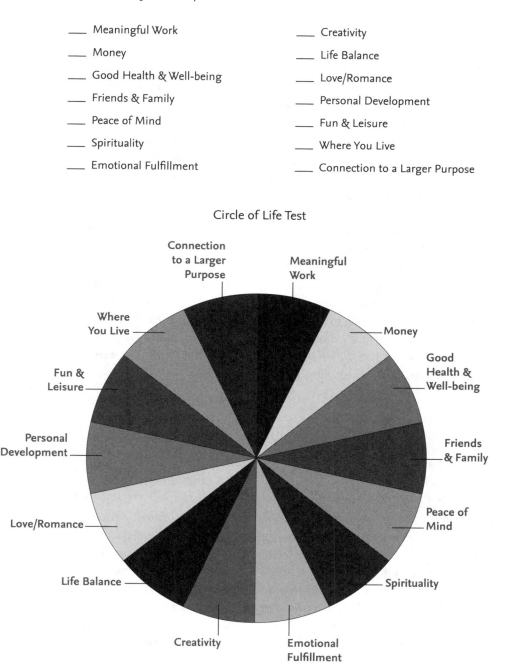

Life Success Circle Test

First, congratulate yourself for the areas where you scored an 8 or above. Write down what would make those areas zoom up to a 10. Then, identify the areas where you have the three lowest scores. These are your transformation targets. Jot down what would need to happen to make these areas evolve into a 10. Review the areas of the circle that you scored in the middle, and note if there is any one thing that you would like to do to boost that score a bit for now, and make a note of those ideas. Put a test date on the circle and then redo it again every six months to review your progress and note down any changes in your goals. We are constantly evolving into new self-awareness and priorities. Now, using the Personal Success Contract in Secret 5, pick your top five goals for the year, complete the form, and follow all of the instructions, including getting the right support systems in place. If you already filled out the Personal Success Contract earlier in the book, you must decide which five goals you value the most right now. All of the women in this book, myself included, are lifelong learners and are always seeking new role models, more knowledge, and bigger risks to take to expand our personal power and serenity, and to make our special contribution to the world. So select the goals that best reflect your intentions and desires. I know this exercise takes some time and some thought, but it will be worth it. We must stop being so busy that we don't create a solid plan about where we are going and what we are trying to create in our lives.

INITIATION RITUAL FOR YOU

Find or buy a big beautiful basket for yourself. It can be open or have a lid. Then get yourself three packages of Post-It Notes in three different colors, preferably colors that you enjoy. Next, think of a place that feels special to you that is quiet, offers you some privacy, feels safe, and is comfortable. Make a time to go there this week. This is your life and there is no time to waste. Cancel something if you have to, but do it now. Bring your basket, your Post-It Notes, your Treasure Map, your journal, your Life Success Circle Test, your Personal Success Contract, and this book with you. You can go to a place outside of your home, like a library or a beach, or simply find a corner or a room in your own home that you don't usually frequent and set up there. Settle into this special place, close your eyes, and imagine that you have manifested the five goals on your Personal Success Contract already. How does it feel? If it feels good, move onto the next step. If not, go back and get rid of anything on your contract that doesn't intuitively feel wonderful and replace that item with something that you deeply know that you want. Take the time to make sure that you have the five goals that you want and that these are the best next steps for you. Okay, you may open your eyes.

Now take your Post-It notes and assign a color to each of these three concepts: Be, Do, or Have. Take as long as you need and write down on the Post-It Notes in the corresponding color, the things that you need to be, to do, and to have to accomplish your goals. For example, you may need to be more aligned with the mission of your business each day (to be), hire a bookkeeper for your finances (to do), and buy a Smartphone so that you can check your email and your messages from anywhere (to have). Think of all the ways that you want to express yourself in the world, actions that you need to take, and things you wish to acquire, which could be skills or knowledge as well as tangible things, in order to ensure that you meet your five goals. Put each item on a Post-It Note in the right Be, Do, or Have color and throw the Post-It Note in your basket. This is your action plan in a basket. You can carry it with you. Once you have completed a Post-It Note task, take the Note out of the basket and put it in a special file for that year or stick it on an accomplishment poster in your office. You want to be able to review and celebrate your achievements each year. Each time you think of a new change that you need to add to the basket, write it on a Post-It Note that says what you need to Be, Do, or Have, and drop it in the basket. When you have completed a goal, replace it with a new goal on your Personal Success Contract. If you are advancing in your life, this process will go on for years. It works. Once you have put all the Post-It Notes that you need to be working on right now into your basket this first time, you are complete for now. Pull out your Treasure Map at this point and see if it is in sync with these new goals. If not, make out a Post-It Note that reminds you of what you need to do to fix your Map and stick it on the Map. In closing, take a moment to close your eyes again and say to yourself, "I am initiated into my Transformation." Open your eyes and go out and begin to gather or experience all the things that you need to do that are noted in your basket. Sit with all these materials for at least fifteen minutes each day and keep fine-tuning.

We have talked in this book about many success strategies. Keep using this book as a reference guide to inspire you on a daily basis. Just try opening to any page and see what pops up. Often we get the perfect lesson or idea out of the blue. One of the most common excuses that we use as a reason to not keep our promises and commitments to ourselves, our businesses, or our relationships is that we do not have the time. As we have discussed before, we are living in a relentless 24/7 culture with amorphous boundaries and endless opportunities to be connected and access the world through the Internet. I think that the time that it takes to keep all this technology backed up, running correctly, and updated is amazing. The number of hours that my husband and I and my team spend on the phone with technology companies and other customer service people is mind-blowing. So while we are saving time with our devices and gadgets, it takes time to keep them working for us.

Successful women know that time is at a premium and that they need to treat it like creative gold. We need to be in touch with our big vision for our life and our business, and simultaneously be crystal clear about what part of that vision we will work on today. It's the macro and the micro perspective being connected. For all of us who want success, or greater success, we simply have to become time management experts. We also have to practice vigorous "subtraction," as I talked about earlier, of anything that is not valuable to us or is a non–goal-enhancing activity. Those activities that we need to subtract, like working with clients we don't like, or cooking for a big gathering when we hate cooking and are not good at it either, I call Junk Time, and it has empty calories like junk food. Stand up for yourself. Get new clients and change your entertaining model and either hire a caterer, have a potluck event, or go out to a restaurant. We don't have any time to waste. I have an old friend who is now a minister, and she loves to have people stay with her at her house. But she makes it very clear that she will not cook for them. They can use the kitchen and she will stock the refrigerator, but she will not make meals. People come to visit her all the time anyway.

THE CREATIVE TIME CATCHER

Twenty-four hours per day is a given. The fact that you have control over that time is also a given. You are the creator of each day with far more leverage over your precious daily portion of twenty-four hours than you may acknowledge at this moment. In order to achieve your own personal success in life, you must activate your individual power to capture time.

Imagine standing on a lovely hillside with a gorgeous view, holding a simple butterfly net. As clouds of time go by, you capture them for yourself with your net. After you have captured your allotted twenty-four hours, then you head back home to craft your time clouds into your own art form. Every day is a gift, and you want to secure it so you can sculpt it to your liking. Every day contains major choice points. Are you going to squander your day with empty calorie TV, relationships that no longer serve you, or work you despise? Or are you going to delete all that and claim a higher standard and fill your day with creative choices that reflect your inner spirit, self-expression, and joyfulness? The choices that you make about how you spend your limited time and energy determine the quality of your life experience. Of course, there are lots of distractions, interruptions, mistakes, disappointing people and projects, chores, and necessary evils that steal your time. Learn to be a better warrior and steal it back. You can learn to steadfastly defend your position and fight those internal and external demons that undermine your intentions and your passions.

You are not defenseless or helpless, even though you may have moments where you feel that way. You are the driver of your own life and you choose the itinerary every day. The route you take changes the outcome, and if someone gives you bad directions or you get lost on your own, you can find the highway once again. Don't give up on yourself and your life. You can change your relationship with your daily twenty-four hours and learn mastery and self-defense. You can start to drill into your real goals and break them into manageable action steps and results. As we have talked about in this book, you can shift out of negative relationships into positive mutual ones. You can also implement filters—structures that keep out pollutants, stressors, and unwanted guck. You need to fight for your time and your life, as no one else will do it. If you dream of painting landscapes in the hills of Montana, want to make a documentary film about cancer survivors, or write a chapbook on ecological psychology, you are the one who is in charge of making it happen. It's not just having more money, a more understanding partner, or a more flexible job. It is about the strength of intention and a plan. It is about learning the dance of addition and subtraction and keeping your commitments to yourself. This is about time recovery and preservation. It is about taking responsibility for our daily quotient of creativity and our other priorities.

In our new twenty-first century work culture, time has a shifted meaning. There is a blur between work and play as well as a loss of important boundaries and limits on when, where, and how we can work. While technology has amazing benefits, it has also massacred many of our tried-and-true time management strategies. For each of us, renegotiating our individual relationship with time and fending off our work and lifestyle saboteurs are essential to our success. You don't need more gimmicks or clutter control suggestions, you need an overhaul of your thinking and your actions.

In a survey of my newsletter audience and in conversations with my clients, as well in the hundreds of emails that I get from the readers of all of my books, the issue of finding time to work on our creative, business, and life transformation is the number one critical issue for which people are seeking ideas and support. As a creative person, I, too, continually try new formulas that stimulate and facilitate my creative ideas and expression, get things done, and then send them out into the marketplace. Many creative people suffer from feeling scattered, trying to do too many projects at the same time, being stuck in right or left brain dominance, languishing without firm deadlines, and so on. Learning to be efficient in a way that supports our work style makes life so much easier.

> *You are the driver of your own life and you choose the itinerary every day.*

So I decided to do some research on what systems were working for people. I posed the question to my LinkedIn contacts a couple of months ago, and my inbox was flooded with responses. The answers were all quite unique. About 75 percent of the respondents used a software tool AND a paper tool. Many people had lost data on their computers, so they wanted a paper copy of client appointments, important addresses, and dates.

The different tools that people were using are as follows:

1. Outlook Calendar

2. Basecamp to manage group projects (*www.basecamphq.com*)

3. Google Calendar and many other Google products

4. David Allen's *Getting Things Done* software (takes a while to learn, but worth it) (*www.davidallen.com*)

5. Planner Pads (*www.plannerpads.com*)

6. Daylite, a Mac productivity tool

7. Franklin Covey Daytimer

8. Microsoft Project for big projects

9. Mind-mapping with Mindjet (*www.mindjet.com*)

10. iPhone Calendar

11. Traxtime for project tracking software (*www.spudcity.com/traxtime*)

12. A hand-written to-do list

13. Two people created their own index card/paper calendar systems

14. Dream Manifesto (*www.dreammanifesto.com*) for making a vision of your goals with pictures and affirmations

15. Levenger Notebooks

16. Appointment scheduling tools: *www.timetrader.com* and *www.Tungel.com*

I was struck by how people responded differently to all the systems out there and often adapted several systems to meet their needs, including incorporating paper into the whole. People talked about how much they enjoyed physically crossing a to-do off their list, which kept them in the paper camp. Many young people are really doing the "green thing" and keeping everything electronic, while we older folks still want to hold a book in our hands and have some kind of a paper planning book.

Just remember, these time management tools are meant to enhance implementation. You need to be sure that you have a set of written personal and professional goals that are accurate and meaningful to you, first. Dream Manifesto can help you to "see" photographs of your goals as a reminder to keep the big picture in mind as you choose your daily focus. Mindjet can help you to brainstorm lots of ideas and put them into a manageable form—but then you must choose what to work on. We all know that life throws us challenges—our car breaks down, people get ill (including us), companies make billing errors that take days to clean up, and so on. Don't succumb to impotence in your life, but instead grasp tightly onto this guaranteed formula for success and regenerate your faith in yourself and the magic of intention. You may cringe from those formidable saboteurs—fear and self-doubt—but they can be resolved. Experimentation and self-awareness have the potential to transform your life and allow your goals and dreams to emerge and manifest. Open your body, mind, and spirit to the quest.

BANISHING TIME WASTERS

1. Keep a list of people, events, and processes that regularly waste your time. You will then have the facts to make decisions about them. Susan realized

that never being able to find anything in her office was her biggest time waster. The $500 she paid a professional organizer to set up a filing system for her was a true stress reducer.

2. Find a quiet place to work. This is often a challenge with today's modular offices. Try some of these solutions: request an office with a door, share an office with someone who's out a lot (like a sales person), sign up for time in the conference room, play classical music softly at your desk to block noise, ask to work at home, come in early or stay late when the office is empty, don't answer your calls so that you can concentrate, or sit in your car or a nearby cafe for a while. Depending on your level of responsibility and your support staff situation, you will have different options. Every hour of focused time is worth it! If you work for yourself, you have loads of options for experimentation.

3. Are there chatty people who interrupt you too often? If so, schedule drop-in hours, close your door, put books or papers on the chair in your office so there's no place to sit, or be assertive and tell them you only have five minutes and stick to it. You can also not answer your phone or your closed door. If you work in the same office, you could also tell them you'll drop by their office later; then you can leave when you want. If you need to collaborate regularly with certain people, schedule virtual or live meetings with them. Sometimes a fifteen-minute meeting every morning prevents interruptions for the rest of the day. Remember that we have email and voicemail for a reason—it's so we can choose when to respond.

4. Protect your productive work time. Determine what time of day you have the most energy for planning and work that requires total concentration, and build your day around that high-energy biorhythm. Do you get the most work done early in the day or does your engine fire up at mid-afternoon? Determine in which block of time you're most productive and try to schedule appointments and meetings at other times of the day. Tanya knows that if she can work straight for three hours at home each morning that she gets an amazing amount of work done.

5. The telephone has the potential to be a great time-saver; it can eliminate the need for a trip or a meeting. Have you learned to take advantage of the free conference lines available to you like *www.freeconference.com,* which I use for interviews, meetings, teleclasses, etc.? It will record the calls and even

transcribe them for you. Speaker phones let you file or do sit-ups while you are talking. Several of the women I interviewed for this book talked to me in their cars while driving on long drives; they said that they get a lot of work done that way, hands free. If you are playing telephone tag with people, set aside specific call in or call back times. With talkative people, tell them up front how much time you have for them. Lastly, have your assistant return as many calls as possible to save you the time. That way, you can personally handle the important calls that will generate revenue for your business or with people that you love to work with.

6. Whenever you or someone else begins to schedule a meeting, ask yourself if there's an easier method. There are numerous new software packages that allow teams of people to communicate with each other and share documents and graphics right from their own work stations. Check with your operations department or software store for information.

7. I keep waiting for our paperless workplace; it's certainly not here yet. Do you have a ruthless paper routing system? If not, try some of these suggestions:

   a. Sort your mail into three piles. The first pile goes in the recycle bin or in the wastebasket. Throw out everything you can. Don't even open it if you know it's junk mail. The second pile is your Action pile, and the third pile is your To-Read pile. Have a To-Read folder either on your computer and/ or keep it by the phone, in front of the television, or in the car, and read from it when you're waiting in line, on hold on the phone, or waiting for an appointment.

   b. Use standard form letters for routine correspondence. You can buy books of forms at your office supply store.

   c. Use an agenda for meetings with second page for a list of tasks that need to be researched or completed before the next meeting, and by whom, and make sure that everyone gets a copy and is accountable.

8. Learn to say "No" to unrealistic timelines, committees you're not interested in, or people you don't want to socialize with. A firm "no" in the first place is much easier than trying to undo your commitment later.

9. Every day, ask yourself if you are doing the most important things for your business and your life and, if you are not, make some decisions about that.

Time is a gift. Protect it and make positive goal-directed choices for each day. Your results will be your reward.

INITIATE TRANSFORMATIONS FOR YOUR TEAM

Now that you have gotten yourself, your business, your creativity, and your life on the creative success path of transformation, it's time to look at your team. If you are a leader in a company other than your own, you may have inherited a team. That can be a real problem if you are in an organization that has little accountability and does not give you full rein to select your own people, and then let them go if they are not working out. If you work in such an organization, watch out. These poor performers will undermine your ability to achieve the success you want. I have worked with a number of managers who have been brought down by an incompetent and/or devious employee. If this is your situation, see what you can do to rectify it or seriously begin to look elsewhere for another opportunity.

If you have your own business or work for a positive organization, then choosing and developing your team can be a joyful and powerful process. You want to choose people who are in alignment with your business and creative goals and who see their job as part of their own personal growth and professional development plan. Many years ago, I used to hire people who were students or in transition to another career. Inevitably, I would end up doing career coaching with them and guide them into another job, and then I would have to start over. You want to hire people who want to be doing what you are hiring them to do, not people who really want to be doing something else. In all the years that I taught my program, Positive Management Techniques, it became clear to me that motivation starts from within. You can be the best manager on the planet, but if the person you are managing is not motivated to do the job and to do it well, none of the proposed "magical" management techniques will work. People have to possess both the willingness and the ability to do the job, or things are not going to work out. You want to empower the right people to engage in the transformational process that you have just experienced for yourself by reading this book.

Obviously this topic of building a transformative and creative team could be a whole book in itself. But, as it is such an important success strategy, I feel the need to mention some key factors here as a guide.

BEFORE YOU HIRE ANYONE

Good hiring decisions are essential to the growth of your business, your peace of mind, and how supported you feel—and they also have legal consequences. Many of the women in this book hired contractors, and many of them were virtual. All the people who work with me—my virtual assistants, my web designer, my accountant, my graphic designer, my editor—are all virtual 1099 employees. Decide what model you want for your business. Write down what specific skill set you need in the person that you want to hire, and then write down what kinds of personal traits, like extreme trustworthiness, are essential to the job or project. Then go on Craigslist, *elance.com*, career websites, and other job ad sites and note down the details of the jobs advertised, rates paid, and any other aspects of the job description. Craft a job description and a job ad so that you are clear on exactly what you need. After that, take a moment to fantasize about an ideal person and the specific attributes that he or she would bring to the job to get you in touch with some of your unconscious desires for that person too. The first time I hired a virtual assistant, I interviewed excellent people all over the country, but in the end, I had to admit that I wanted someone in Boston who could come over to my office to pick things up and file for me. While she and I only met in person a dozen times, it was what I wanted at the time.

When you interview people, tell them about your goals for your company or department, and then talk to them at length about their best strengths, their aspirations, their willingness to learn new things, and their interest in your business. If they really want to be a vet and you are a consultant, then they really ought to go work for a vet. Sometimes we just need someone for a project and it may not matter. But ideally we want to have people in our inner circle who have both the knowledge that we need them to have and a real passion for learning about the industry, or even better, previous experience in the industry. Finally, listen to your gut and look for red flags. If there is something that you don't like about a person, even if it seems ridiculous, do not hire that person. Wait for the right person. We talked about how valuable your time is, and you don't want to have to train two people. Be patient—don't be desperate. In my years of running a business, I have learned that if my intuition is cautioning me in any way in the midst of a decision, it's a "No."

TRANSFORM YOUR TEAM BY BEING A
POSITIVE MANAGER

Outstanding interpersonal or people skills are essential for your effectiveness as a leader. Learning to listen, training, coaching, advising, and inspiring become essential communication skills for notable managers. Your management style expresses your genuineness and integrity as a person. If you are dishonest, you will not be trusted for long. Successful managers, above all, treat their employees with respect.

In my training sessions with managers, everyone can recall being the victim of a lousy manager. But not everyone has been fortunate enough to work under a positive one. If you have had a great manager, think back to why the person was likable and effective. For sure, this person made a personal connection with you. That's what you want to do with your employees; make them feel important to you and the company. If you don't have the experience of a constructive role model, look for admirable managers in other parts of your company or among your peers. Good managers demonstrate achievements in planning, recruiting, organizing, directing, training, and conflict resolution. Technical competence in your field is vital, but interpersonal excellence really counts.

Good leaders are not necessarily always nice. There's a good reason for that old expression "it's lonely at the top." You can't gossip in the same way with your cronies or disclose "all you know." One of the women who I interviewed for this book wept when she talked about how lonely it can be to for her as CEO of her company. We talked about how much she needs other CEOs as peers and a coach who she can be totally open with. So we're going to do some work together. Disciplining employees and enforcing policies and quality standards are all key ingredients of your job. You can be fair and professional, but you won't always be popular. If you are a solo manager in your company, find other managers at your level inside or outside the company and share expertise. If that's not possible, get a management coach or take advantage of the available books, videos, audiotapes, and training programs. Also, as a manager, you become a role model. If you're late every day, how can you complain when Sherry is too? You have a responsibility to the managers of the future to demonstrate the best management skills that you can. You are being watched.

Whatever your strengths and weaknesses, being a manager will put them to the test. If you are disorganized, watch out! Your employees may take advantage of the fact that you don't remember when a project is due. If you are insecure, your employees may try to manipulate you. If you're too laid back, people may take advantage of you. To become a positive manager, you must be very self-aware. Play on your strengths and experience and make a plan to manage your weaknesses. Karen was a superb manager, but she was weak in the budget department. She bounced checks, overspent on supplies, and once had paychecks delayed because the account was overdrawn. Her forgetfulness around money worried her employees and lowered her esteem in their eyes. She either needed to learn these financial management skills or delegate these responsibilities to a competent other. She chose to take classes and meet regularly with the comptroller of her company to earn back the respect she wanted. Admit to yourself what you need to work on and then do it.

THE POWER OF POSITIVE RECOGNITION

In job satisfaction surveys of employees, the number one wish is for positive recognition for their work. People want authentic praise for their efforts. Make a point of acknowledging your employees regularly. A "thank you" or a congratulatory memo on a job well done work like a charm for morale and motivation. In addition, you need to analyze your work culture. Are you getting positive accolades from your boss or your employees? Are people in the organization upbeat or demoralized? Is the company growing or stagnant? Is management well organized and strategically on the mark? Is company communication clear or secretive? How is the company viewed by the community? Are people proud to be affiliated with this company? You are not managing in a vacuum. It's hard to be a great manager in a lousy company. You generally can't create a total oasis for yourself and your employees. If you're feeling unappreciated and resentful of a high percentage of management practices, then how can you be a cheerleader for that team? You are an advocate for your employees and while you can't expect to win every battle, you want to at least feel that you have a fighting chance.

Unhappy managers cannot inspire much except job turnover. So ask yourself the following questions:

- What are your personal and professional goals and are they being met in your current job?

- How would you reorganize your job/department to better meet your goals?

- Do you agree with the goals of your organization, especially if it is your own?

- Is your organization a positive work environment that rewards employees and fosters their career development?

- How equipped is your company and your industry to compete successfully in the global marketplace?

- What are the major challenges/problems in your company and department?

- What changes can you propose to improve the work environment for your employees?

If you feel like a fraud every time you implement a new policy, your employees will feel it too. It's best to work for a company in alignment with your goals and values so you can support its direction and mandates.

MANAGEMENT COMMUNICATIONS

To be a positive manager, you need to deepen your knowledge of management communications in the areas of discipline, coaching for improved job performance, delegation, and coaching for career development. Start with a plan for your department. Then hire and train employees to perform specific job descriptions. By monitoring performance, you communicate regularly with employees, giving them both positive and negative feedback. Then you coach them with the goal of either improving their performance or enhancing their career growth. Annually, you review this cycle with a performance review. If you don't talk to your employees all year and then try to conduct a meaningful performance review, you've missed a year of building a relationship with each other.

DISCIPLINE

Managers often hesitate to discipline an employee. Yet if you don't, the rest of the team resents your cowardice. For example, Becky continuously took overly long lunches. As a customer service representative, this meant that Becky was not handling her fair share of customer calls. Her coworkers kept waiting for her manager to intervene. It is your job to make sure that work is distributed fairly. Becky's manager, an empathic woman, knew that Becky was using her lunch break to run errands for her elderly mother. Yet, Becky's personal dilemma was compromising the morale and coverage for the entire department. Disciplinary action was in order. To help you feel more confident, follow these six steps:

1. Meet with the employee in private as soon after the incident as possible. Don't let the problem fester.

2. Outline the specific job responsibility the employee has not performed up to the expected standard. If this is an ongoing problem, keep track of what you have noticed, with dates and times, if you can.

3. Refer to the employee's job description or the company manual to clarify why this behavior is unacceptable.

4. State clearly the required behavior in specific behavioral language. For example, you could say "Company policy states that lunch break is only thirty minutes daily."

5. State the reasons for the expected behavior.

6. Let the employee know that his/her performance will be evaluated and cite the consequences of not performing the required behavior. For example, you could say "As of today, you must be back at your desk from lunch in thirty minutes or you will be required to make up the time each week. If you continue to abuse the lunch policy, you will receive a written warning."

Discipline, unlike coaching, is meant to be swift and precise. Certainly, you can sympathize with Becky's personal need to help her mother with errands. Your job as manager is to ensure that the company's customers can reach a customer service representative quickly. If Becky's at the drugstore, your customers are not getting the service they deserve, and her coworkers are being swamped with calls. You may want to take this opportunity to talk with Becky about alternatives. But it's Becky's job to manage her personal affairs. Always remember that if you make an exception for one person, other employees will want the privilege. So you are not free to tell Becky that she can have longer lunches unless you adjust her entire schedule. Then you can expect that her coworkers will be knocking on your door for the same flexibility. Keep in mind what's best for the department as a whole.

PREPARING TO COACH

A coach is a guide as well as a teacher and a motivator. Your job is to help your employees do the best job they can for the company and themselves. Balancing those two sets of needs can sometimes be tricky. A good coach converses regularly with her team. You must do the same. With a disciplinary intervention, hopefully one discussion is enough. Coaching is a longer process. Coaching can either be for improving an employee's job performance for an ongoing problem or it can help an employee reach a new goal or learn an advanced skill.

Let's first begin by identifying the steps to coaching employees for poor performance. Before you meet with the employee, fill out this pre-coaching questionnaire:

1. Identify the specific job performance behavior you want changed. It is not your job to the change personal characteristics of your employee. Be certain that your goal relates to a job task.

2. Is the problem important enough to warrant your time and energy to correct it? If not, then don't waste your time on it. For example, if Susan's idea of a planning book is a pocketful of papers but she's meeting all her timelines, then let it go. If the problem is important to the goals of the department, then tell the employee that you are going to meet with him or her to work on this specific problem.

3. In your opinion, does the employee agree that this behavior is a problem? If not, then that is your first agenda item. Refer to the employee's job description for support. If the employee agrees that he or she has a problem, then you must gain his/her commitment to resolve it. We can't coach people who don't want to change.

4. Prior to the coaching interview, review these issues:

   a. Are there obstacles outside of the employee's control that prevent him/her from performing the desired behavior?

   b. Does the employee have both the ability and the willingness to do the desired behavior?

   c. Has the employee received enough training?

d. If the employee does not improve his/her performance, what will be the consequences?

e. If the employee improves his/her behavior, what will be the rewards?

STEPS FOR A COACHING MEETING FOR IMPROVED JOB PERFORMANCE

Assumption: This employee understands and agrees that there is a job performance problem to be resolved.

1. In a private meeting with the employee, introduce the problem in a positive manner, acknowledging the employee's other strengths in the job. (If you have nothing positive to say about this employee, why are you keeping him or her?) Describe the problem specifically, including both the undesired and desired behaviors, and give examples. Ask the employee to verify and clarify the problem. Negotiate a mutual agreement on the exact problem and the desired outcome. Do not proceed until you have agreed on the goal.

2. Identify and write down all possible solutions to the problem together, making sure to address the causes of the problem. Listen intently to the employee's comments; don't assume you have all the answers.

3. Agree on a solution to the problem and write down the specific actions each of you will take and the completion dates.

4. Schedule a follow-up meeting within two weeks and include how progress will be measured.

5. Reinforce and review all written mutual agreements and commitments. Discuss the consequences for both the resolution and the non-resolution of this performance problem. Close on a positive note.

If you communicated clearly and listened carefully to your employee's comments, you should have learned something.

DELEGATION

Delegation is not dumping. Be careful not to delegate a component of your management role. Delegation can be a career opportunity for the recipient to learn new skills and diversify their career portfolio. Beware, though, that if your employees are already overloaded or on the verge of burnout, their response may be less than enthusiastic. Also, be careful not to delegate all the choice assignments to one employee. Spread out the challenges and try to match tasks with skill sets. Be honest with your employees about whether or not this is a job assignment which they have a choice about. Also, when you delegate, be prepared to spend the time with the employee to insure that the task is completed to your expectations. Delegation often requires a period of training to educate the employee about all the components.

Follow this framework to help the process to go more smoothly:

- Decide on the task to be delegated and select a person who has the capability to do the task or the ability and interest to learn it.

- Meet with the person selected and describe in detail the task to be done and the standards and time line you expect. Ask the person if he or she is willing to perform the task and what assistance/training/change of responsibility he or she would need to complete the task.

- When the person has agreed to do the task, ask them to outline the sequence of activities with estimated completion dates and then review the plan together and make any necessary changes.

- Decide with the person how much assistance or freedom he or she needs and then set up interval check points as needed.

- Be sure to build in positive recognition for a job well done!

COACHING FOR CAREER DEVELOPMENT

Delegation is often an opportunity for you and your employee to assess talents and areas for growth. In addition, meet regularly with your employees to discuss career goals. Don't assume that you know what your employees want; ask them. A positive manager asks key development questions such as the following:

- What do you like best and least about your job?

- What skills do you have the most and least confidence in?

- What are your goals for this job?

- What other jobs in the organization interest you and why?

- Why did you choose this career? Is it what you expected?

- Do you have long term goals in this career or an interest in changing careers in the future?

- How can I and the organization best support you in meeting your goals and/or resolving current job problems?

- How do you learn best? What kinds of training experiences have you had? What kinds of training and coaching experiences would you like in the future?

- Are you active in professional organizations or taking courses to advance your career?

- What motivates you right now?

If you have established yourself as a manager your employees can trust, you can benefit greatly from this discussion. If the two of you agree on a set of goals, meet regularly to implement them.

In addition, the following suggestions will help you to create a career enhancing environment in your department:

- Encourage your employees to become active in professional organizations. Coach them to volunteer for leadership positions, committees, and speaking engagements. The visibility and networking contacts will be beneficial for all.

- Have your employees keep an ongoing list of their accomplishments to remind them of their achievements.

- Make certain that your employees have the training and support to succeed at their jobs. Also, encourage them to take advantage of all internal training opportunities and tuition reimbursement options. No one can have too many skills in today's marketplace.

- Recruit a diverse staff to help your employees learn to manage teams and workplace diversity. By 2020, three-fourths of all people entering the job market will be women and minorities.

- Discuss career development strategies regularly with your employees as a group and encourage them to support each other's goals (allowing for confidentiality where appropriate).

- As entrepreneurial skills are assets for everyone, be certain that your employees are aware of the bottom line issues in your company. Also, see if there are opportunities for employees to run their own profit centers for the experience.

- Initiate team-building activities, such as task forces, group research, or problem-solving meetings to foster an improved ability to work in teams. Also initiate alliances with other departments in your organization to further increase these skills.

- Lastly, if you don't like being a manager, chart your career path elsewhere. Not everyone feels comfortable dealing with the intensity of relationships that being a positive manager demands. If you are a CEO, hire a general manager, so that you are only managing one person or create a business that has no other employees. But, if managing others fulfills your mentoring and leadership longings, use the guidelines we just talked about to help you to build a strong and cohesive work group and enhance your professional growth as well.

If you work for yourself, do not hesitate to have your team read this book and do the Challenges for themselves, including the Transformation Initiation exercises in this chapter. Let them know that you are invested in their success and are available to assist them, if you enjoy that role. If not, you can send them to workshops, coaching, industry conferences, including Creative Success Circles, to help to foster their professional growth and loyalty to the company. If you work for someone else, you will need to judge what kind of professional development guidance and advice is acceptable in your work culture. But you can always direct them to other mentors, if you are not able to fulfill that role.

EMPOWERING YOURSELF AND SHARING THE WEALTH

So there you have it: all 12 secrets of highly successful women. The path has been laid out for you. What you as an individual creative woman make of your life impacts everyone around you. Claim your unique gifts and your personal power, use them for the common good, prosper, and be generous with others. The next generation of women is counting on you. Show them the possibilities for personal, heartfelt success, and then share with them these secrets, so that they can seek out their own fulfillment.

Resources

WEB ADDRESSES OF WOMEN FEATURED IN THIS BOOK

Ali Brown *www.alibrown.com*

Baeth Davis *www.yourpurpose.com*

Brenda Michaels *www.conscioustalk.net/brenda.php*

Caroll Michels *www.carollmichels.com*

Chellie Campbell *www.chellie.com*

Cindy Morrison *www.cindywmorrison.com*

Debora George Tsakoumakis *www.wireacake.com*

Dr. Elizabeth Stewart *www.mayoclinic.org/bio/14879786.html*

Dr. Madeleine Randall *drmadeleinerandall.com*

Gillian Drake *www.capeartsreview.com*
    www.casadellaquercia.com
    www.gilliandrake.com

Jean Sifleet *www.smartfast.com*

Jeanne Carbonetti *www.crowhillgallery.com*

Jennifer Robenalt *www.robinhillmedia.com*

JJ Virgin *www.jjvirgin.com*

Katherine Ann Hartley *www.katherineannhartley.com*

Kathleen Dudzinski *www.dolphincommunicationproject.org/main*
www.aquaticmammalsjournal.org

Lesley Bohm *www.bohmphotography.com*

Lisa Sasevich *www.theinvisibleclose.com*

Lynn Robinson *www.lynnrobinson.com*

Marilyn Tam *www.howtousewhatyouvegot.com/book.htm*

Mary Hayden *www.nar.ucar.edu/2008/ASP/catalog/mary_hayden.php*

Olga Aura *www.OlgaAura.com*

Pat Schroeder *womenincongress.house.gov/member-profiles/profile.*
html?intID=220

Patricia Aburdene *www.patriciaaburdene.com*

Pearl Kaufman *www.pearlkaufman.com*

Peggy Whitson *www.jsc.nasa.gov/Bios/htmlbios/whitson.html*

Pele Rouge Chadima *www.resonance.to/about.htm*

Shama Hyder Kabani *www.Shama.Tv*

Sheri McConnell *www.sherimcconnell.com*

Sheryll Hirshberger Reichwein *www.thebeachroseinn.com*

Victoria Moran *www.victoriamoran.com*

Bibliography

Aburdene, Patricia, *Megatrends 2010: The Rise of Conscious Capitalism*, Hampton Roads Publishing, 2007.

Aburdene, Patricia, *The Power of Conscious Money* (to be published in 2011).

Asserof, John, *The Secret*, The Power Within Inc., 2007 .

Blum, Ralph H., *The Book of Runes: A Handbook for the Use of an Ancient Oracle, the Viking Runes*, St. Martin's Press, 1993.

Campbell, Chellie, *The Wealthy Spirit*, Sourcebooks, Inc., 2002.

Campbell, Chellie, *Zero to Zillionaire*, Sourcebooks, Inc., 2006.

Carbonetti, Jeanne, *The Heart of Creativity*, Eden Center Press, 2009.

Carbonetti, Jeanne, *The Tao of Watercolor* DVD, Jeanne Carbonetti, November, 2002.

Carbonetti, Jeanne, *The Zen of Creative Painting* DVD, Jeanne Carbonetti, June 2010.

Dyer, Wayne, *Excuses Begone, How to Change Lifelong, Self-Defeating Thinking Habits*, Hay House, 2011.

Dyer, Wayne, *The Shift* DVD, Hay House, 2009.

Godin, Seth, *The Dip, a Little Book that Teaches When to Quit (and When to Stick)*, Portfolio Hardcover, 2007.

Hill, Napoleon, *Think and Grow Rich*, Tribeca, 2011.

Hirschberger Reichwein, Sheryll (with Miller, Olivia), *The Feng Shui Deck: 50 Ways to Create a Healthy and Harmonious Home*, Chronicle Books, 2003.

Kabani, Shama, *The Zen of Social Marketing*, Ben Bella Books, 2010.

Kelley, Tim, *True Purpose, 12 Strategies for Discovering the Difference You Are Meant to Make*, Transcendent Solutions Press; First Edition, 2009.

LeClaire, Ann, *Listening Below the Noise*, a *Meditation on the Practice of Silence*, Harper, 2009.

Marson, Bonnie, *Sleeping with Schubert*, Random House, 2004.

McConnell, Sheri, *Smart Women Know Their Why: The Guide for Discovering Your Life Purpose While Owning a Business So You Can Create Positive Change In the World and . . . Make Big Profits*, Butterfly Women Press, imprint of Wyatt-MacKenzie, 2010.

McConnell, Sheri, *The Smart Woman's Business and Marketing Planner: A Daily Companion for the Female Entrepreneur*, Sheri McConnell Companies Inc., 2010.

McMeekin, Gail, *Creativity Courage Cards*, Creative Success, 2009.

McMeekin, Gail, *Positive Choices: From Stress to Serenity*, workshop on tape, Guided Growth, 1990.

McMeekin, Gail, *The 12 Secrets of Highly Creative Women: A Portable Mentor*, Conari Press, 2000.

McMeekin, Gail, *The Power of Positive Choices*, Conari Press, 2001.

Michaels, Brenda, *The Gift of Cancer: Awakening the Healer Within* (to be published in 2011).

Michels, Caroll, *How to Survive and Prosper as an Artist*, Holt Paperbacks, 2009.

Moran, Victoria, *Creating a Charmed Life*, HarperOne, 1999.

Moran, Victoria, *Fat, Broke & Lonely No More*, HarperOne, 2007.

Moran, Victoria, *Living a Charmed Life*, HarperOne, 2009.

Moran, Victoria, *Younger Every Day, 365 Ways to Rejuvenate Your Body and Revitalize Your Spirit*, HarperOne, 2005.

Morrison, Cindy, *Girlfriends 2.0*, Yorkshire, 2010.

Muller, Robert, *Most of All They Taught Me Happiness*, Doubleday, 1985.

Ponder, Catherine, *Open Your Mind to Prosperity*, DeVorss & Company; revised edition, 1984.

Robinson, Lynn, *Divine Intuition*, DK Adult, First Edition, 2001.

Robinson, Lynn, *Listen: Trusting Your Inner Voice in Times of Crisis*, GPP Life, 2009.

Sasevich, Lisa, *The Invisible Close System*, *www.theinvisibleclose.com*.

Shaughnessy, Susan, *Walking on Alligators: A Book of Meditations for Writers*, HarperOne; 1st edition, 1993.

Sifleet, Jean, *Advantage IP: Profit from Your Great Ideas*, Infinity, 2005.

Stewart, Elizabeth, *Uterine Fibroids: The Complete Guide*, The Johns Hopkins University Press, 2007.

Tam, Marilyn, *How to Use What You've Got to Get What You Want*, Select Books, 2010.

Virgin, JJ, *Six Weeks to Sleeveless and Sexy: The 5-Step Plan to Sleek, Strong, and Sculpted Arms*, Gallery, 2010.

Williamson, Marianne, *A Return to Love, Reflections on the Principles of A Course in Miracles*, Harper Paperbacks, 1996.

"Women with High Job Strain Have Increased Risk of Heart Disease," *www. brighamand womens.org/about_bwh/publicaffairs/news/pressreleases/ PressRel*, Brigham and Women's Hospital, Boston, MA, November 14, 2010.

"Women-Owned Businesses: America's New Job Creation Engine," Mark D. Wolf, *Forbes.com*, January 12, 2010, contains link to *The Guardian Life Small Business Research Institute Report*.

About the Author

Gail McMeekin, LICSW, is the CEO of Creative Success, LLC. She is a national executive, career, and creativity coach as well as a licensed psychotherapist and writer in Boston. She has over thirty years of experience helping people to vision and achieve their personal, professional, and creative goals. She coaches clients on how to leverage their creative ideas into heartfelt, prosperous businesses and fulfilled lives.

Gail is the author of *The 12 Secrets of Highly Creative Women: A Portable Mentor* (Conari Press, 2000), which sold out its first printing in eight weeks, and *The Power of Positive Choices* (Conari Press, 2001), which won the *Living in Balance* magazine Award in 2001. She is also the author of two e-books: *Boost Your Creativity, Productivity, and Profits in 21 Steps* and *The Path to Creative Success;* and a deck of *Creativity Courage Cards.*

Her work has been featured on television and radio as well as in major publications such as *Investor's Business Daily, Boston Business Journal, Redbook, Shape, Woman's Day, Health, The Boston Globe,* One Spirit Bookclub, and the *New York Times.*

Gail has a BA from Connecticut College, an MSW from Boston University, and a certificate in Human Resource Management from Bentley College. She also completed the coursework for The Coaches Training Institute. Check out her website at *www.creativesuccess.com* for a free offer.

To Our Readers